Grammar, Usage & Style

The essential guide for writers

Steve Moline

OXFORD
UNIVERSITY PRESS

253 Normanby Road, South Melbourne, Victoria 3205, Australia

Oxford University Press is a department of the University of Oxford. It furthers the University's objective of excellence in research, scholarship, and education by publishing worldwide in

Oxford New York

Auckland Bangkok Buenos Aires Cape Town Chennai Dar es Salaam Delhi Hong Kong Istanbul Karachi Kolkata Kuala Lumpur Madrid Melbourne Mexico City Mumbai Nairobi São Paulo Shanghai Singapore Taipei Tokyo Toronto

First published 2002

National Library of Australia

Cataloguing-in-Publication data:

Moline, Steve. (Author)

A student's A to Z of grammar, usage & style: the essential guide for writers.

ISBN 019 551504 8.

1. Grammar, Comparative and general—Dictionaries—Juvenile literature.
2. Style, Literary—Dictionaries—Juvenile literature. I. Title.

808.02

Edited by Kath Selkirk and Jocelyn Hargrave
Text design and typeset by Black Cockatoo Publishing Pty Ltd 2002
Cover designed by Olga Lavecchia
Illustrated by Black Cockatoo Publishing Pty Ltd 2002
Printed through Bookpac Production Services, Singapore

OWLS
OXFORD DICTIONARY WORD AND LANGUAGE SERVICE

Do you have a query about words, their origin, meaning, use, spelling, pronunciation, or any other aspect of international English? Then write to OWLS at the Australian National Dictionary Centre, Australian National University, Canberra ACT 0200 (email ANDC@anu.edu.au). All queries will be answered using the full resources of *The Australian National Dictionary* and *The Oxford English Dictionary.*
The Australian National Dictionary Centre and Oxford University Press also produce OZWORDS, a biannual newsletter which contains interesting items about Australian words and language. Subscription is free – please contact the OZWORDS subscription manager at Oxford University Press, GPO Box 2784Y, Melbourne, VIC 3001, or ozwords@oup.com.au

Photograph on page 148 © Hugo Moline
Photograph on page 206 © Axel Moline

What's in this dictionary?

The words defined in this dictionary are the basic terms used in:

• traditional school grammar
• functional grammar
• usage and commonly confused words and spellings
• style (personal, publishing and word processing)

as they apply to:

• written or keyboarded texts
• websites, emails, mobile text messages
• formal and informal contexts
• visual literacy

How to read this dictionary

The type in this dictionary is intended to help define the words visually. Any example of a headword (the word to be defined) is set in ***bold italic like this***. For example, in the entry "common noun" we read:

common noun

The name of anything that is *not* a particular person or thing.

> Most ***frogs*** live in ***water*** but some are found in ***trees*** or below the ***sand*** of the ***desert***.

Here the type tells us that all the words in ***bold italic*** are examples of the term that is being defined. So the words ***frogs***, ***water***, ***trees***, ***sand*** and ***desert*** are all examples of common nouns.

Sometimes words other than the headword are defined using other kinds of type, such as <u>underlining</u>. For example, in the same entry about common nouns <u>underlined type</u> is used to identify a different kind of noun:

The names of particular people or things are proper nouns. The following sentence includes ***common nouns*** and <u>proper nouns</u>:

> My ***sister*** <u>Alison</u> arrived on a ***plane*** from <u>Sydney</u>.

Here the type tells us that ***sister*** and ***plane*** are common nouns but that <u>Alison</u> and <u>Sydney</u> are other kinds of nouns called proper nouns.

About this dictionary

This dictionary is intended as a quick reference for students who hesitate over the meaning of some of the common terms of grammar, usage or style and who need a straightforward definition and example of each of those terms.

Formal or informal?

This is not a dictionary of pedantic rules. Many points of grammar and usage are disputed, and the appropriate word or phrase may vary depending on the context. For these reasons a distinction is often made between formal and informal writing.

Writing and drawing

Writing also includes drawing. Sometimes we write a diagram or map because these visual forms can make our meaning clearer than if we had written the information in sentences; so this dictionary also includes the key terms of visual literacy.

A student dictionary

This is intended as a dictionary for student writers. Students are now expected to know the conventions of various specialised forms of writing, both for the print media (such as newspaper and book publishing) and for the electronic media (such as film, TV, video and websites). Students are expected to write in various non-fiction genres, as well as narrative and poetry. Many of the common terms in all of these fields of writing are therefore included.

Does grammar matter?

Grammar is useful only where it helps the reader to understand the writer. Agreed conventions of grammar, usage and style serve a practical purpose where they make the meaning clearer to an unknown reader.

"Correct" or "accepted"?

Notions of "correct" usage are also continually changing—driven by the forces of repeated use in conversation, radio and TV, advertising and so on. At some point an expression that was once "wrong" (in the eyes of some people) becomes accepted by many. There are no rules for acceptance and no one makes a decision about it.

Acceptance varies not only between social groups but also between English-speaking countries. "Correct" punctuation in Australia is in some cases "incorrect" in the United States.

In this dictionary where there is a disagreement on usage both points of view are summarised and the decision is left to the reader. As with any social convention, a decision about usage may vary depending on context. How we compose a letter in answer to a job application is likely to be very different from how we write a mobile text message to a friend.

Language is social

Appropriate language is just one aspect of the social relations between writer and reader. Social conventions change. Sometimes it is in the writer's interest to form sentences according to traditional grammar, if only to avoid offending the grammatical expectations of the reader. When we are writing for an unknown reader, it is often a help to that reader if we use conventional grammar, usage and publishing style (including conventional spelling). For these reasons this dictionary recognises formal writing as a social convention, the rules of which a writer will need to know in certain situations.

abbreviation

A shortened version of a word.

If the abbreviation ends with the same letter as the full word, no full stop is required:

Dr = Docto<u>r</u>   ***Rd*** = Roa<u>d</u>

If the abbreviation ends with a different letter, a full stop is usually added:

Prof. = Professor

Abbreviations made of capital letters do not need full stops:

TV = television

Metric units of measurement do not need full stops:

mm = millimetre

Some abbreviations (called ***clippings***) are formed from one or two syllables from the full word. These are often written without a full stop:

ad = <u>ad</u>vertisement

net = inter<u>net</u>

sitcom = <u>sit</u>uation <u>com</u>edy

See *also* **acronym** • **apostrophe** • **contraction** • **slash** [/]

abbreviations, list of

An alphabetical list of all the abbreviations used in the book in which the list appears. It is usually placed at the front or back of the book.

See *also* **front matter** and **end matter**

absolute words

See **gradable** and **non-gradable**

abstract noun

A noun that stands for something that you cannot see, such as an idea, feeling or action.

the ***cause*** of her ***anger***

a ***voyage*** of ***discovery***

See *also* **concrete noun**

accept or *except?*

- ***accept*** means "to receive"
- ***except*** means "excluding"

He ***accepted*** all our gifts ***except*** the last one.

acronym

A word made from the first letters of other words. Often the word is written in capital letters. No full stops are used.

NIMBY = ***n****ot* ***i****n* ***m****y* ***b****ack* ***y****ard*

See *also* **abbreviation**

active text

See **interactive text**

active voice

A verb form in sentences that follow the pattern

subject—verb—object

or

agent—process—effect

Subject (agent)	Verb (process)	Object (effect)
The dog	stopped	the traffic.

See *also* **passive voice**

additive conjunction

IN FUNCTIONAL GRAMMAR

A form of sentence cohesion in which ideas are brought together by adding them on. Often used in information reports to build up a large number of facts.

Crabs have a carapace for protection ***as well as*** legs for walking ***or*** swimming. ***In addition,*** most crabs have four tentacles ***and*** two eyes. They have no scales, ***nor*** do they have skin.

See *also* **cohesion**

adjectival clause

See **adjective clause**

adjectival phrase

See **adjective phrase**

adjective

A word that accompanies or describes a noun or pronoun. There are several kinds of adjective.

Descriptive adjective

An adjective that describes a *noun* or pronoun. Many adjectives are descriptive:

a ***green*** *cicada*
Some *cicadas* are ***green***.
Those are ***green***.

Some descriptive adjectives are also called ***epithets*** and others are called ***classifiers***. Both are kinds of ***pre-modifier***.

Demonstrative adjective

Any of the words ***this***, ***that***, ***these*** or ***those*** followed by a *noun* or noun phrase:

I bought ***this*** *video*.
She owns ***that*** video game.
Can you put away ***these*** *clothes*?
We met ***those*** people in the bus.

Demonstrative adjectives are also called ***pointers***, a kind of pre-modifier.

Distributive adjective

An adjective that refers to the separate items in a group. The main ones are ***each***, ***every***, ***either*** and ***neither***:

> Join ***each*** wire to its own battery.
> ***Every*** person had a different idea.
> ***Either*** of us can go, but not both.
> ***Neither*** dog was wearing a collar.

Indefinite adjective

An adjective that indicates an approximate amount:

> We ate ***a few*** chips.
> ***Most*** birds can fly.
> ***Some*** people can afford to buy a home; ***many*** people can't.

Interrogative adjective

An adjective (or *determiner*) that asks a question. These are the so-called ***wh-*** words + ***how***:

> ***How*** can I help?
> ***Where*** is it? ***What*** is it?
> ***When*** do we start?
> ***Why*** are they here?

Number adjective

An adjective that uses numbers to indicate ***how many*** or in what order:

> The Solar System has ***nine*** planets. Earth is the third planet from the Sun.

Number adjectives are also called *numeratives*, a kind of pre-modifier.

Possessive adjective

Any of the words ***my***, ***your***, ***her***, ***his***, ***our*** or ***their***:

	Singular	*Plural*
1st person	***my***	***our***
2nd person	***your***	***your***
3rd person	***her/his/its***	***their***

Demonstrative, distributive, numeral and possessive adjectives are also called *determiners*.

See *also* **classifier • degree • determiner • epithet • interrogative words • number adjective • personal pronoun • pre-modifier**

adjective clause

See **relative clause**

adjective group

IN FUNCTIONAL GRAMMAR

A group of words based on an ***adjective***.

> Tyrannosaurs were moderately to highly ***intelligent***.

adjective phrase

A ***phrase*** that does the job of an adjective, describing the *noun* that goes with it.

> The *shells* were ***easy to find***.

In this sentence ***easy*** is an adjective and ***easy to find*** is an

☞

adjective phrase describing the noun *shells*.

Adjective phrases can also describe a pronoun:

They were ***easy to find***.

See *also* **phrase**

ad. or ad?

See **abbreviation**

AD or BC?

• ***AD (anno domini)*** is used for all dates *after* the birth of Christ. The date goes *after* **AD**.
• ***BC (before Christ)*** is used for all dates *before* the birth of Christ. The date goes *before* **BC**.

AD 650   *512 BC*

You can also use:
• ***CE (common era)* = *AD***
• ***BCE (before common era)* = *BC***
The date always goes *before* **CE** or **BCE**.

650 CE = AD 650
512 BCE = 512 BC

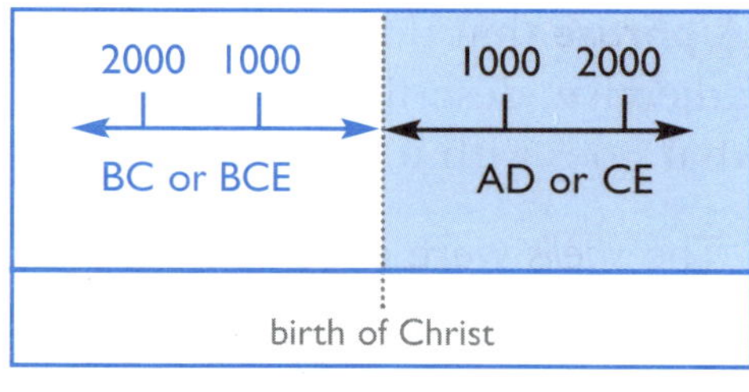

• ***BP (before the present)*** can be used to count *backwards* from the present year. An event that occurred five thousand years ago can be written ***5000 years BP***.

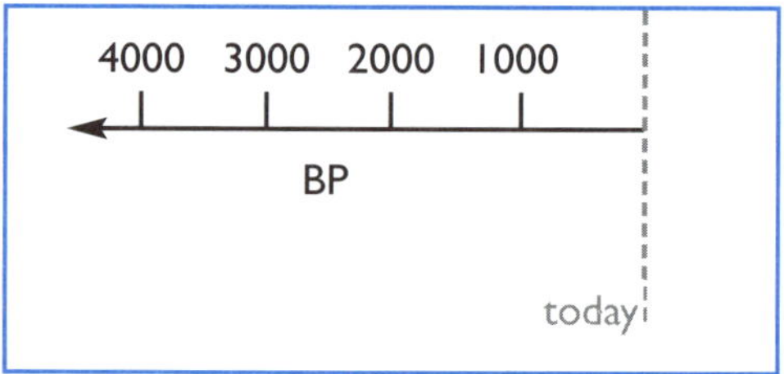

No full stops are needed.

adverb

A word that modifies a verb, an adjective or another adverb.

Adverb modifying a verb:
to act ***stupidly***

Adverb modifying an adjective:
completely new

Adverb modifying an adverb:
too often

Most common adverbs

The most common adverbs indicate how, when, where, how often or how much.

Adverb of manner (how?):
Icebergs melt ***slowly***.

Adverb of time (when?):
It rained ***yesterday***.

Adverb of place (where?):
We swam ***there***.

Adverb of number (how often?):
The computer crashed ***twice***.

Adverb of degree (how much?):
We will be ***very*** hungry.
The bottle was ***almost*** empty.
Those clothes are ***too*** small.

Interrogative adverbs

These adverbs are used to form questions:

How does it work?
When will the bus arrive?

Other adverbs

Adverbs can express doubt:
Life ***possibly*** exists on Mars.

Adverbs can make a sentence negative:
A spider is ***not*** an insect.

See also **degree • interrogative words • *negative adverb*** *or* ***negative particle?***

adverb clause

A clause that does the job of an adverb.

Most common adverb clauses

These clauses state how, when, where or why:

Clause of manner (how?)
"Do ***as I say*** not ***as I do***!"

Clause of time (when?)
The lava hardens ***while it cools***.

Clause of place (where?)
Sit ***wherever you wish***.

Clause of reason (why?)
We did not see the stingrays ***since they were camouflaged***.

Other adverb clauses

Other adverb clauses state a result, purpose, comparison, condition or concession:

Clause of result
The plastic became ***so*** hot ***that it melted***.

Clause of purpose
Some birds collect seaweed ***in order to make nests***.

Clause of comparison
She swims ***as*** fast ***as I can walk***.

Clause of condition
I will see you at the game ***unless I am late***.

Clause of concession
Although they may look like fish, dolphins are mammals.

adverb group

IN FUNCTIONAL GRAMMAR

A <u>group of words</u> based on an ***adverb***.

She left ***<u>almost immediately</u>***.

In this sentence both ***almost*** and ***immediately*** are adverbs. They form an adverb group.

adverb phrase

A phrase that does the job of an adverb, usually stating how, when, where or why.

Fossils form ***on the seabed***.

In this sentence **on the seabed** states where fossils form.

See also **adverb • phrase**

adverbial clause

See **adverb clause**

adverbial phrase

See **adverb clause**

adversative conjunction

IN FUNCTIONAL GRAMMAR

A form of sentence cohesion in which contrasting or opposite ideas are brought together. Used in information reports and discussions.

A pet show would be fun for pet owners ***but*** most of us don't own a pet. It might raise money for the school. That is not guaranteed, ***however***. Some people say that the pets could escape and get lost; ***nevertheless*** I doubt that would really happen. ***On the other hand***, you can't rule out the possibility. ***Despite all this***, it is likely we will go ahead anyway.

See also **cohesion • discussion**

advertese

Spellings used in advertising that have spread into English more generally.

Common examples of advertese are:

lite = light ***nite*** = night
thru = through

These are usually avoided in formal English but are accepted elsewhere, such as in emails and mobile text messages.

See also **email shorthand • mobile shorthand**

advice or *advise*?

- ***advice*** is a noun (or thing)
- ***advise*** is a verb (or action)

Take my ***advice***: don't let anyone ***advise*** you.

advisor or *adviser*?

Both mean "someone who gives advice" and both are accepted.

advisory or *advisery*?

- ***advisory*** means "giving advice" or "warning"

• ***advisery*** is a misspelling

Parental ***advisory***: the language in this book may lead your child to think for herself.

a few or *a little*?

• ***a few*** is used with things that *can* be counted
• ***a little*** is used with things that *cannot* be counted

This recipe calls for ***a few*** eggs and ***a little*** milk.

Countable things are usually identified with ***count nouns***. Uncountable things are usually identified with ***mass nouns***.

See *also* **count noun** and **mass noun** • ***fewer*** *or* ***less?***

affect or *effect*?

• ***to affect*** means "to alter"
• ***to effect*** means "to enable" or "to cause" a result
• ***an effect*** means "a result"

Smoking can ***affect*** your health.
Applying heat will ***effect*** a rise in temperature.
Fire was an ***effect*** of the earthquake.

affix

Part of a word that has been added either before or after a base to form a new word.

The word ***unbreakable*** is made up of a base ***break*** and two affixes ***un-*** and ***-able***. An affix that starts a word is a ***prefix*** and one that ends a word is a ***suffix***.

Prefix	*Base*	*Suffix*
un	break	able

See *also* **base** • **prefix** and **suffix**

agent

IN FUNCTIONAL GRAMMAR
The participant that "causes the process" in a sentence.

Our team won the cup.
The cup was won by ***our team***.

See *also* **participant**

agentless passive

See **passive voice**

agreement

The agreeing of two parts of a sentence in number, person or gender.

Agreement occurs between ***verb and subject*** or between ***noun and pronoun***.

Agreement of verb and subject
If a subject is singular, the verb is usually singular as well. The ***verb***

☞

agrees in number with the subject:

A crab ***has*** ten legs.
All crabs ***have*** ten legs.

In the first sentence both crab and ***has*** are singular.
In the second sentence both crabs and ***have*** are plural.

Agreement of noun and pronoun

If a pronoun refers to a noun (or noun phrase) it is usually the same number and the same person as the noun:

Lake Baikal is the world's deepest lake. ***It*** is also the oldest.

In these two sentences the noun phrase ***Lake Baikal*** is third person, singular number. The pronoun ***It*** is also third person, singular number and agrees in both person and number.

A ***pronoun*** also agrees in gender with its noun in the rare cases in English where gender is shown:

Kate lent me ***her*** CD.

Some exceptions

Some expressions do not agree:

All I have ***is*** ten dollars.

See also **gender** • ***everybody/ everyone + is*** *or* ***are?*** • ***he or she + they?*** • ***it is + plural?*** • **number** • ***one*** *or* ***you?*** • **person**

alignment (of text)

The arrangement of the words and lines of a text. Alignment can be ***left***, ***centred***, ***right*** or ***justified***.

Text can be aligned ***left***.

The text can be ***centred***.

Text can be aligned ***right***.

Text can be ***justified***, which means that it is aligned on both left and right sides.

allegory

A narrative that has a more general meaning or "message".

See also **symbol**

alliteration

A series of words in which some words start with the same sound.

fast and ***f***urious   ***st***em to ***st***ern
knots and ***gn***arls

allograph

See **grapheme**

allomorph

See **morpheme**

allophone

See **phoneme**

all ready or *already*?

• ***all ready*** means "everything prepared"
• ***already*** means "previously"

Having packed our bags we were ***all ready*** to leave.
When they started packing I had ***already*** finished.

all right or *alright*?

• both ***all right*** and ***alright*** can mean "OK" or "satisfactory"
• ***all right*** can mean "all correct"

I felt ***alright*** because my exam answers were ***all right***.

all together or *altogether*?

• ***all together*** means "all in the same place"
• ***altogether*** means "completely"

Join the pieces ***all together***.
You are ***altogether*** mistaken.

a lot of or *plenty of*?

See ***lots of*** or ***a great deal of***?

alphabetical order

There are two ways to arrange words in alphabetical order.

Letter by letter

Sort the letters and ignore the spaces between words:

catastrophe
cat owners
cattle
cat trainers

This method is used in most dictionaries (such as this one).

Word by word

Group the same words together, then sort the letters that follow them:

cat owners
cat trainers
catastrophe
cattle

This method is used in some library catalogues and book indexes.

alphanumeric key

See ***keyboard***

A

alternate or *alternative*?

• ***alternate*** means "every second one"
• ***alternative*** means "other" or "offering a choice"

Last week it rained on ***alternate*** days.
We preferred to travel by train, but our ***alternative*** plan was to take the car.

The adverb ***alternatively*** can also be used as a conjunction to mean "on the other hand" or "otherwise":

We could go by car. ***Alternatively*** we could catch the train.

alternative question

See **question**

although or *though*?

Both mean "yet" or "however". Both are accepted and are interchangeable in *most* cases.

It was hard work, ***although*** it was interesting.
= It was hard work, ***though*** it was interesting.

Though can end a sentence, but ***although*** cannot:

It was hard work. It was interesting, ***though***.

In the last sentence ***though*** is accepted, whereas ***although*** would sound "unfinished" at the end of this sentence.

ambiguity

(Also called ***double meaning***)
Having an uncertain meaning, or having two or more meanings. Ambiguity can be deliberate or accidental.

The koala has ***grey, furry ears and teeth***.

This sentence is ambiguous because it could mean that the koala's teeth are grey and furry.

among or *amongst*?

Both these words are accepted and mean the same.

one ***among*** many
= one ***amongst*** many

a.m. or *p.m.*?

• ***a.m. (ante meridiem)*** means "before noon" and includes all times after midnight and before noon
• ***p.m. (post meridiem)*** means "after noon" and includes all times after noon and before midnight

12.00 noon (not a.m. or p.m.)
12.00 midnight (not a.m. or p.m.)
12.01 p.m. (a minute past noon)
12.01 a.m. (a minute past midnight)

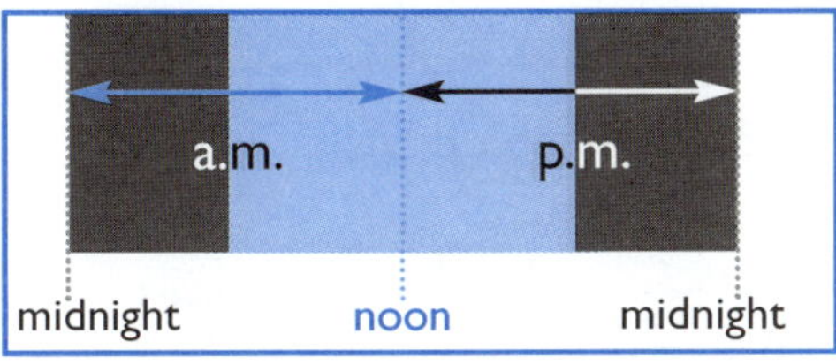

ampersand [&]

A symbol that stands for ***and***.

Totter **&** Lean, Architects

The ampersand is used with names in formal situations, but is more common in informal shorthand such as in emails and text messages:

CU **&** Ben @ 4

See also **email shorthand** • **mobile shorthand**

analogy

(1) A comparison of two things which are in one respect similar.

The heart works like a pump.

(2) The formation of new words based on similarities with existing words.

She ***faxed*** her ***filmography***.

Fax is a shortened form of ***facsimile***. The ending ***-ed*** has been added by analogy with words like ***taxed*** and ***relaxed***.

A ***filmography*** is a list of films. This word is derived by analogy with the word ***bibliography***. The word ***film*** replaces ***biblio-*** (which means "book") and ***-graphy*** means "writing about".

See also **bibliography**

analysis

The breaking down of sentences (or clauses, phrases or even words) into their parts to describe their grammar.

and + comma [,]?

See **comma**

and/or

See **slash** [/]

And starting a sentence?

Generally ***and*** is used to join two parts within a sentence.

fish ***and*** chips
into the house ***and*** up the stairs
He turned around ***and*** saw me.

However, there are occasions when we can use ***And*** to start a sentence, creating the effect of an afterthought, a return to an idea in an earlier sentence, a pause or a refrain:

"I was not sure if I should go back to the house alone," he said.
"And did you?" I asked.
"Yes, I did. And that's when I noticed the lights were still on."

"I'll bake it myself," said the Little Red Hen. And she did.

angular brackets [< >]

Punctuation marks used to identify a computer command or to indicate an internet address.

Type a word, then press <ENTER>.

Visit us at <www.noname.org.au>.

See also **brackets • names • quotation marks**

ante- or *anti-*?

- ***ante-*** means "before"
- ***anti-*** means "against" or "the opposite of"

antedate = to happen before
anti-war = against war
anticlockwise = opposite of clockwise

antonym

A word with the opposite meaning of another word. The following pairs of words are antonyms of each other:

good, bad
pleasant, unpleasant
trust, distrust

Some words have more than one antonym:

old—young old—new

voluntary—compulsory
voluntary—involuntary

See also **chain • synonym**

anybody/anyone + *is* or *are*?

See ***everybody/everyone* + *is* or *are*?**

apostrophe [']

A punctuation mark used to show either contraction or possession.

Apostrophe of contraction

This apostrophe shows that one or more letters are left out:

don't = do not
you've = you have
o' clock = of the clock

Some abbreviations (called ***clippings***) have come to be "words in their own right" and usually have *no* apostrophe:

flu = influenza
phone = telephone

Apostrophe of possession

An apostrophe (with or without ***-s***) is also used to show ownership or belonging (= ***of***):

sharks = more than one shark
shark's = of one shark
sharks' = of more than one shark

The way we use the apostrophe may be changing. At present the rule is:

s = more than one
's = of one
s' = of more than one

Where a plural word does not have an ***s***, add ***'s***:

men = more than one man
man's = of *one* man
men's = of *more than one* man

Where a singular word ends in ***-s*** or ***-x***, add ***'s*** or just ***'***:

Cyprus's capital
Cyprus' capital
= the capital of Cyprus

Alex's nose
Alex' nose
= the nose that belongs to Alex

In Australia the apostrophe is omitted from place names, with some odd results:

Frenchs Forest
Rosss Creek
Duffys Forest
Coxs River

In other countries the apostrophe is retained in place names:

Land's End, England
Martha's Vineyard, USA

A plural is formed with an **s** but no apostrophe:

We ate ice creams.
NOT We ate ice cream's.

However, letters used as words can take a plural using ***'s***:

Dot your ***i's*** and cross your ***t's***.

Plural numbers are sometimes written with an ***'s*** (as in ***the 1990's***) but the simplest rule to remember when writing these plurals is simply to add the usual plural-forming **s**:

since the ***90s***
in the ***sixties***
Four ***fives*** are twenty.
They came in ***twos*** and ***threes***.

The vanishing apostrophe?

The apostrophe may be "disappearing" from printed and electronic texts. Many newspapers, billboards and websites contain examples of words that "should" have the possessive apostrophe but don't. Usually these examples are in contexts where the meaning remains clear. The question arises whether the possessive apostrophe may eventually be dropped altogether if it rarely clears up a real ambiguity.

See also **its** *or* **it's***?*

appendix

Additional information placed at the end of a reference book. An appendix provides background information that relates to one or more parts of the main text of the book. An appendix is often a list, table or map.

The plural can be written as ***appendices*** or ***appendixes***. Both are accepted.

See also **front matter** and **end matter** • **plural nouns**

argument

A form of persuasive text.
See **persuasion**

arrow [→]

A mark used in visual texts:

- to show direction
- to link labels to a graphic
- to show movement

Arrows that show direction

Arrows can be used to show the order in which we should read a graphic such as a storyboard or flow chart.

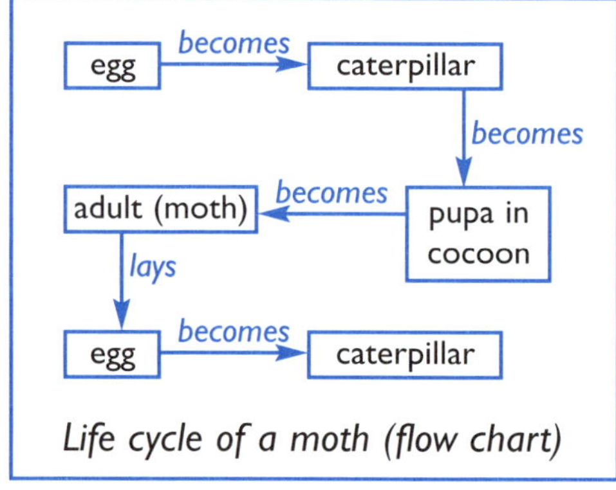

Life cycle of a moth (flow chart)

Arrows that link labels to a graphic

In a diagram the names (labels) of different parts of the graphic can be connected with arrows or leader lines:

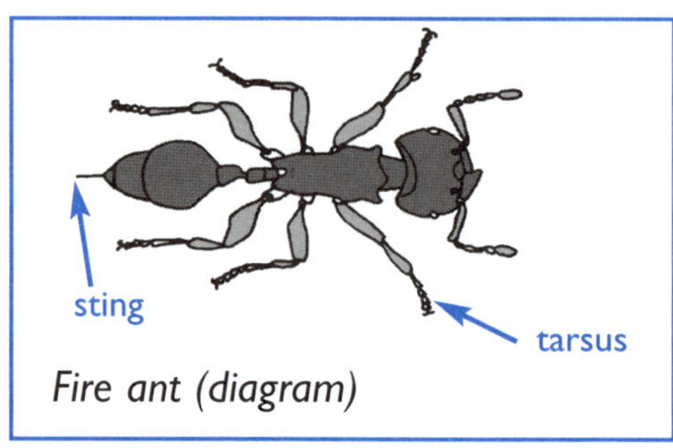

Fire ant (diagram)

Arrows that show movement
Arrows can be used in a map to show a journey line.

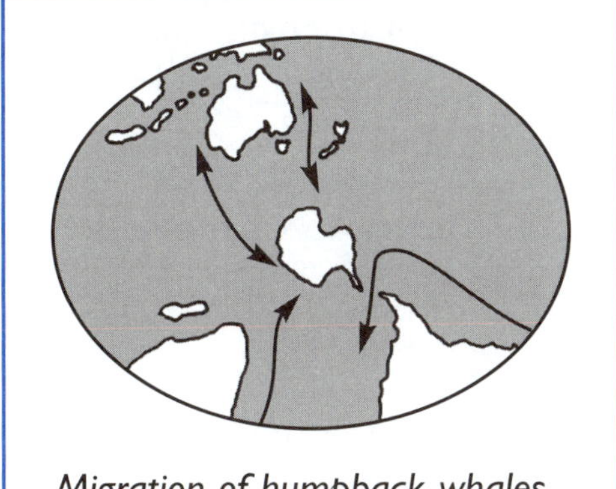

Migration of humpback whales

See *also* **journey line • leader line**

arrow of time

See **time line**

article

One of the words ***a***, ***an***, ***the***.

Definite article: the
The is used with a particular thing that has just been mentioned, or is familiar to the reader or listener:

> We arrived at Carl's place. ***The*** house was deserted. Soon afterwards ***the*** rain began to fall.

Indefinite article: a, an
A or ***an*** is used with "things in general":

> ***An*** ant is ***a*** kind of insect.

We generally use ***a*** in front of a consonant and ***an*** in front of a vowel:

> ***a*** banana   ***an*** apple

You can use ***an*** in front of the consonant ***h*** if this is how you say the words (both are accepted):

> ***a*** hotel
> if you pronounce the /h/
> ***an*** hotel
> if you don't pronounce it

You can use ***a*** in front of the vowel ***u*** when it is pronounced as if it starts with a ***y-***:

> ***a*** uniform   ***an*** uncle

See *also* **determiner • vowel** and **consonant**

as far as + is concerned?

- ***as far as*** means "as distant as"
- ***as far as … is concerned*** means "with respect to"

> We will walk ***as far as*** Mt K—.
> We are equipped to go camping ***as far as*** a tent ***is concerned***.

In conversation some people omit the phrase ***is concerned***.

See *also* **insofar** *or* **in so far***?*

A

as or *like*?

See ***like, as, as if*** or ***such as***?

assonance

Words in a poem that do not rhyme but have similar sounds.

sit and sing

See also ***rhyme*** or ***rhythm***?

assure, ensure or *insure*?

• ***to assure*** means "to encourage [someone] to feel confident"
• ***to ensure*** means "to make sure" that something happens
• ***to insure*** means "to buy insurance for"

I ***assure*** you that her car is safe.
Check the doors to ***ensure*** that the car is locked.
It is expensive to ***insure*** her car.

asterisk [*]

A mark that connects part of the text to a footnote. The asterisk is placed after the word or phrase to be explained, and in front of the footnote that explains it.

Cybershopping* was invented in 1994.

* Shopping on the internet.

An asterisk works as a signpost that redirects the reader to another part of the text. Asterisks are used in printed texts but not in electronic texts where they are replaced by hyperlinks.

See also **footnote** • **hyperlink**

at [@]

A shorthand symbol used in email addresses.

max@uhavenomail.org.au

atmosphere

See **setting** (in a narrative)

attachment

A digital file attached to an email message.

attribute

IN FUNCTIONAL GRAMMAR

A ***word*** or ***phrase*** that describes a participant in a sentence.

Our uniforms were ***blue***.
Jupiter is ***the largest planet***.
Flowering plants have ***fruits and seeds***.

See also **participant**

aural or *oral*?

- ***aural*** refers to hearing
- ***oral*** refers to talking

Was the exam written or ***oral***?
Her ***aural*** test showed that she was slightly deaf.

auxiliary verb

(Also shortened to ***auxiliary*** and sometimes called a "helping verb") A verb that is used to form the tense, voice or mood of other verbs which are called lexical verbs.

The main auxiliaries

(Also called ***primary verbs***) The main ***auxiliaries*** are:

The verb ***to be***

The world ***is*** becoming warmer.
Was it snowing yesterday?

The verb ***to have***

I ***have*** arrived. = I***'ve*** arrived.
Has anyone found my keys?

The verb ***to do***

I ***do*** sing.
I ***do not*** sing. = I ***don't*** sing.
Doesn't he know you?

The modal auxiliaries

(Also called ***modals***) These auxiliaries express degrees of certainty or doubt:

Couldn't they stay?
They ***must*** stay.
He ***mightn't*** win.

In all these sentences the main (lexical) verbs are underlined and the auxiliaries are in ***bold*** type.

Other modals include:

can
may
will
shall
would
should
ought (to)

See also **lexical verb** • **modal auxiliary** • **mood** of a verb • **primary verb** • **tense** of a verb • **verb** • **voice** of a verb

B

backslash [\ ]

See **slash** [/]

bar graph

A graph that arranges amounts along the foot of the graph and items to be compared down the side. Each row forms a "bar". Bar graphs can be used to illustrate explanations and factual recounts.

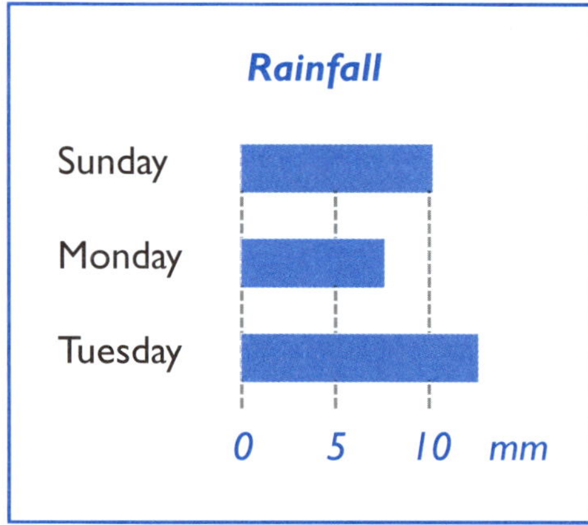

See *also* **column graph**

bare infinitive

See **finite verb** and **non-finite verb**

base

(Also called ***base morpheme*** or ***base word***) The part of a word to which a prefix or suffix is added. For example, ***answer*** is the base in un***answer***able:

Prefix	*Base*	*Suffix*
un	answer	able

See *also* **morpheme** • **prefix** and **suffix**

BC or AD?

See **AD or BC?**

began or begun?

• ***began*** is the past tense of "begin": they ***began***
• ***begun*** is the past participle of "begin": they have ***begun***

Use ***begun*** with have, has or had. Use ***began*** alone:

he ***began***
we had ***begun***
they ***began***
she has ***begun***
they have ***begun***

See *also* **past participle** • **past tenses**

behavioural process

See **process**

beneficiary

IN FUNCTIONAL GRAMMAR
The ***participant*** that benefits from a process.

I gave the video ***to Mark***.

I <u>gave</u> ***Mark*** the video.
I <u>gave</u> ***him*** the video.

See *also* **participant • process**

beside or *besides?*

• ***beside*** means "next to"
• ***besides*** means "in addition to"

We waited ***beside*** the gate.
Besides losing her ticket, she had no money.

Besides, (***Besides*** + *comma*) means "Furthermore" or "Anyway":

She did not want to go to the game. ***Besides,*** she had lost her ticket.

between or *among?*

See ***among*** or ***between?***

between you and me or *between you and I?*

Like other prepositions, ***between*** is followed by an indirect object (***me***) not a subject (***I***).

between you and ***me***
NOT between you and ***I***

The phrase ***between you and I*** is an example of ***hypercorrection***.

See *also* **hypercorrection • *I*** *or* ***me*** *(after* ***is****)?* **• *object*** *(of a sentence)* **• *subject*** *(of a sentence)*

biannual or *biennial?*

• ***biannual*** means "two times a year" = every 6 months
• ***biennial*** means "every two years" = every 24 months

bibliography

A section of a reference book that lists other books on the same topic. The list is usually placed at the end of the book before the index, and the entries are arranged alphabetically by author's surname (last name).

Day, R. *Volcanoes*. Nupress, 2001.
Lee, K. *Lava Lakes*. D Books, 1998.
Tan, L. *Volcano Facts*. Scientia, 2003.

Each entry in a bibliography is usually written in this order and with this punctuation:

Author. *Title*. Publisher, date.

When using handwriting use <u>underlining</u> instead of using *italic*:

Author. <u>Title</u>. Publisher, date.

Different writers use different bibliographic systems. The main rule is to be consistent.

Lists of films are sometimes called ***filmographies***.

Films can be quoted in a similar way (Director. *Title*. Studio, date.):

Welles, Orson. *Citizen Kane*. RKO Pictures, 1941.

Web pages can be quoted as: "Page heading." *Site name*. <URL> (date when accessed):

"Volcanoes." *Encyclopedia Titanica*. <www.encyclopediatiticanica.net/volcanoes> (21 June 2003).

See also • **front matter** and **end matter** • **names** • **references** • **underlining** or ***italic*?** • **URL**

bimonthly and *biweekly*

• ***bimonthly*** can mean *either* "twice a month" *or* "once every two months"
• ***biweekly*** can mean *either* "twice a week" *or* "once every two weeks"

This is very confusing. Avoid these words to ensure that you are understood. Instead, write "twice a …" or "every two …":

She visited us ***twice a week***.
The magazine appeared ***every two months***.

block letter

See **capital letter**

blurb

The text on the back cover of a book, describing the book and its author. The blurb is usually not written by the book's author, but by its publisher as a form of promotion for the book.

bold type

A kind of typeface or ***font*** that is thicker and appears blacker than ordinary type. **Bold type** is used to highlight important words. It can also be used for headings.

Fish without bones

Most fish have bony skeletons. However, some fish have no bones. These **cartilaginous** fish include the sharks and stingrays.

In this paragraph **Fish without bones** is the heading and **cartilaginous** is a key word that is defined in context: the sharks and stingrays.

See also **font**

bookmark

(1) Any item such as a cardboard strip for marking a place in a book.
(2) A file giving the name and address (URL) of a web page.

See also **URL**

both *or* ***each?***

• ***both*** refers to *two* things as a group
• ***each*** refers to *two or more* things, individually

Both *flags have the same design.*

Each *flag has a different design.*

Both is plural, but ***each*** is singular:

> ***Both*** girls have ten dollars.
> ***Each*** of the girls has ten dollars.

But in the next sentence have agrees with **girls** (both are plural) and ***each*** is an adverb:

> The *girls* ***each*** have ten dollars.
> = The *girls* have ten dollars ***each***.

See also ***each + is*** *or* ***are?***

bought *or* ***brought?***

• ***bought*** is past tense of "buy"
• ***brought*** is past tense of "bring"

> They ***bought*** ice creams with the change.
> They ***brought*** ice creams in the esky.

boxed text

See **breakout**

brace [{]

A printer's mark that links two or more lines of type, indicating that they belong together in a group.

planets	{	Jupiter Saturn Neptune

A brace is *not* a kind of bracket and is *not* a punctuation mark. Braces are used like leader lines in a tree diagram.

See also **brackets** ( ) and [ ] • **leader line** • **tree diagram**

brackets ( ) and [ ]

Punctuation marks enclosing words that interrupt the flow of a sentence. There are two kinds of brackets: round and square.

Round brackets ( )

These brackets are used:

- to define or name a word
- to explain why or how
- to make a comment

Defining or naming

Insects **(**which have six legs**)** do not include spiders.

The smallest planet **(**called Pluto**)** has a moon that never sets.

Explaining why or how

I unlocked the box **(**using the key I found**)** but it was empty.

Commenting

Yesterday I went skiing **(**though I am not a very good skier**)**.

Square brackets [ ]

These brackets are used to enclose words that have been added to a quotation.

Original sentence

Most birds have wings but some have flippers.

Quotation

According to one source, "some **[**birds**]** have flippers".

See also **angular brackets** [< >] • **brace** [{] • **parenthesis**

breakout

(Sometimes called ***boxed text***) Part of an article in a magazine or reference book that is separated from the main text using a box or colour panel.

Breakouts like this one are used to explain an idea or to provide background information.

See also **sidebar**

breath or *breathe*?

- ***breath*** is a noun (or thing)
- ***breathe*** is a verb (or action)

Breathe in and hold your ***breath***.

broke or *broken*?

- ***broke*** is the past tense of "break": they ***broke*** the record
- ***broken*** is the past participle of "break": they have ***broken*** it

Use ***broken*** with have, has or had. Use ***broke*** alone:

he ***broke***	they had ***broken***
we ***broke***	she has ***broken***

See also **past participle • past tenses**

brought or *bought*?

See ***bought*** *or* ***brought****?*

***browse, find** or **search**?*

These internet terms have slightly different meanings:
• ***browse*** means "to look through the main topics" and is similar to looking up a table of contents
• ***find*** means "to locate all instances of a word on the current web page"
• ***search*** means "to locate all instances of a word on a whole website or search engine"

See also **search field**

bullet [•]

A mark used when making lists. Each item starts with a bullet.

Shopping List
• ice cream
• batteries
• film for camera

bulletin board

A location on the internet where visitors can post information or comments on a particular topic.

***but** ending a sentence?*

In conversation people sometimes use ***but*** at the end of a sentence.

> We went to the beach on Sunday. It rained all day, ***but***.

IN FORMAL WRITING

Avoid using ***but*** at the end of a sentence:

> We went to the beach on Sunday. It rained all day, ***however***.
>
> We went to the beach on Sunday, ***but*** it rained all day.

See also **however** + *comma?*

***But** starting a sentence?*

You can use ***But*** to start a sentence where the sentence stands in opposition to more than one preceding sentence, or for dramatic effect:

> She pushed open the door and ran up the stairs. On the table was the ivory box. She lifted the lid. The money was still there. ***But*** the jewels were missing.

IN FORMAL WRITING

Use ***However,*** (***However*** + **comma**) to start a sentence:

> Dear Sir,
> Thank you for your letter inviting me to … I appreciate your kind offer. ***However,*** I regret that …

Here ***However*** means "On the other hand". Use a comma after ***However*** when it means this.

See also **however** + *comma?*

call for action

In an argument a call for action invites the reader to do something if he or she agrees with the argument. The ***call for action*** comes immediately after the argument's conclusion.

> ... In conclusion, electric trains are cleaner and safer than cars. ***For this reason everyone should use trains instead of cars.***

See also **persuasion**

camera angle

In both movie and still photography, the position from which a camera views the subject.

Camera angle can affect the viewer's attitude to a character or setting. A face viewed from below may seem more threatening, while a setting seen from overhead may give the viewer a sense of distance, serenity or control.

can or may?

- ***I can*** means "I am able to"
- ***I may*** means "I am allowed to"

> ***I can*** operate the computer, but ***I may*** not use it.

The same rule applies to ***could*** and ***might***, where they are the past forms of ***can*** and ***may***:

> As ***I could*** operate the computer, they told me that ***I might*** use it.

May is also a modal auxiliary that suggests possibility or doubt:

> Aliens ***may*** exist somewhere in our galaxy.

See also **modal auxiliary**

can't hardly or can hardly?

Hardly means "almost not at all" or "with difficulty". In English two negatives are thought to cancel each other out, forming a positive statement.

> I can't hardly move
> = I can't move with difficulty
> = I can move easily

This is presumably the opposite of what the speaker intended. In formal writing, write ***can hardly***:

> After the marathon yesterday I ***can hardly*** walk today.

For the same reason, instead of ***couldn't hardly***, write ***could hardly***:

> Her little brother ***could hardly*** reach the shelf.

See also **double negative**

capital letter

(Also called ***capital***, ***block letter*** or ***upper case letter***) A letter used to start a sentence or a proper name.

Next week **D**r **S**tein will leave for **M**t **E**rebus.

Sometimes **HEADINGS** and **LABELS** are written wholly in capital letters:

WARNING
Do not enter

See also **lower case** and **upper case**

caption

Words or sentences that accompany a visual text such as a photograph or diagram. The caption can be used to explain or describe parts of the graphic.

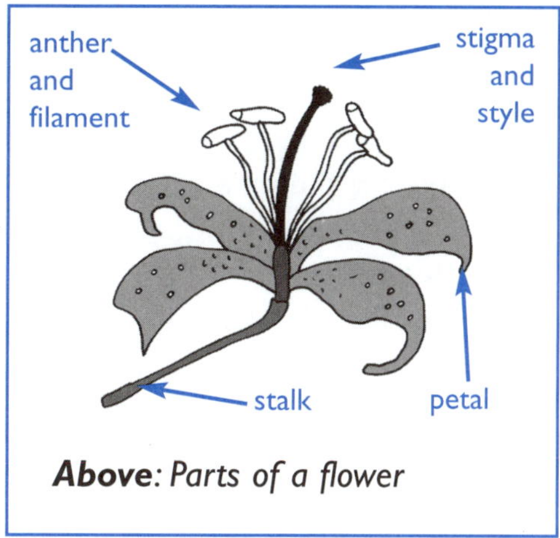

Above: *Parts of a flower*

The part of a caption that links it to the visual text is called the ***indicator***. Here the indicator is ***Above***.

See also **indicator**

cardinal

See **number adjective**

case

(1) The form of the alphabet letters, either UPPER CASE or lower case.

See **lower case** and **upper case**

(2) The function of a noun, pronoun or noun phrase. There are three main cases in English: ***nominative***, ***objective*** and ***possessive***.

Nominative case

The case of the ***subject***, usually

the first part of a sentence, the part that "does" the action of the verb:

My bike hit the tree.

Objective case

The case of the ***direct object***, the noun, pronoun or noun phrase that is affected by the action of the verb:

My bike hit ***the tree***.

Possessive case

The case of a ***noun*** or ***pronoun*** that owns something:

Maria's bike hit the tree.
My bike hit the tree.

Other cases

Other cases include the ***vocative*** case, where a person or thing is addressed:

Maria, could I borrow your bike?

See also **lower case** and **upper case** • **objective case** • **possessive case** • **subject** (of a sentence) • **vocative**

causal conjunction

IN FUNCTIONAL GRAMMAR

A form of sentence cohesion in which a cause is linked to its effect, or a reason to its conclusion. Used especially in explanations and arguments.

We have no money ***so*** we can't catch the bus. ***If*** we had thought of it earlier ***then*** we could have asked Kim for some. ***Because*** we can't afford the bus we will have to walk. ***For this reason*** we will be late. ***Consequently*** the others will miss us and ***as a result*** they may go to the game without us.

See also **cohesion**

cell (in a table)

A rectangular "box" in a table. The contents of a cell belong to the column heading above it *and* the row heading alongside it. In this table the cell ***pink*** belongs to the column heading ***Mars*** and the row heading ***sky***.

	Earth	***Mars***
Moons	1	2
Sky	blue	***pink***
Life	✓	?

We can read a table by putting these elements (cell + headings) together in a sentence:

On ***Mars*** the ***sky*** is ***pink***.

See also **column** (in a table) • **row** (in a table) • **table**

centred text

See **alignment** (of text)

centre on or centre around?

• ***centre on*** is preferred where you mean "has its centre at"

Hitler's air raids were ***centred on*** London.

chain

(Also called a ***word chain***)

IN FUNCTIONAL GRAMMAR

A series of words or phrases in a text that have related meanings and give ***lexical cohesion*** to a text. There are several kinds of chain.

Repeated words

Repeated words help to connect (or give ***cohesion*** to) the text:

Igneous ***rocks*** can be volcanic or *plutonic*. Volcanic ***rocks*** form at the surface, whereas *plutonic* ***rocks*** originate deep in the Earth.

Synonyms and antonyms

Words with the same meaning are synonyms. Words with opposite meanings are antonyms.

In the next sentence ***form*** is a synonym for ***originate***, while *plutonic* is the antonym of *volcanic*:

Volcanic rocks ***form*** at the surface, whereas *plutonic* rocks ***originate*** deep in the Earth.

Hyponyms

The name of something that belongs in a group is a hyponym of that group: "cat" and "dog" are hyponyms of "animal".

In the next sentence *volcanic* and *plutonic* are hyponyms of ***igneous***:

Igneous rocks can be *volcanic* or *plutonic*.

Meronyms

The name of a part: "tail" and "paw" are meronyms of "cat".

In the next sentence *crater* and *vents* are meronyms of ***volcano***:

A ***volcano*** usually has a *crater* and one or more *vents*.

See *also* **cohesion**

character

(1) A person in a narrative such as a novel or a movie.

Harry is my favourite ***character***.

(2) A letter of the alphabet.

The option key changes the ***character*** X to the symbol ≈.

See *also* **narrative**

chart

A general term covering a number of different visual texts, chiefly graphs and tables.

See **graph** • **table**

chronological report

See **factual recount**

circumstance

(1) The context in which something happens.

(2) *IN FUNCTIONAL GRAMMAR*
One of the three main parts of a sentence:
- ***participant***: refers to a *thing*
- ***process***: refers to *what happens*
- ***circumstance***: refers to the *context* in which things happen (usually a time or place)

Participant	*Process*	*Circumstance*
Fossils	are found	***in rocks.***

Circumstance	*Participant*	*Process*
In 1851	gold	was discovered.

Process	*Participant*	*Circumstance*
Pour	the cement	***before it sets.***

circumstances: *in* or *under*?

Both ***in the circumstances*** and ***under the circumstances*** are accepted and they mean the same thing.

> She had measles and ***under the circumstances*** she stayed home.
> = She had measles and ***in the circumstances*** she stayed home.

classifier

A noun or adjective that classifies the noun that follows it. To classify something is to describe the *kind* of thing it is, or the *group* it belongs to.

> a ***meat-eating*** dinosaur
> some ***raspberry*** yogurt
> a ***2MB high-density floppy*** disk

A classifier is a kind of ***pre-modifier***.

See *also* **pre-modifier**

clause

A part of a sentence that includes a verb. A clause is usually identified as:
- a ***main*** clause, a ***subordinate*** clause or a ***coordinate*** clause
- a ***finite*** clause or a ***non-finite*** clause

Main clause

(Also called a ***principal clause***)
A clause that can make sense by itself:

> ***The Nile***, which flows through several countries, ***is the world's longest river***.

Subordinate clause

(Also called a ***dependent clause***) This kind of clause depends on another clause in the same sentence, and does not make complete sense alone:

> The Nile, ***which flows through several countries***, is the world's longest river.

Coordinate clauses

(Also called ***parallel clauses***) Clauses that are of equal importance, neither being subordinate to the other. The following sentences contain only coordinate clauses, and they are joined by ***conjunctions***:

> He swam ashore ***and*** so did they.
>
> She went ***but*** I stayed home.
>
> Add the milk, ***then*** heat it gently.
>
> ***Either*** he goes ***or*** I do.
>
> ***Not only*** do they speak French ***but*** they speak Chinese ***as well***.

Finite clause

A finite clause includes a ***finite verb*** (a verb that has tense, such as past or present tense):

> Arriving in 1980, ***they lived with relatives*** already settled here.

Non-finite clause

A non-finite clause has no finite verb, but may have a ***non-finite verb*** (ending in ***-ing***, ***-ed*** or ***-en***). A ***non-finite verb*** has no tense, number or person:

> ***Arriving in 1980***, they lived with relatives ***already settled here***.

Verbs ending in ***-ing*** or ***-ed*** are also called ***participles***, so a non-finite clause is sometimes called a ***participial clause***.

See also **conjunction • number • participial clause • person • tense**

---

clause complex

IN FUNCTIONAL GRAMMAR

A combination of clauses that make up a sentence.

> She opened the envelope | which was addressed to her | but there was nothing inside.

The clauses in this sentence are separated by a blue line (|).

See also **clause**

---

cliché

A phrase that has been used many times before.

> ***Slowly but surely*** he dragged the boat ***high and dry*** above the stream. Finally, ***sick as a dog***, he walked home ***sadder but wiser***.

C

climax

See **crisis** (in a narrative)

clipping

See **abbreviation**

closed question

See **question**

close-up shot

In film and TV a frame which shows a close or detailed view of the subject. For example, a close-up of a person might show only her/his face.

See also **two-shot • wide shot**

cloths or *clothes*?

- ***cloths*** are fabrics
- ***clothes*** are what you wear

> We polished the windows with some clean ***cloths***.
> None of his ***clothes*** fit him.

cohesion

Cohesion includes all the grammatical connections between parts of a text. There are several kinds of cohesion.

Reference

Reference pronouns can be used to refer forward or backward to nouns in the text.

Backward reference

In the following sentence the ***pronoun*** directs us back to the underlined noun:

> The boys said ***they*** would stay.

Forward reference

In the next sentence the ***pronoun*** directs us forward to the underlined noun phrase:

> Once ***it*** melts the ice on our path is very dangerous.

Ellipsis and substitution

Ellipsis is the omission of words. ***Substitution*** is adding new words in their place. Often these devices are used in persuasive texts to convey attitude:

> What are banks for? ***Making money***. Do they care? **No**.

In the ellipsis ***Making money*** some words were omitted: Banks are for ***making money***.

The word **No** is a substitution for They do not care.

Lexical cohesion

Repeated words (***repetition***), words that mean the same thing (***synonyms***) or words that have opposite meanings (***antonyms***) can form ***chains*** that connect ideas in the text. Lexical cohesion can also be formed with examples of a topic (***hyponyms***) and parts of a topic (***meronyms***). All are illustrated in this passage about rainforests:

> Tropical rainforests include lowland and montane forests. Lowland forests have the tallest trees, whereas montane rainforests (sometimes called cloud forests) have many ferns but few if any trees. Lowland forests have three layers: canopy, understorey and the forest floor.

In this information report about rainforests we can find:

- ***repetition***: repeated use of the words *rainforest* and *forest*
- ***synonyms***: *montane forest* means the same as *cloud forest*
- ***antonyms***: *many* is the opposite of *few*
- ***hyponyms***: *lowland forest* and *montane forest* are included within the more general term *tropical rainforest*
- ***meronyms***: *canopy, understorey and forest floor* are all parts of a *lowland forest*

Conjunction
Joining of clauses or sentences in any of the following ways:

Additive conjunction
We're having fish ***and*** so are they.

Adversative conjunction
Frogs have lungs ***but*** tadpoles have gills.

Causal conjunction
It rained all day ***so*** the game was cancelled.

Temporal conjunction
There were few mammals ***when*** the dinosaurs became extinct.

See *also* **additive conjunction** • **adversative conjunction** • **chain** • **causal conjunction** • **ellipsis** and **substitution** • **temporal conjunction**

collective noun

A noun that refers to a group of individuals.

> The ***crowd*** rushed ahead.
> We accept the ***majority's*** decision.

Collective nouns are usually singular as they refer to *one group* of individuals. They usually have a singular verb:

> Our ***family*** comes from Vietnam.

However, if you are thinking of the individuals in the group, use a plural verb and *plural pronouns*:

> Our ***team*** keep losing *their* uniforms.

You could also write:

> Members of our team keep losing *their* uniforms.

collocation

IN FUNCTIONAL GRAMMAR

A group of words that usually go together. There are two kinds: ***grammatical*** and ***lexical***.

Grammatical collocation

A construction in which one word must follow another to make sense:

Don't be ***afraid of*** spiders.
NOT Don't be ***afraid*** spiders.

Lexical collocation

Any familiar pairing of words:

We never use ***knives and forks*** when we have ***fish and chips***.

colloquialism

Informal language. Often but not only used in conversation.

Colloquial
I grabbed a bunch of CDs off the the shelf.

Formal
I took some CDs from the shelf.

colon [:]

A punctuation mark joining two parts of a sentence where the first part leads to the second.

Sharks are fish**:** they have gills.
Hurry up**:** the boat is sinking.

You can also use a colon to introduce an example or a list:

You will need**:**
3 eggs
1 cup of milk
2 cups of flour

In some play scripts a colon follows the name of a speaker:

1ST PRISONER**:** Where are you?
2ND PRISONER *(whispering)***:** Here!

colour coding

The use of colour in a map, graph or diagram to stand for something. Sometimes a key is provided to explain the meaning of the different colours.

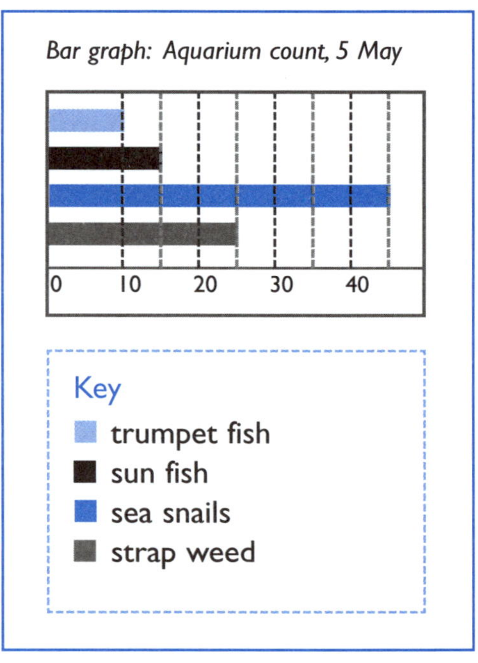

column graph

A graph that arranges items to be compared along the foot of the graph and the amount of each item down the side. Each item is shown as a "column".

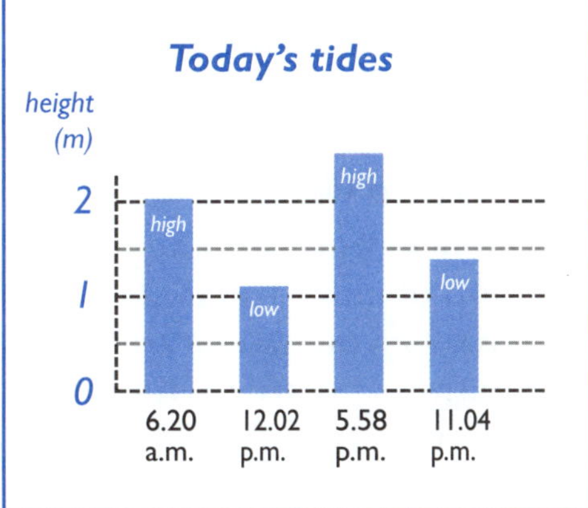

Column graphs are often used to illustrate explanations or factual recounts.

See also **explanation • factual recount • graph**

column (in a table)

Part of a table that is read from the top down. All cells in a column belong to the ***COLUMN HEADING***.

	REPTILES	*BIRDS*
Legs	4	**2**
Covering	scales	***feathers***
Warm blood	✗	✓

See also **cell** (in a table) • **row** (in a table) • **table**

comma [,]

A punctuation mark used to link or separate a series of words or clauses.

Commas linking words

In North America commas are used with ***and*** or ***or***. Elsewhere the comma just before ***and*** or ***or*** is omitted:

American and Canadian style:

> Paper, glass bottles, steel cans, and some plastic bottles can be recycled. Collect them in boxes, bins, or bags.

Australian style:

> Paper, glass bottles, steel cans and some plastic bottles can be recycled. Collect them in boxes, bins or bags.

Commas separating clauses

Use commas to separate long clauses, in order to help the reader follow your sentence:

> Perhaps the most well-known of all clouds are cumulus clouds, which have a flat base and "cauliflower" domes.

Commas used instead of brackets

Commas can also be used to enclose a parenthesis (words that

☞

interrupt the flow of a sentence) instead of brackets. Use a comma at each end of the parenthesis, just like brackets:

> Cumulus clouds, which have a flat base and "cauliflower" domes, are perhaps the most well known.

If the parenthesis is short, *both* the commas are omitted:

> Cirrus clouds or "mare's tails" bring no rain.

See *also* **comma** *or* **full stop?**

comma *or* full stop?

- ***commas*** separate clauses
- ***full stops*** separate sentences

IN FORMAL WRITING

Use a full stop and a new sentence for each new idea:

> The caterpillars hatch from eggs. They start to eat leaves. After a few weeks they make cocoons. Finally a moth emerges from the cocoon.

IN FORMAL WRITING

Use commas only where clauses have been connected with a conjunction:

> As soon as the caterpillars hatch, they start to eat leaves. After a few weeks they make cocoons, from which a moth emerges.

Commas are sometimes used instead of full stops to convey excitement or fast-moving events:

> He hit the brakes, I heard the tyres squeal, the car skidded, it hit the barrier, then suddenly …

See *also* **comma • full stop**

command

A sentence which has the function of an instruction or an order. Most commands are imperatives and are used when writing procedures.

Imperative command

This kind of command starts with the verb and its subject (you) is omitted:

> ***Attach*** the wire to the battery.

This kind of sentence is also called an ***imperative***, and its verb is said to be "in the imperative mood".

More urgent commands (usually spoken) take an exclamation mark:

> ***Shut*** the door***!***
> ***Look out!***

Question command

These commands look like questions but their function is to give an instruction. They are usually spoken:

Could you shut the door please***?***

Statement-command
These commands look like statements but they are really instructions:

Passengers ***will remain*** seated.

See *also* **direct** and **indirect questions** and **commands** • **mood** (of a verb) • **sentence**

common noun

The name of anything that is *not* a particular person or thing.

Most ***frogs*** live in ***water*** but some are found in ***trees*** or below the ***sand*** of the ***desert***.

Common nouns do not start with a capital letter unless they begin a sentence:

Bats that fly at night, such as vampire ***bats***, have radar.

The names of particular people or things are proper nouns. The following sentence includes ***common nouns*** and proper nouns:

My ***sister*** Alison arrived on a ***plane*** from Sydney.

See *also* **proper noun**

comparative degree

See **degree**

comparison

A sentence in which one thing is compared with another.

Your dog is ***the same as*** ours.
Frogs are ***different from*** toads.
Emus run ***faster than*** we can.
She is ***more*** talented ***than*** …
These are ***less*** expensive ***than*** …

See *also* **degree** • ***different from, to*** *or* ***than?*** • ***than me*** *or* ***than I?***

compass rose

A mark on a map used to show the direction of north and often the other compass points: east, west and south. Used when interpreting relationships and journeys on a map.

Sendai ***is north of*** *Tokyo.*

complement

Part of a sentence that follows a verb describing a relationship, such as the verb *to be*. A complement can be a **word**, phrase or **clause**.

That's ***him***.
He is *the new football coach*.
The fact is ***we don't know his name***.

See *also* **object** (of a sentence)

complement or *compliment*?

- ***to complement*** means "to complete"
- ***to compliment*** means "to praise"

He was ***complimented*** on how the frame ***complemented*** the photograph.

complex preposition

See **preposition**

complex sentence

See **sentence**

complex verb

A verb phrase made up of more than one verb.

I ***might have lost*** my keys.
We ***will have wasted*** our time.
I ***am trying to remain*** calm.

A complex verb is *not* the same as a compound verb.

See *also* **compound verb**

complication (in a narrative)

Part of the storyline of a narrative in which a new element occurs that leads to a crisis.

When the Friar's message does not reach Romeo [*complication*], he decides to take poison [*crisis*].

See *also* **crisis** • **narrative**

compliment or *complement*?

See ***complement*** *or* ***compliment***?

compound sentence

See **sentence**

compound verb

A verb phrase made up of a **verb** and a particle.

You can ***look*** up the answers.
Can I ***try*** on that jacket?
Look out! You'll get ***run*** over!

A compound verb is *not* the same as a complex verb.

See *also* **complex verb • particle**

compound word

A word made of two other words.

download = down + load
handlebar = handle + bar
backup = back + up

See *also* **portmanteau word**

concept map

See **web diagram**

conclusion (in an argument or a discussion)

A statement that follows logically from the reasons preceding it in an argument (a form of ***persuasion***) or in a ***discussion***.

Save our rainforest plants!
Some rainforest plants are rare or endangered. Some have not even been named or discovered yet. Many of these plants may contain new medicines and they may have economic value. ***Therefore we should protect these plants.***

See *also* **discussion • persuasion**

concrete noun

The name of something you can normally see or touch.

The ***rain*** that falls from the ***clouds*** fills the ***lakes***.

A ***concrete*** noun is the opposite of an abstract noun. Words like anger and fear are abstract nouns because they are the names of things you cannot see or touch:

The ***girls*** felt anger but not fear.

See *also* **abstract noun**

conjunction

(1) ***IN FUNCTIONAL GRAMMAR***
A form of cohesion.
See **causal conjunction • cohesion**

(2) ***IN TRADITIONAL GRAMMAR***
(Also called a ***connective***) A word used to join two words, phrases or clauses. There are two main kinds of conjunction: ***coordinating*** and ***subordinating***.

Coordinating conjunction

These conjunctions join two equal units (words, phrases or coordinate clauses):

He remained angry ***but*** silent.
We came by bus ***or*** on foot.
Scroll down ***and*** click "Search".

☞

Subordinating conjunction

These conjunctions join a main clause to a subordinate clause:

I'm the one ***who*** found your dog.
Click "save" ***before*** you close.

See also **clause • paired conjunction • phrase**

connective

See **conjunction** (2)

consonant

See **vowel** and **consonant**

contents page

See **table of contents**

context

See **text and context**

continual *or* continuous?

• ***continual*** means "repeated many times"
• ***continuous*** means "going on without a break"

Her sleep was ***continually*** interrupted by phone calls.
All day we heard the ***continuous*** sound of the rain.

continuous tenses

(Also called ***progressive tenses***)
Verb tenses that indicate that the action continues for a period of time. Continuous tenses are formed using the verb ***to be*** + ***-ing***. These tenses can be present, past or future.

Present continuous tense

Indicates an event that is continuing now:

He ***is eating*** a pizza.

Past continuous tense

Indicates an event that was continuing in the past:

He ***was eating*** a pizza.

Future continuous tense

Indicates an event that will be continuing in the future:

He ***will be eating*** a pizza.

See also **tense** (of a verb)

contraction

A shortened form of a word or phrase, usually replacing some letters with an apostrophe (**’**).

isn’t = is not
he’ll = he will
she’d = she had *or* she would
they’re = they are

Double contractions are often

heard in direct speech:

couldn't've = could not have

See *also* **abbreviation** • **apostrophe** • ***could have, could've*** *or* ***could of?*** • **direct** and **indirect speech**

cooperate, coöperate or *co-operate?*

These are three spellings of the same word. All are accepted. The spellings ***coöp-*** and ***co-op-*** are designed to avoid mispronouncing the first two syllables. The ***dieresis*** (¨) can be used to separate vowels.

See *also* **dieresis [¨]** • ***no-one*** *or* ***no one?***

coordinate clauses

(Also called ***parallel clauses***) Two or more clauses in the same sentence that are of equal importance.

Either he goes ***or*** I do.

These clauses are joined by one of the ***coordinate conjunctions***:

and	***either ... or***
but	***neither ... nor***

See *also* **clause**

coordinate conjunction

See **coordinate clause**

coordinates (in maps)

Letters and numbers that can be combined to indicate a place on a map. The coordinates are written along the sides of the map. Grid lines show the area that is named by each pair of coordinates.

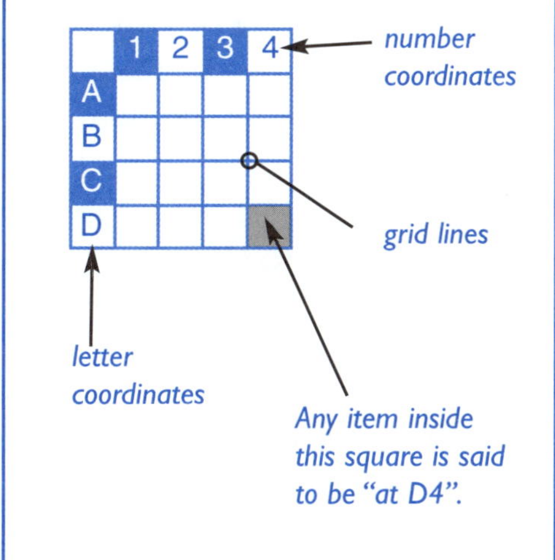

See *also* **grid lines**

coordination

Linking of any two equal parts of a sentence, using ***or***, ***and*** or ***but***.

See *also* **conjunction** • **coordinate clause**

C

could have, could've or could of?

• ***could have*** is the form used in formal writing
• ***could've*** means "could have" in direct (quoted) speech
• ***could of*** makes no sense; it is a mistaken hearing of ***could've***

Birds ***could have*** evolved from dinosaurs.

"I ***could've*** helped him!" she said.

The same applies to these forms:

would have or ***would've***
should have or ***should've***
NOT ***would of*** or ***should of***

could or might?

See **can** or **may**?

couldn't hardly?

See **can't hardly** or **can hardly**?

countable

See **count noun** and **mass noun**

count noun and mass noun

Nouns can be grouped into either ***count nouns*** or ***mass nouns***, depending on whether they can take a plural form.

Count noun

(Also called ***countable***) A count noun is one that refers to something that *can* be counted. They can be either ***singular*** or plural:

Put this ***cup*** with the other cups.

Mass noun

A mass noun *cannot* take a plural form. Mass nouns are the names of things that can sometimes be measured but *cannot* be counted. Examples include milk and pain.

The following sentences include ***count nouns*** and mass nouns:

The ***people*** in our ***town*** have too much leisure and not enough happiness.

NOT

too many leisures and not enough happinesses.

Some words are used in both ways:

As a count noun
There have been too many ***wars***.

As a mass noun
War is hell.

crisis (in a narrative)

(Also called a ***climax***) Part of a narrative in which complications need to be resolved.

Complications

... Romeo believes that Juliet is dead and the Friar's message, explaining that Juliet is really alive, does not reach Romeo.

Crisis

Romeo decides to take poison. When Juliet finds Romeo dead she stabs herself.

Resolution

On hearing of their deaths and recognising that their families' rivalry has led to this crisis, the Montagues and Capulets are reconciled.

See also **narrative**

---

criterion *or* ***criteria?***

These are two forms of the same word, which means "a standard by which things may be judged".

- ***criterion*** is the singular form
- ***criteria*** is the plural form

"Honesty is the only ***criterion*** by which politicians should be judged."

"I disagree. Other ***criteria*** should be considered, such as loyalty and integrity."

See also **plural nouns**

---

critical literacy

The ability to analyse the ways in which a text has been presented, revealing the writer's attitudes and purposes. Critical literacy can be applied to any text, such as books, the media, websites, advertising, performance or environmental print.

Some of the questions that can be asked when looking at a text in this way are:

Who wrote (or made) the text?
What is the writer's purpose?
Who is the audience (or market)?
How does the text try to influence the reader or viewer?
Do I agree or disagree with the author?

---

cross-reference

A part of a text that refers the reader to another part of the same text or to a different text.

The world's deepest lake is in Russia ***(see* Lake Baikal*)***. Lakes are sometimes confused with inland seas.
***See also* Inland seas**

In electronic texts, such as websites or CD-ROM encyclopaedias, a cross-reference often takes the form of an underlined blue hyperlink.

See also **hyperlink**

cross-section

A diagram that shows its subject as if "cut in half". Cross-sections name parts that are normally hidden, and show relationships between them. Used to illustrate reports and explanations.

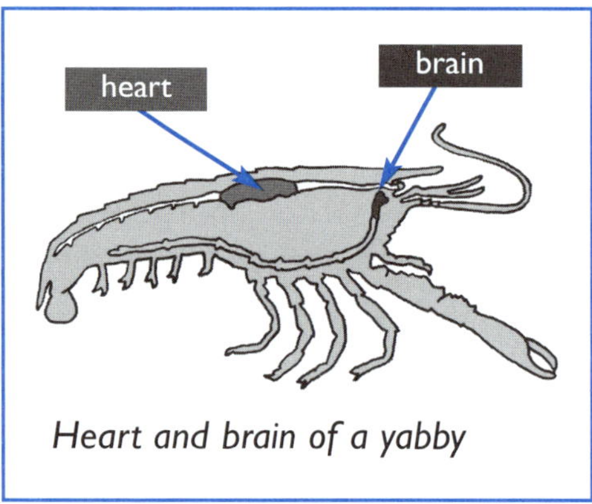

Heart and brain of a yabby

cutaway diagram

A diagram in which part of the surface of the subject is "peeled away" to reveal hidden details.

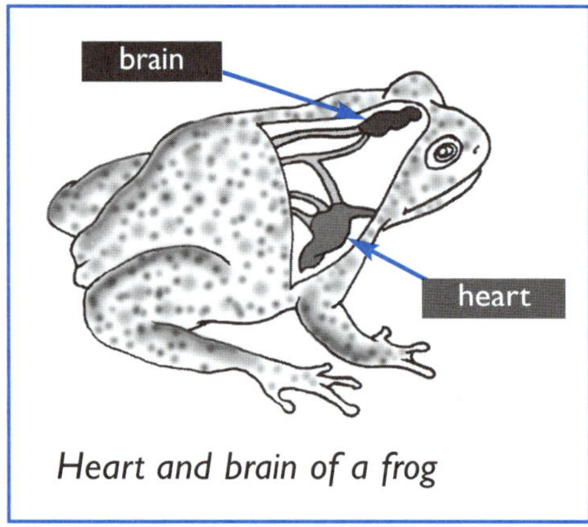

Heart and brain of a frog

See also **cross-section**

cut or *fade*?

These words are used in audio (radio, music) and video (film, TV to indicate how one sound or image is changed to the next.

Cut

A ***cut*** is a sudden change in sound or vision. Originally the tape or film was cut and joined, but the concept also applies to digital production. A ***jump cut*** is caused by removing frames from a scene to give the illusion of people or objects suddenly changing position.

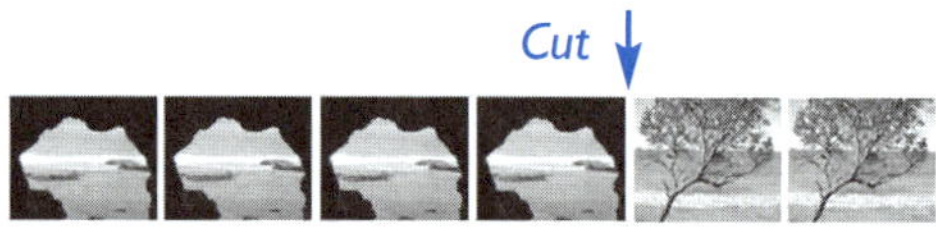

Fade

A ***fade*** is a gradual change in sound or vision. A scene may open with a ***fade-in*** or close with a ***fade-out***. These two effects may overlap to create a merging of scenes or ***cross-fade***.

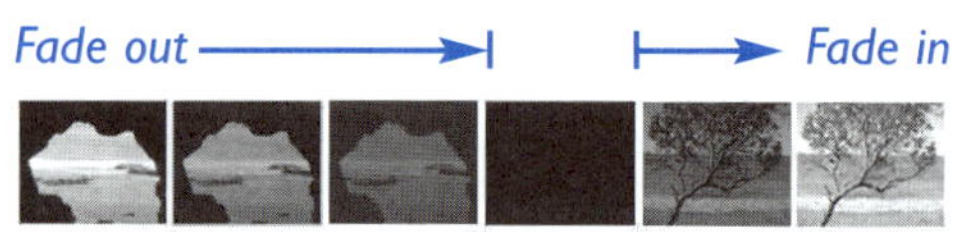

Movies often end with a ***fade to black***.

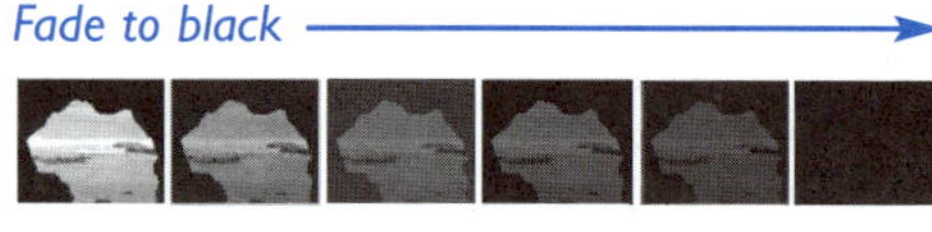

dangling participle

A participle is a verb ending in ***-ing***, ***-ed*** or ***-en***. Participles sometimes refer to a noun (or pronoun or noun phrase) that comes after it.

> ***Looking up,*** my sister saw me.
> ***Frightened,*** he started to run.

A ***dangling participle*** *seems* to refer to the noun or phrase that follows it, but really it refers to something else:

> Kim walked out the door.
> ***Looking up,*** the sun was directly overhead.

Looking up in this sentence is a dangling participle because it is "left hanging"— it is not attached to the following noun sun. (The sun is not looking up.) Instead, ***Looking up*** really belongs with *Kim*. The sentences could be rewritten:

> *Kim* walked out the door.
> ***Looking up,*** she saw the sun was directly overhead.

In the next sentence ***Frightened*** is called a dangling participle because it *seems* to be attached to the words the runaway train. It really belongs with *him*:

> ***Frightened,*** the runaway train was heading straight towards *him*.

The sentence could be rewritten:

> ***Frightened,*** he realised that the runaway train was heading straight towards *him*.

See also **participle**

dash [—]

A punctuation mark that can indicate a break in the sentence, an omission or a parenthesis.

Dash indicating a break

A dash can indicate that the sentence is interrupted. It is often used in quoted speech:

> "I have a message for—"
> "What did he say? I can't—"
> "—for your leader. You must—"

Dash indicating an omission

A dash can show that something has been left out:

> The next witness, Mr M—, entered the box. The judge quietly addressed Mr M—.

Dash indicating a parenthesis

A dash can also indicate words that interrupt the flow of the sentence, often to explain something. They work like brackets:

> The carnosaurs—or meat-eating dinosaurs—include *Allosaurus*.

This kind of dash is *not* used in front of a full stop:

☞

Allosaurus was a carnosaur
—or meat-eating dinosaur.

NOT *Allosaurus* was a carnosaur
—or meat-eating dinosaur—.

See *also* **hyphen**

declarative mood

See **mood** (and residue) • **mood** (of a verb)

definite article

See **article**

degree

Gradable adjectives and adverbs can take three degrees: ***positive***, ***comparative*** and ***superlative***.

Positive degree

The usual form of an ***adjective*** or adverb is its positive form:

a ***fast*** car
a ***complicated*** sentence
he walked slowly

Comparative degree

This form includes **-er** or ***more ...*** and indicates a higher degree (more of something, or a greater amount):

a ***faster*** car
a ***more complicated*** sentence
he walked more slowly than us

Superlative degree

The superlative form includes ***the ... -est*** or ***the most ...*** and indicates the highest degree (the most or the greatest amount):

the fastest car
the most complicated sentence
he walked the most slowly of all

See *also* **gradable** and **non-gradable**

demonstrative adjective

Any of the words ***this***, ***that***, ***these*** or ***those*** when followed by a *noun* or noun phrase.

I bought ***this*** *book*.
She painted ***that*** old green door.
Do you want ***these*** *shoes*?
We saw ***those*** hot-air balloons.

Demonstrative adjectives are also called ***identifying determiners***.

See *also* **demonstrative pronoun** • **determiner**

demonstrative pronoun

Any of the words ***this***, ***that***, ***these*** or ***those*** when used instead of a noun or noun phrase.

I bought ***this***.
She painted ***that***.

Do you want ***these***?
We saw ***those***.

See *also* **demonstrative adjective**

dénouement

See **resolution** (in a narrative)

dependant clause

See **clause**

description

IN FUNCTIONAL GRAMMAR

A kind of text in which the subject is described in detail. A description is similar to an information report, but does not classify a topic into groups as a report does.

A description usually has:

- a ***main statement*** that names the topic and gives it a context
- a series of ***descriptive facts***, often in no particular order

The Empire State Building

Main statement

The Empire State Building was the tallest skyscraper in the world when it was completed in 1931.

Descriptive facts

The building has 102 floors and 1860 steps from the street to the top floor. Its water pipes extend over 100 kilometres and there are more than 600 kilometres of power cables. When the building was completed, few people wanted to rent office space, so it became known as the Empty State Building.

A description can be planned using a word wheel.

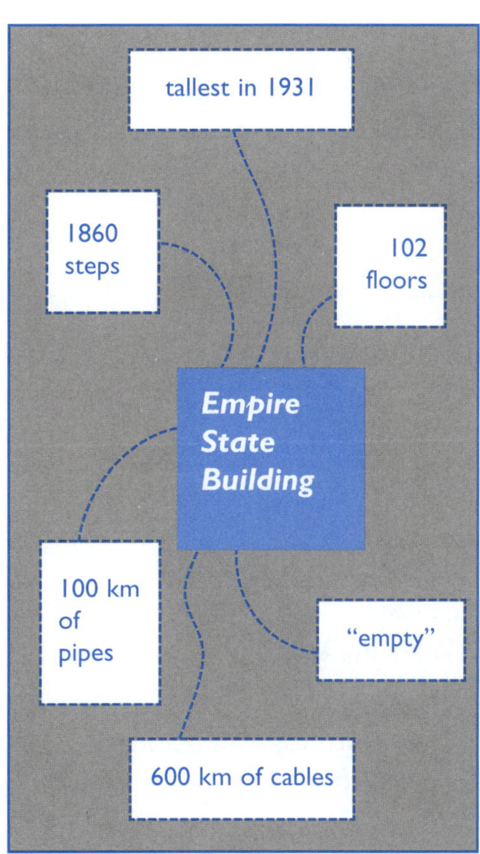

See *also* **diagram • information report • word wheel**

D

descriptive adjective
See **adjective**

desert or *dessert?*
• ***desert*** (with the stress on the first syllable) means "arid land"
• ***deserts*** (with the stress on the second syllable) means "reward"
• ***dessert*** means "sweet course at the end of a meal"

Most of Australia is ***desert***.
He got his ***just deserts***.
There's ice cream for ***dessert***.

design (of a text)
See **graphic design**

determiner
A word that precedes a noun and limits its meaning. Determiners can query or identify a participant, or they can show ownership.

Querying
Whose bike will you borrow?

Identifying
The white caravan belongs to us.
I'd like ***that*** pizza.

Showing ownership
Our cat climbed up ***their*** tree.

See also **adjective • article • personal pronoun**

diaeresis
See **dieresis [¨]**

diagonal
See **slash [/]**

diagram
A graphic in which parts of the subject are labelled with their names or brief explanations. Diagrams simplify (or leave out) some details and they make generalisations about the subject.

Parts of a saxophone

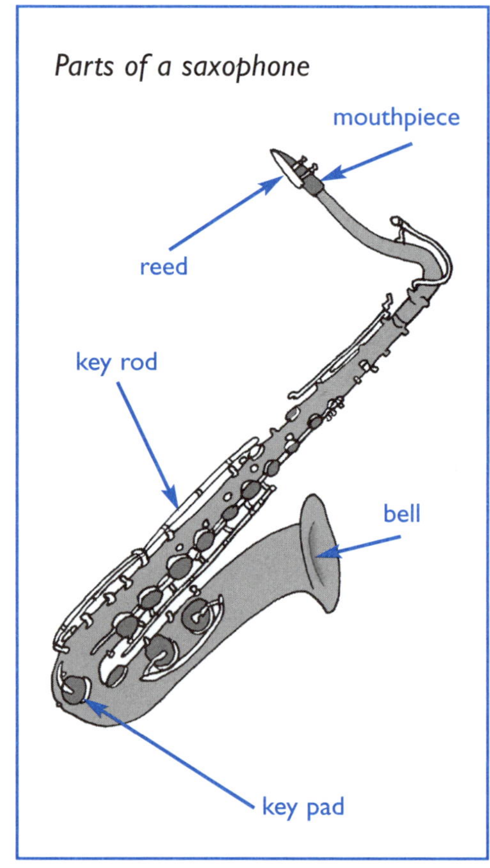

Often the function of a diagram is similar to a glossary. Diagrams:

• *name* parts of a subject

• *define* the meanings of those names by showing what the named parts look like and where they belong

In the diagram of the saxophone the label *mouthpiece* names a part of the diagram and the graphic defines the meaning of the word "key pad".

Diagrams are often used to illustrate information reports, descriptions and explanations.

See also **picture glossary**

diary entry

A kind of ***personal recount***. A text in which recent personal experiences are recorded, with comments, and the date. Words are sometimes shortened and sentences often omit "I".

> *Sunday, 4th March.*
> Stayed o/night @ M's. Went walking on the beach & found some shells. Wish I cd stay another week here.

See also **personal recount**

did or *done?*

• ***did*** is the past tense of "do": I ***did*** it

• ***done*** is the past participle of "do": I ***have done*** it

Use **done** with *have*, *has* or *had*. Use **did** alone:

> He ***did*** everything.
>
> We have ***done*** all we could.

dieresis [¨]

A mark that indicates that two adjacent vowels are pronounced separately.

> naïve is pronounced
> *ny-eve*, ***not*** *nave*

Also spelled ***diaeresis***. Both spellings are accepted.

See also **cooperate, coöperate** *or* **co-operate***?*

different from, different to or *different than?*

• ***different from*** is preferred to ***different to*** in formal writing; this agrees with the expression **to *differ from***

• ***different than*** is widely used in the USA

direct and **indirect questions** and **commands**

Question and commands are said to be either direct or indirect.

Direct question

A direct question is expressed in the form of ***direct speech*** and requires quotation marks (" ") and a question mark (**?**):

> "Where are they now**?"** she asked. I replied, **"**Don't you know**?"** and she said: **"**No! Can't you tell me**?"**

Use a comma (**,**) or colon (**:**) *before* a question:

> I replied**,** … she said**:** …

Use a question mark (and omit the comma) *after* a question:

> … now**?"** she asked

Indirect question

An indirect question is a form of ***indirect speech*** and is expressed without a question mark:

> He asked me what I was doing.
> I asked her if I could come.

Compare the following sentences which include **direct questions** and indirect questions:

> He asked me, ***"Who are you?"***
> He asked me who I was.
>
> ***"Can we stay?"*** she asked.
> She asked whether they could stay.

Direct and indirect commands

Direct and indirect commands follow the same principles as direct and indirect questions. Compare the following sentences which include ***direct commands*** and indirect commands:

> He shouted, ***"Go away!"***
> He ordered me to go away.
>
> ***"Come in!"*** she said.
> She told me to come in.

See also **command • direct** and **indirect speech • quotation marks**

---

direct and **indirect speech**

Direct and indirect speech are two ways of recording what someone said.

Direct speech

(Also called ***quoted speech***)
Direct speech records the speaker's exact words enclosed in quotation marks (" "). Use a comma (**,**) to separate quoted speech from the rest of the sentence:

> She said**,** ***"I've lost my dog."***
> ***"It's in that shop,"*** he replied.

Other punctuation marks (such as **. , ? !**) are placed inside the quotation marks *only if* they belong with what was actually said:

> ***"Sofia! Where are you?"*** her friend cried.

However, punctuation should show clearly who is asking the question in sentences like these:

> ***"Are you there?"*** she asked.
> Did you answer ***"yes"*** or ***"no"*** ?

A full stop at the end of direct speech is changed to a comma if it is followed by the *reporting verb*:

> Her friend *said*, ***"Go on ahead."***
> ***"Go on ahead,"*** her friend *said*.

This rule does *not* apply to other punctuation marks:

> ***"Where are the tickets?"*** I *asked*.
> ***"Stop!"*** she *shouted*.
> ***"What did you—"*** he *began*.

Indirect speech

(Also called ***reported speech***)
Indirect speech reports what was said by using a *reporting verb* followed by a subordinate clause. Quotation marks are not used:

> She *said* that she was lost.
> Her friend *told* us to go ahead and she would catch us up.
> She *asked* if anyone was there and we *replied* that we were.

See *also* **direct** and **indirect questions** and **commands** • **quotation marks**

direct object

See **object** (of a sentence)

disc or *disk*?

Both spellings are accepted. However, CD is usually written out as compact disc.

discussion

A kind of text in which two or more points of view are compared. The writer attempts to summarise each point of view without taking sides.

A discussion usually has:
- a ***statement of the topic***
- some ***background information***
- the ***arguments for and against*** with reasons, and expressed without taking sides
- a ***conclusion***, which could recommend one side over another, or offer a new position

> *Should we kill sharks?*

Statement of the topic

> Some people believe that the killing of sharks is cruel, while others say that sometimes it is necessary to kill them.

Background information

Millions of sharks are killed each year. Some are killed deliberately, but most are caught by accident in fishing nets.

Argument for

Sharks occasionally kill swimmers. When this happens there may be good safety reasons for killing the shark. If human life is threatened we would have good reason to kill the shark.

Argument against

Many sharks are caught and have their fins removed, as this is a popular food in some countries. Some people say that this is cruel because the sharks cannot swim without their fins, causing them to die slowly. After all, we don't need to eat sharks. There are plenty of other things that we can eat.

Conclusion

On balance it seems that sharks should not be killed in a cruel way for food. However, when sharks are a danger they should be caught if not actually killed.

A discussion is different from an argument (a form of ***persuasion***). In an argument the writer is usually committed to only one side of a dispute.

Persuasion (argument)

I think it is simply cruel.

Discussion

Some people say that it is cruel.

A discussion can be planned using a table, which can organise the arguments for and against:

Reasons for	*Reasons against*
Sometimes sharks kill people. For our own safety we may sometimes need to kill sharks.	Some sharks have their fins removed. This kills the shark slowly. This is cruel. We don't need to eat sharks. We can eat other food.

A Venn diagram can show where people in a discussion agree and disagree:

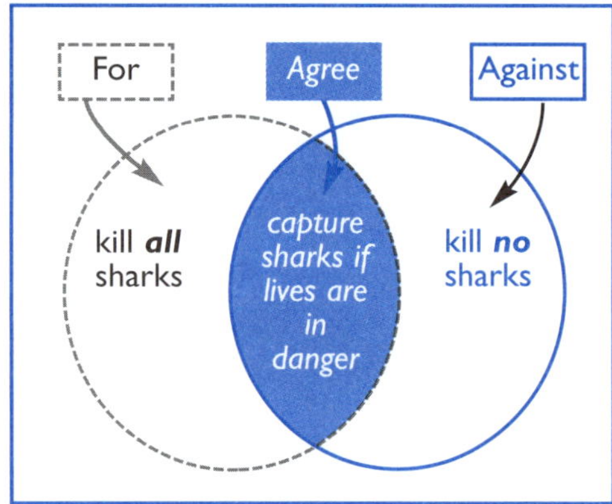

See also **persuasion • table • Venn diagram**

disinterested or *uninterested*?

- ***disinterested*** means "not taking sides"
- ***uninterested*** means "bored"

Their website had a ***disinterested*** discussion of global warming, but he was simply ***uninterested*** in the topic.

These two words come from two very different meanings of ***interested***:

- having an interest (or a stake) in something
- being engaged by something (finding it interesting)

disk or *disc*?

See ***disc*** or ***disk***?

distributive

A word that refers to the separate items in a group. The distributives are ***each***, ***every***, ***either***, ***neither*** and ***none***.

Distributives can be *adjectives* or *pronouns*.

Distributive adjective

These distributives are followed by a *noun* or noun phrase:

Put ***each*** *fork* next to a plate.
Every *flag* was blue.
Either *girl* can go, but not both.
Neither black dog wore a collar.

Distributive pronoun

Distributive pronouns stand in place of nouns:

Each was a different colour.
Either can go, but not both.
Neither can go.
None wore a collar.

See also ***both*** *or* ***each***? • ***each*** + ***is*** *or* ***are***? • ***everybody/everyone*** + ***is*** *or* ***are***?

documentary

A film or radio/TV program that is intended to present information on a topic, such as an event in history or a science subject.

Documentaries often adopt a recount or narrative structure and may also have a persuasive purpose as well. No documentaries are entirely objective.

See also **critical literacy • factual recount • narrative • persuasion**

dolly shot

See **tracking shot**

domain name

The name of a website. A domain name includes the top-level name and the ***second-level name***:

www. ***washingonline***.net.au

The top-level name includes an entity name (such as net) and sometimes a geographic name (such as au for Australia).

done or did?

See **did** or **done**?

double meaning

See **ambiguity**

double negative

A sentence which includes two negatives. In English two negatives cancel out each other.

I did ***not fail*** to finish the test.
= I did finish the test.

A double negative can also be used as a *lukewarm* positive:

I was ***not unhappy***.
= I was (fairly) happy.

Many double negatives are not intended by the speaker:

I ***don't*** know ***nothing***.
= I do know something.

IN FORMAL WRITING avoid this kind of double negative.

A double negative can also be used to avoid taking sides:

I ***don't deny*** it.
= I neither confirm nor deny it.

See also ***can't hardly*** or ***can hardly***?

download or upload?

• ***download*** means "to copy *to* a computer to an internet site"
• ***upload*** means "to copy *from* a computer to an internet site"

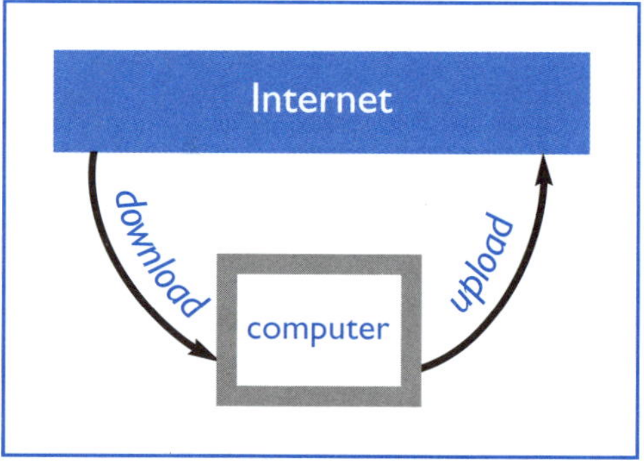

due to or owing to?

Both expressions can mean "because of" or "caused by" and both are now accepted.

I was late ***owing to*** a traffic jam.
= I was late ***due to*** a traffic jam.
= My lateness was ***due to*** a traffic jam.

each + ***is*** or ***are***?

Each, ***every***, ***either***, ***neither*** and ***none*** are distributives. A distributive refers to the separate items in a group. Each item is treated as a single thing, so ***each***, ***every***, ***either***, ***neither*** and ***none*** take a singular verb.

> ***Each*** of the answers is correct.
> ***Every*** box of apples was sold and ***none*** of them was broken.
> ***Either*** parent is welcome.
> We invited the twins. ***Neither*** was able to come.

Agreement of ***each***, ***every***, ***either***, ***neither*** and ***none*** with a "double" relative pronoun (such as he or she) is not so strict. To avoid a crowd of pronouns, some writers use the plural they instead:

> ***Every*** passenger had his or her ticket taken from him or her.
> ***Every*** passenger had their ticket taken from them.

You can also make the whole sentence plural:

> ***All the*** passengers had their tickets taken from them.

See also **agreement** • ***both*** *or* ***each***? • **distributive** • **everybody/everyone** + ***is*** *or* ***are***? • **gender** • ***he*** *or* ***she*** + ***they***?

each or ***both***?

See ***both*** *or* ***each***?

each other or ***one another***?

These two expressions can be treated as if they mean the same.

> The dancers faced ***each other***.
> The dancers faced ***one another***.

However, some people use these two expressions in different situations. They use:

- ***each other*** for *two* items
- ***one another*** for *more than two*

> The Earth and the Moon attract ***each other***.
> The Earth, the Moon and the Sun attract ***one another***.

ebook

(Also spelt ***eBook*** and ***e-book***)

> ***ebook*** = *electronic* ***book***

A computer device that displays pages of a book, which can be loaded as a software program.

A survey of the internet in 2002 found that spellings *without* the hyphen are preferred.

See also ***email*** *or* ***e-mail***?

effect

IN FUNCTIONAL GRAMMAR

The participant that is the result of the process in a sentence.

We lit ***a fire***.
Heat is produced by fire.

An effect is also the participant that is affected by a process:

The fire warmed ***us***.
We were warmed by the fire.

See *also* **participant • process**

effect or affect?

See ***affect*** *or* ***effect****?*

e.g. or i.e.?

- **e.g.** means "for example"
- ***i.e.*** means "that is"

Most mammals (**e.g.** wolves and foxes) have fur. However, one sea-going mammal (***i.e.*** the whale) appears not to have any fur.

The letters **e.g.** and ***i.e.*** stand for Latin words:

e.g. = **e***xempli* **g***ratia*
i.e. = ***i****d* **e***st*

Full stops can be used to show that **e.g.** and ***i.e.*** are abbreviations. However, no comma is needed:

e.g. wolves and foxes
NOT **e.g.,** wolves and foxes

either + is or are?

See ***each*** + ***is*** *or* ***are****?*

elder or older?

- ***elder*** means "older" but is generally used only with family members
- ***older*** does not have this limitation and can be used in place of ***elder***

She is his ***elder*** sister.
= She is his ***older*** sister.

He has an ***older*** computer.
NOT He has an ***elder*** computer.

The use of ***elder*** seems to be disappearing. Writers may prefer to use ***older*** in all situations, avoiding ***elder*** completely.

The same applies to ***eldest*** and ***oldest***:

He is the ***eldest*** son.
= He is the ***oldest*** son.

We have the ***oldest*** car.
NOT We have the ***eldest*** car.

electronic text

See **text**

ellipsis [...]

A punctuation mark used to indicate a silence, an interruption or an omission.

Indicating a silence

An ellipsis can indicate a silence or pause:

> I listened again **...** but there was no sound.

Indicating an interruption

In direct speech an ellipsis shows that the speaker did not finish the sentence:

"I tried to phone, but **...**"
"Where is the **...** ?"

Indicating an omission

In quoted writing an ellipsis shows that some words have been omitted:

Original sentence:

> Bats and dolphins both use echo-location to find their prey.

Quotation:

> "**...** dolphins **...** use echo-location to find their prey".

ellipsis and substitution

IN FUNCTIONAL GRAMMAR

Ellipsis is the omission of words that are "understood" by the reader or listener. ***Substitution*** is the adding of new words in their place. Both give cohesion to a text.

Ellipsis and substitution often occur in spoken texts:

> "Where's the TV program?"
> ***"On the table."***
> "Are you sure?"
> ***"Yes.*** I put it there."

In the ellipsis ***On the table*** some words were omitted:

> The TV program is ***on the table***.

The word ***Yes*** is a substitution for I am sure.

Ellipsis and substitution are sometimes used in persuasive texts for dramatic effect:

> Where is the Mayor? ***Overseas.***
> Will he listen to us? ***No***.

See also **cohesion**

email or *e-mail*?

Both spellings are accepted. A search of the internet in 2002 found 66 million examples of ***email*** and 43 million examples of ***e-mail***.

> ***email*** = electronic ***mail***

See also **ebook**

email shorthand

Email shorthand is part of the informality of email style, and in some cases speeds up keyboarding.

CU L8r
= see you later
meet U @ 6 4 10-S
= meet you at six for tennis

These shorthand expressions are used for the same reasons in mobile phone text messages.

Some visual symbols are email inventions:

smile ***:-)***
scowl ***8-(***
wink ***;-)***
cry ***(:,-<***
groan ***:-|***
aargh ***):-@***

See also **mobile shorthand**

embedded clause

A clause which is included in a noun group and which helps to define other words in the group.

That's the town ***where I was born***.
The fact ***that she lied*** amazed us.
The man ***you met*** is my dad.

Embedded clauses can be ***finite*** or ***non-finite*** clauses:

The house ***that was destroyed in the storm*** has since been rebuilt.
The house ***destroyed in the storm*** has since been rebuilt.

See also **clause • embedded phrase • noun group • projection**

embedded phrase

A phrase which is included in a noun group and which helps to define other words in the group.

Melissa is the girl ***with dark hair***.
That horse ***over there*** is hers.

See also **embedded clause • phrase • noun group • projection**

embedded projection

See **projection**

emigrate or *immigrate*?

- ***to emigrate*** means "to leave [a country]"
- ***to immigrate*** means "to enter [a country]"

They hope to ***emigrate*** from Canada and may ***immigrate*** to Australia.

emphatic pronoun

A pronoun which is used to give emphasis to a *noun* or pronoun in the same sentence.

The *driver* ***herself*** was unhurt.
They ***themselves*** were mistaken.

The emphatic pronouns look the same as the reflexive pronouns:

myself
yourself
herself, himself, itself, oneself
ourselves
yourselves
themselves

Their difference lies in their use. They are "emphatic" *only* when they emphasise other words. The following *reflexive pronouns* do not emphasise other words:

My dog has hurt *itself*.
We helped *ourselves*.

See *also* **personal pronoun** • **reflexive pronoun**

end matter

See **front matter** and **end matter**

enquire or inquire?

See ***inquire*** or ***enquire?***

ensure or insure?

See ***assure, ensure*** or ***insure?***

entity

IN FUNCTIONAL GRAMMAR

A participant that is part of an ***existential*** or ***relational*** process.

Existential process

An existential process asserts that an **entity** exists (or does not exist):

There are ***two kinds of mammal***.
There is no ***simple answer***.

Relational process

A relational process usually states what an **entity** is, has, belongs with or lacks. It identifies an entity's relationship with something else:

The shark's skin is very rough.
Sharks have ***a very rough skin***.
Dolphins are not ***a kind of fish***.
Dolphins belong with ***mammals*** and ***they*** lack ***scales*** and ***gills***.

See *also* **participant** • **process**

E

epithet

An adjective or phrase that describes the qualities of a nearby noun.

Store in a ***warm***, ***dry*** place.
On ***wet*** days the walls are ***damp***.

Epithets can also indicate the writer's attitude:

a ***cool*** game ... a ***boring*** movie
The exam was too ***hard***.

See *also* **pre-modifier**

-er or -re?

See **-re** or **-er**?

et cetera, etc. or &c.?

All of these expressions mean "and the others". They are used when the writer wishes to indicate that many other examples are possible.

Browser toolbars include icons for actions such as refresh, stop, print, search, **etc.**

Generally **etc.** is more widely used than ***et cetera*** or **&c**.

Some writers also use **etc.** to mean "and so on":

Every day I get up, get dressed, have breakfast, **etc.**

etymology

(1) The study of the origin and history of words.

(2) The origin and history of a particular word.

Dictionaries may show a word's *etymology* as well as its definition:

sandwich [noun] Two slices of bread with food between them [*named after the 4th Earl of Sandwich who wanted a meal he could eat while playing cards*]

every + is or are?

See ***each*** + ***is*** or ***are***?

everybody/everyone + is or are?

Everyone and ***everybody*** are distributives. A distributive refers to the separate items in a group.

Each item is treated as a single thing, so ***everybody*** and ***everyone*** are singular and take a singular verb.

Everyone has a vote.
Everybody is in the bus.

Agreement of ***everybody*** or ***everyone*** with a double pronoun (such as he or she) is not so strict. To avoid a crowd of pronouns, some writers use they:

Everyone has his or her ticket with him or her.
Everyone has their ticket with them.

The same rules applies to:

anybody/anyone
somebody/someone
nobody/no-one ***none***

See *also* **agreement** • **distributive** • ***each*** + ***is*** *or* ***are***? • ***he or she*** + ***they***?

everybody/everyone + *they*?

See ***everybody/everyone*** + ***is*** *or* ***are***?

except or *accept*?

See ***accept*** *or* ***except***?

exclamation

A word, phrase or sentence that expresses strong feeling.

That hurts! No way!
That's excellent! Get a life!

Single-word exclamations are also called ***interjections***:

Ouch! Cool!

See *also* **exclamation mark** • **interjection**

exclamation mark [!]

A punctuation mark that indicates an exclamation, an interjection or an urgent command.

Exclamations and interjections

That's awful! Mmmm!
Yuk! Yes!
Hey! Nice one!

Urgent commands

Look out! Take cover!
Hurry up! Careful!
Stop! Don't!

See *also* **exclamation** • **interjection** • **mood** (of a verb)

existential process

See **process**

explanation

IN FUNCTIONAL GRAMMAR

A kind of text in which a process is explained, usually as a series of steps. Each step is often the result of the previous step.

An explanation usually has:
• a ***phenomenon to be explained***
• an ***explanatory sequence***, presented as a series of causes and effects

How is Bread Made?

Phenomenon to be explained

How do large bakeries produce bread?

Explanatory sequence

Flour, salt, yeast and water are trucked to the bakery. All the ingredients are mixed to form a dough, which is kneaded to release excess air bubbles. The dough is placed in trays after which it is heated in ovens at 175°C. After 40 to 50 minutes the bread is removed and allowed to cool. Loaves are sometimes sliced and wrapped by a machine, then stamped with a batch code and a date.

An ***explanation*** is different from a ***procedure***.

Explanation

An explanation shows *how something is done* and is usually arranged as a series of sentences, often using passive verbs:

> The dough is placed in a tray after which it is heated in an oven . . .

Procedure

A procedure shows *how to do something* and is arranged as a series of commands, using verbs in the imperative mood:

> Place the dough in a tray.
> Then heat it in an oven . . .

An explanation can be planned using a flow chart or storyboard.

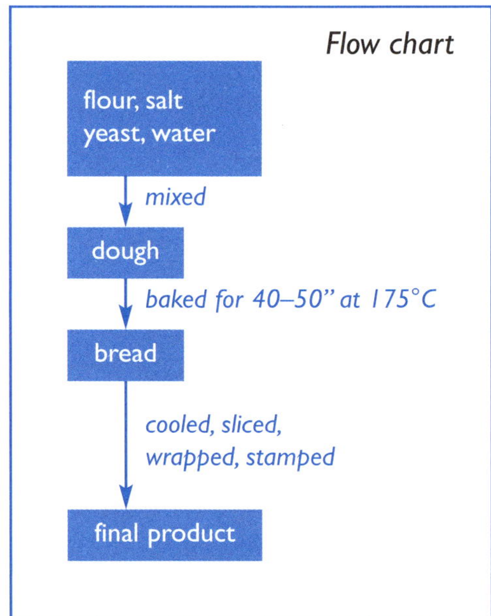

See also **flow chart • imperative mood** (of a verb) **• passive voice • procedure • storyboard**

exposition or expository text

(1) A general term for "factual text" or "information text".

(2) A more specific term that is sometimes used instead of "persuasive text".

See also **factual text • persuasion**

factual recount

(Also called a ***chronological report***)

IN FUNCTIONAL GRAMMAR
A kind of text in which events are recalled, usually in the order in which they occurred. Examples of factual recounts include history, biography, news reports and records of science experiments.

A factual recount usually has:
- an ***orientation*** answering the questions: What is the subject? When and where (or why) did the events take place?
- a ***series of events*** arranged in chronological order
- an ***outcome*** that results from the series of events

Conduction Experiment

Orientation
Today we tested a number of materials to see if they conducted electricity.

Series of events
First a battery, light bulb and three wires were used to form an electric circuit. Items made of steel, zinc, copper, plastic, wood and paper were tested in turn and the results recorded.

Outcome
We found that items made of steel or copper conducted electricity. The others did not.

News reports often state the outcome in the headline and the opening paragraph.

A ***factual recount*** is different from a ***personal recount.***

Factual recount

A factual recount attempts an impersonal tone and is limited to statements of what happened:

We found that items made of steel or copper conducted electricity.

Personal recount

A personal recount includes the <u>personal responses</u> of the writer:

<u>I was surprised</u> that zinc didn't conduct electricity.

A factual recount can be planned using a flow chart (see below and next page).

Electric circuit (simple flow chart)

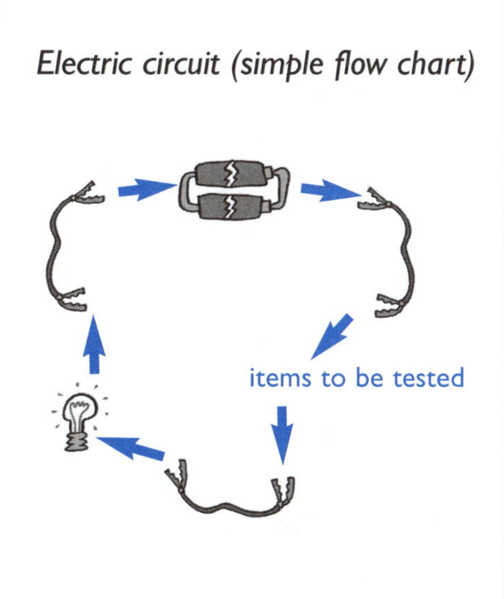

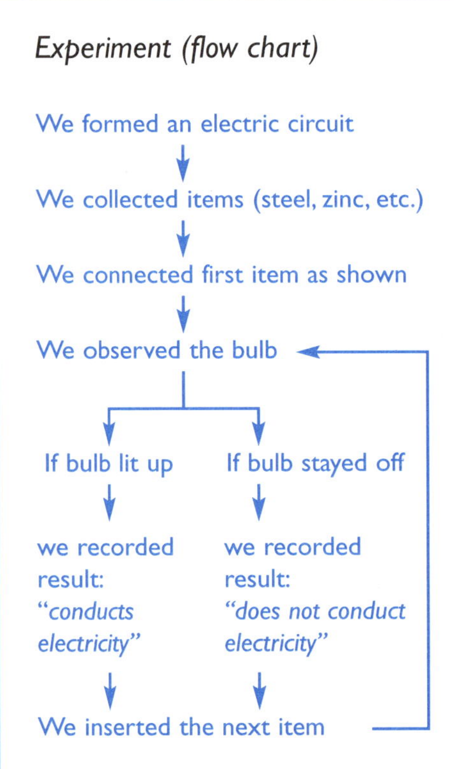

See also • **personal recount**

factual text

(Also called an ***expository text***, ***non-fiction***, ***information text*** or ***exposition***) Any text that provides information, as opposed to a fictional text. A factual text can take various non-fiction forms, such as explanation, discussion, report and recount.

See also **fiction**

fade or *cut*?

See ***cut*** or ***fade***?

FAQ

(**F**requently **A**sked **Q**uestions)
A page of questions and answers on a website that provide information for users.

farther or *further*?

• ***farther*** means "more distant"
• ***further*** can mean "more distant" *or* "additional"

Which is ***farther*** from Canberra: Melbourne or Sydney?
Which is ***further*** from Canberra: Melbourne or Sydney?
My essay needs ***further*** work.

In Australia ***further*** is much more common than ***farther***. Many Australians use ***further*** in *all* situations.

fax

Short for ***facsimile*** which originally meant "exact copy".

A ***fax machine*** copies text and images digitally and transmits them over phone lines.

See also **analogy** (2)

feminine

See **gender**

fewer or *less?*

• ***fewer*** is used with things that *can* be counted
• ***less*** is used with things that *cannot* be counted

This recipe calls for ***fewer*** eggs and ***less*** milk.

Countable things are usually identified with ***count nouns***. Uncountable things are usually identified with ***mass nouns***.

See also **a few** or **a little?** • **count noun** and **mass noun**

fiction

A text that recounts imagined events, usually in a narrative form. Opposite of non-fiction or factual text.

See also **factual text** • **narrative**

field

(1) *IN FUNCTIONAL GRAMMAR*
The social context in which language is used.

See **text and context**

(2) A box on a web page in which the user adds information.

Search for: echidna GO

The information is then used by the website to perform a task.

Type the word you are looking for in the ***search field*** and click "go".

See also **browse, find** or **search?**

figure of speech

A literary expression such as a simile, metaphor, personification, onomatopoeia or irony.

Simile

A comparison of two things, with the construction ***A is like B***:

My love ***is like*** a red red rose
— Robert Burns

Metaphor

A comparison of two different things, often in the form ***A is B***:

She ***is*** all States, and all Princes, I
— John Donne

A metaphor can also describe one thing as if it were another, very different thing. Here money is as plentiful as water:

He is ***drowning*** in money.

Personification

A presentation of a thing as if it were a person:

O rose thou art sick!
— William Blake

F

Onomatopoeia
Words that are thought to sound like the thing they name (such as ***kookaburra*** or ***currawong***).

See also ***irony*** or ***sarcasm***? • ***literally***, ***virtually*** or ***metaphorically***? • **mixed metaphors**

filmography
See **bibliography**

find or *search*?
See ***browse***, ***find*** or ***search***?

finite clause
See **clause**

finite verb and non-finite verb
Verbs are said to be ***finite*** or ***non-finite***. One kind of non-finite verb is the ***infinitive***.

Finite verb
Any verb that shows when the action occurs (in the past, present or future). Such a verb is said to have tense:

> Ice ***has*** ***formed*** on the pond.
> Ice ***was*** ***forming*** on the pond.
> Water ***freezes*** at 0° Celsius.
> The ice ***will*** ***melt*** when heated.

In English, tense is often shown by the ***auxiliaries***. These are underlined in the above examples.

Non-finite verb
The form of a verb which does not show person (who did it), number (how many) or tense (when it happens).

Non-finite verbs can be grouped into ***infinitives*** (the *to*-infinitive and the bare infinitive) and ***other non-finite verbs***.

Infinitive
Most infinitives start with **to**:

> She wants **to go**.

This is called the ***to-infinitive***.

Some infinitives omit **to**:

> She must **go**.

This is called the ***bare infinitive***.

To-infinitive
This form of the verb usually follows verbs such as want, like, have and begin:

> He likes ***to play*** hockey.
> We want ***to stay*** home.
> The snow began ***to fall***.

The **to**-infinitive is also used to make a verb work like a noun (nominalisation):

> ***To go back*** now would be a mistake.

Bare infinitive

This form of the verb usually follows verbs such as see, feel, make or let, and modal auxiliaries such as must, should, would and will (or shall or -'ll):

> You should **see** that movie.
> You would ***like*** it.
> She said we must ***stay*** outside.
> We'll ***take*** some sandwiches.

Other non-finite verbs

These verbs also show no person, number or time, but are formed with ***-ing***, ***-ed*** or ***-en***:

> ***Having*** no fare, he walked home.
> No goods ***refunded*** if ***broken***.

See *also* **modal auxiliary** • **number** • **person** • **split infinitive** • **tense** (of a verb)

first or *firstly?*

Both forms are accepted when organising a sequence of events or reasons:

> We have called this meeting ***first*** to put our case and ***second*** to answer your questions.

All these forms are accepted, but the first is perhaps the simplest:

> first … second … third …
> first … secondly … thirdly …
> firstly … secondly … thirdly …

first person

See **person**

flashback

A plot device in which the scene shifts back into the past, then returns to the time where the story was interrupted. The word was first used in movies but can apply to text narrative as well.

See *also* **narrative**

flammable or *inflammable?*

Both words mean "able to be set on fire".

> ***flammable = inflammable***

Inflammable is derived from the verb *to inflame* which means "to set on fire". However, it might be mistaken for the opposite of "flammable" (just as *incapable* is the opposite of *capable*). To avoid this confusion, ***flammable*** is used on warning labels.

> Petrol is ***flammable*** but water is ***not flammable***.

Note that ***inflammable*** is **NOT** the opposite of ***flammable***.

The only opposite of ***flammable*** is ***not flammable***.

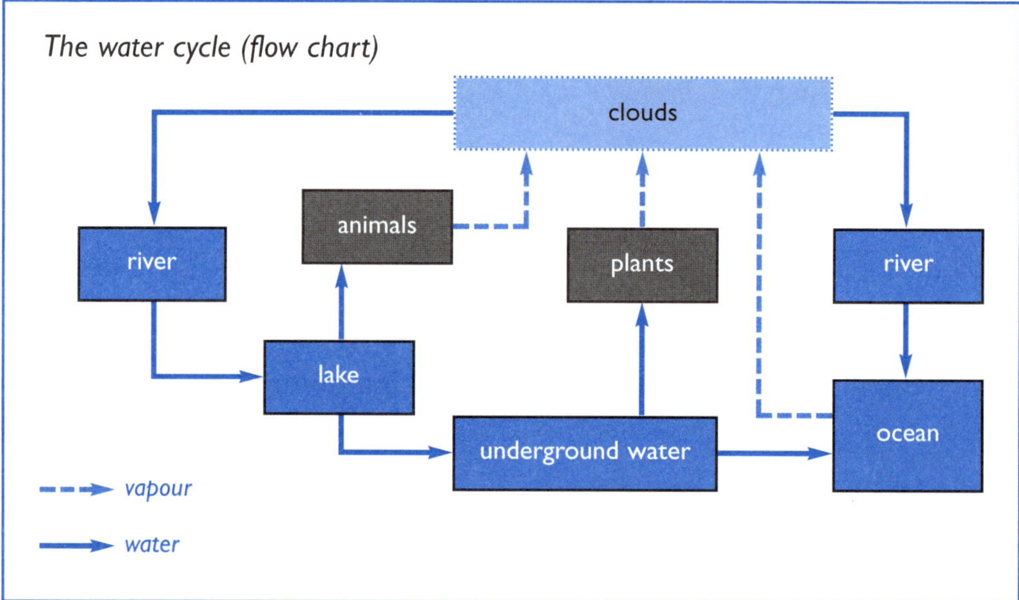

flow chart

(Also called a ***flow diagram*** or ***system diagram***) A diagram that arranges events or reasons in a sequence using arrows. Sometimes several parallel or alternative sequences are shown.

Flow charts can be used to plan explanations, factual recounts, personal recounts and procedures.

See *also* **explanation • factual recount • personal recount • procedure • web diagram**

folio

See **page number**

font

(Also called a ***typeface***) A style of type used in printing and word processing. Fonts can be serif or sans serif.

Serif fonts

These fonts have small straight lines (called serifs) at the ends of most letters:

Sans serif fonts

These fonts do not have serifs. ***Sans serif*** means "without serif":

Fonts (or typefaces) can also be roman, **bold**, *italic* or ***bold italic***:

Serif fonts	*Sans serif fonts*
roman	roman
bold	**bold**
italic	*italic*
bold italic	***bold italic***

• Roman fonts are used in general printing and word processing.
• *Italic* fonts are used to emphasise a word or phrase and also for the names of books.
• **Bold** fonts are used for headings and to highlight key words.

In this dictionary:
• the headwords are in a **bold sans serif font**
• the definitions are in a serif font
• the examples are in a sans serif font
• the key words are highlighted in ***bold italic sans serif***

The words ***type***, ***face*** or ***typeface*** can be used instead of ***font***:

italic **font** = *italic* **type**

See *also* **names**

footer

See **header** and **footer**

footnote

A note that is printed at the foot (or lowest part) of a page, or at the end of a book or chapter.

Footnotes[1] contain remarks that are secondary to the main ideas in the text and are too long to be placed in parentheses[2].

[1] A single footnote can be attached to the text with an asterisk (*).

[2] Where two or more footnotes are used, they can be organised with numbers, as here. Footnotes are also used to explain a detail more fully.

Footnotes are also used to acknowledge the source of information. For example, in an article about sharks you may need to state your sources[3] using footnotes.

[3] Day, D. *Sharks*. Predator Press, 2000; <www.greatwhitesharks.org>

See *also* **asterisk** • **bibliography** • **names** • **parenthesis**

foreign plurals

See **plural nouns**

formally or *formerly*?

- ***formally*** means "in a formal way"
- ***formerly*** means "in the past"

He addressed her ***formally*** as Professor Li.
Today we send emails whereas ***formerly*** we would have sent a telegram.

formatting

A general term used in word processing. Formatting includes *layout* and *typography*.

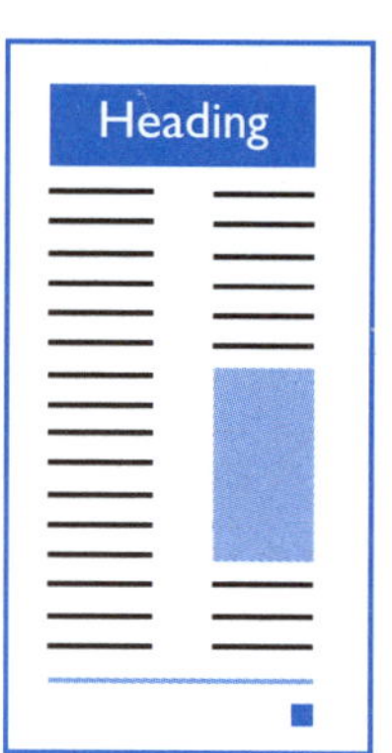

- Layout is the placing of headings, text and graphics on a printed page or website.
- Typography is choosing the size and style of the type.

Formatting is usually the job of a graphic designer who selects the font or type size and arranges the paragraphs in columns, positions the photographs, etc.

See *also* **font** • **graphic design**

former or *latter*?

- ***former*** means "the *first* thing I just mentioned"
- ***latter*** means "the *second* thing I just mentioned"

The next day I met the poodle again but this time it was with its owner. The ***latter*** was being dragged along by the ***former***.

Using ***former*** and ***latter*** forces the reader to re-read and check the meaning by substituting the words they stand for. This can sound clumsy. You can avoid this problem by using a **who** clause:

The next day I met the poodle again but this time it was with its owner, ***who*** was being dragged along by the ***dog***.

forward slash [/]

See **slash** [/]

French plurals

Words borrowed from French which sometimes have plurals other than ***-s***. These plurals include ***-x*** as in ***plateaux***.

See **plural nouns**

from or *off*?

See ***off*** *or* ***from****?*

front matter and **end matter**

The pages at the front and back of a book, particularly a reference book.

Front matter

Front matter includes the title page, copyright notice, acknowledgements, table of contents, list of illustrations and preface (usually in that order).

End matter (or back matter)

End matter includes the appendices, glossary, notes, references, bibliography and index (usually in that order).

See also **abbreviations, list of • appendix • bibliography • glossary • illustrations, list of • index • references • table of contents • title page**

---

ftp

(***f***ile **t**ransfer ***p***rotocol)
The coding used to construct files that can be downloaded from the internet.

A URL that ends with ***ftp*** is likely to be a download file (and can be a text, image, movie, sound, application or other file).

See also **URL**

---

full stop [.]

A punctuation mark that indicates either the end of a sentence or an abbreviation.

Full stops and sentences

Full stops can indicate that a sentence is complete:

> There are three classes of compound lever**.** An example of the first class is a pair of scissors**.**

Full stops and abbreviations

Abbreviations that end with a letter other than the last letter of the original word usually have a full stop:

> ***Trafalgar Sq.***
> = Trafalgar <u>Sq</u>uare
>
> ***temp.***
> = <u>temp</u>erature

Abbreviations that end with the same letter as the full word do not need a full stop:

> ***Main St***
> = Main Stree<u>t</u>
>
> ***Mt St Helens***
> = Moun<u>t</u> Sain<u>t</u> Helens

See also **abbreviation • sentence**

---

full stop or comma?

*See **comma** or **full stop?***

F

functional grammar

A system of grammar which considers the social function of language.

See *also* **text and context**

further or *farther*?

See ***farther*** *or* ***further?***

fused participle

A ***participle*** joined to a pronoun.

> Do you mind me ***sitting*** here?

Traditionally this would be corrected to:

> Do you mind my ***sitting*** here?

However, both forms are now accepted.

future tenses

Various forms of a verb that refer to an event that has not yet happened.

Future simple

This tense is the most common future tense. It is formed from ***will*** or ***shall*** + the verb:

> The train ***will*** arrive at 2 p.m.
> We ***shall*** leave at 2 p.m.

Future continuous

This tense is used for events that continue over a period of time in the future. It is formed from ***will*** or ***shall*** + ***be*** + a verb ending in -ing:

> They ***will be*** eating lunch on the train.

Future perfect

This tense is used for events that will have been completed when we remember them in the future. It is formed from ***will*** or ***shall*** + ***have*** + a verb ending in -ed or -en:

> We ***will have*** eaten lunch by the time we get there.

There are two other ways of forming the future tense in English.

The "going to" future

This tense is formed from ***am/is/are*** + ***going to*** + the verb:

> We ***are going to*** leave at 2 p.m.

The present tense used as a future tense

The present simple and present continuous tenses are sometimes understood by the listener to refer to the future:

> The train ***arrives*** in two hours.
> I ***am seeing*** my dad tomorrow.

See *also* ***shall*** *or* ***will?***

gateway

An entrance point into a text.

Printed examples include a book's index and table of contents or a newspaper's headlines.

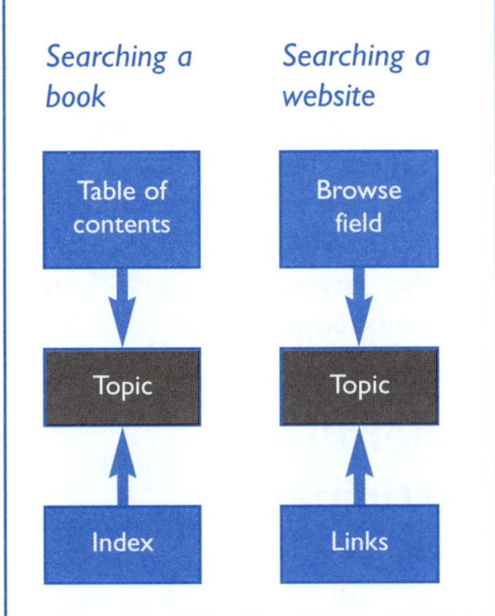

Electronic examples include a website's browse field and its interactive hyperlinks.

See also ***browse, find** or **search?***
hyperlink • signpost

gender

The grouping of nouns or pronouns according to whether they are feminine, masculine, either, both or neither.

Feminine and masculine nouns

Some nouns (often job or career names) have a masculine and a feminine form, such as actor and actress. Many writers now prefer to use the traditionally "masculine" form to refer to either women or men or both:

My sister is an ***actor***.

New words have been coined to avoid suggesting a job belongs only to men or to women:

chairman — ***chairperson***
waitress — ***server***

Neuter nouns

Nouns that are neither masculine nor feminine are usually neuter. These include the names of ***non-living things*** and abstract ideas:

Heat turns ***ice*** into ***water***; evaporation turns ***water*** into ***steam***.

Nouns without gender

Many nouns in English do not indicate gender, except when given a context:

Our ***cat***
could be masculine or feminine

Our ***cat, Thomas***
is likely to be masculine

Our ***cat*** had kittens
is feminine

Feminine pronouns

These pronouns refer to female people (and some animals):

Kim found ***herself*** separated from ***her*** friends who could not hear ***her***. Then ***she*** noticed that the backpack she held wasn't ***hers***.

My cat has lost ***her*** collar.

Masculine pronouns

These pronouns refer to male people (and some animals):

Kim found ***himself*** separated from ***his*** friends who could not hear ***him***. Then ***he*** noticed that the backpack ***he*** held wasn't ***his***.

My cat has lost ***his*** collar.

Pronouns that are both, either or neither gender

These are the pronouns ***it***, ***its***, ***itself*** and ***they***, ***them***, ***their***, ***themselves*** and ***theirs***.

These pronouns can refer to people or animals that may be *either* male *or* female (we simply don't know from the context):

All my friends have ***their*** results.
My cat has lost ***its*** collar.

See also **agreement • *everybody/ everyone + is*** *or* ***are?*** **•** ***he*** *or* ***she + they?***

generalisation

A statement that defines members that belong to a group. Used especially in information reports, a generalisation does not refer to particular individuals.

Some birds cannot fly.
Not all birds have wings.
Most fish have scales.
Many fossils have been found.
All reptiles have a skeleton.
No animals exist on the Moon.

See also **generalised participant • information report**

generalised participant

A ***participant*** is a word that refers to a person or thing. A ***generalised participant*** is a word or phrase that refers to "people or things in general" rather than particular individuals.

Passengers must remain seated.
Oxygen is produced by ***plants***.
Most ***bats*** fly at night.

Generalised participants are often used to form generalisations in explanations and reports:

The nest of ***the termite*** is made of ***mud***.
Caterpillars eat ***leaves***.

The whale is not a fish.
Some ***birds*** cannot fly.

Generalised participants can be singular or plural:

The bat is a ***mammal***.
= ***All bats*** are ***mammals***.

See *also* **explanation • generalisation • information report • nominalisation**

genitive

See **possessive case**

genre

(1) A literary form.

Traditional literary ***genres*** include novels, plays and poems.

(2) *IN FUNCTIONAL GRAMMAR*
(Also called **text type**) A kind of text, either fictional or informational. The main text types are said to be:

- description
- discussion
- explanation
- factual recount
- information report
- narrative
- personal recount
- persuasion
- procedure

See *also* **text and context**

gerund

(Also called a ***verbal noun***) A verb ending in ***-ing*** that is used to name a thing, as a noun does. The process of turning a verb into a noun is called ***nominalisation***.

She prefers ***drawing***.
No ***smoking***.
They oppose the ***hunting*** of seals.

Gerund or participle?
Participles are also words that end in ***-ing***. However, participles do not name anything. ***Participles*** work as verbs; ***gerunds*** work as nouns.

Participle
We were ***fishing*** on the rocks.

Gerund
Fishing is his favourite sport.

See *also* **nominalisation • participle**

get *and* got

These words are often discouraged in formal writing, but they are accepted in conversational speech.

IN FORMAL WRITING
Get (or **got**) is usually avoided in favour of more specific or formal words, such as become (or became), collect(ed) and arrive(d).

Informal

I've **got** to **get** home to **get** the gift Bob **got** for me.

Formal

I must return home to collect the gift Bob bought for me.

The* get*-passive

When forming the passive voice **got** is a stronger word than ***was***:

The kite ***was*** caught in the tree.
The kite **got** caught in the tree.

By adding a reflexive form the *get*-passive can suggest that the subject helped bring about the action.

The burglar ***was*** caught

is not the same as

The burglar **got** herself caught.

See also **got** *or* **gotten?** • **passive voice**

get-passive

See **passive voice**

gif

(**g**raphics ***i***nterchange ***f***ormat) The coding used to construct a picture file on a website. Gifs are usually diagrams, maps or drawings rather than photographs.

A URL that ends with ***gif*** is likely to be a picture file.

See also **jpeg** • **URL**

giga- *or* mega-?

See ***mega-*** *or* ***giga-?***

given and new

The ideas in a sentence can be labelled according to whether they are given or ***new***.

A given idea is one that has already been introduced in a previous sentence, while a ***new*** idea has not already been introduced in the text.

The following paragraph includes both given and ***new*** ideas:

Are sharks dangerous?
Some sharks are dangerous but ***90%*** of them ***are harmless.*** In fact ***most*** sharks ***are too small*** to harm us.

glossary

Part of a reference book in which technical terms are arranged in alphabetical order and defined.

bullet (•) A printer's mark used in lists to indicate a new item (called a *dot point*).

cutaway A diagram that shows part of the inside of an object.

dot point See bullet.

A glossary usually comes in the ***end matter*** of a book before the index.

See also **front matter** *and* **end matter**

goal

IN FUNCTIONAL GRAMMAR

The aim or purpose of an instructional text (also called a ***procedure***). The goal may be expressed in the text's ***heading*** or in its opening paragraph:

> ***Testing for magnetism***
> Follow these steps to find out which items are magnetic: …

See also **procedure**

got or gotten?

These two words mean the same and both are accepted. Some writers see **gotten** as "American".

See also **get** *and* **got • passive voice**

gradable and non-gradable

Adjectives and adverbs can be grouped as either gradable or non-gradable.

Gradable words

Adjectives and adverbs that *can* be ranked with degrees of comparison are gradable. Degrees of comparison are ***positive***, ***comparative*** and ***superlative***.

Positive	*Comparative*	*Superlative*
simple	simpler	simplest
good	better	best
seriously	more seriously	most seriously

Gradable words can also be used with intensifiers, such as ***very***, ***too***, ***less***, ***hardly***, ***extremely*** and ***somewhat***.

very dark	***less*** dark
too slow	***somewhat*** slow
hardly clever	***extremely*** clever

Non-gradable words

Adjectives and adverbs that *cannot* be ranked with degrees of comparison and cannot take intensifiers are non-gradable. Lists of such words often include the following, although many writers would doubt whether some of these words were always non-gradable:

☞

perfect	equal
married	supreme
identical	dead

See also **adjective • adverb • degree • intensifier**

grammar

A description of a language system that attempts to explain how the language works. There are many different systems of grammar, such as ***functional*** (or systemic) grammar, ***traditional*** (school) grammar and ***visual*** grammar.

Grammar is different from usage or style.

Usage considers the various ways in which words or phrases are used. "Accepted" usage depends on the social context. Formal usage is not always the most appropriate usage.

Style includes personal style (such as tone of voice and choice of vocabulary), publishing style (spelling, punctuation, layout and design) and word processing style (fonts and basic design).

See also **functional grammar • style • traditional grammar • usage • visual grammar**

grammar checker

Part of a word processing program that is intended to "correct" the user's (traditional) grammar. Grammar checkers can only find patterns of words that *may sometimes* be a problem. They cannot (yet) identify a pattern that makes sense in one context but not in another. Grammar checkers often identify apparent "mistakes" that are in fact correct.

See also **spelling checker**

graph

A visual text that arranges items and quantities so that they can be measured and compared easily. These texts can be used to support writing in all subject areas, not just mathematics.

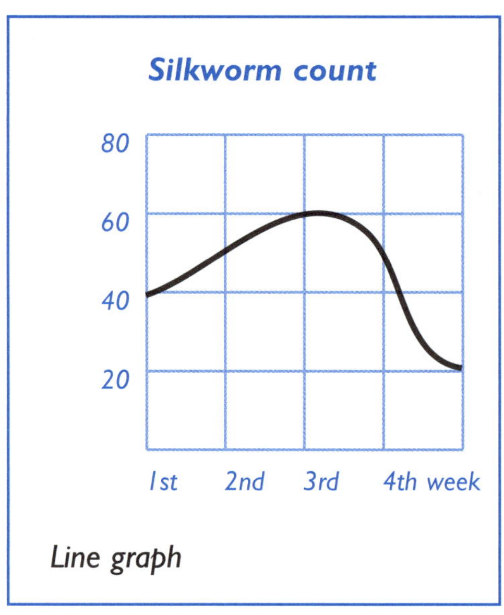

Line graph

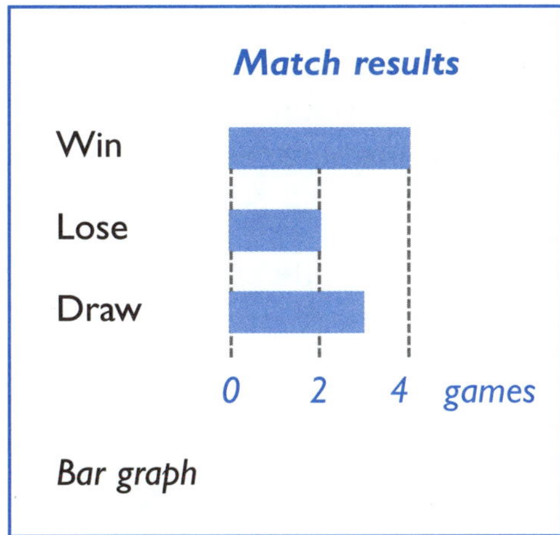

Bar graph

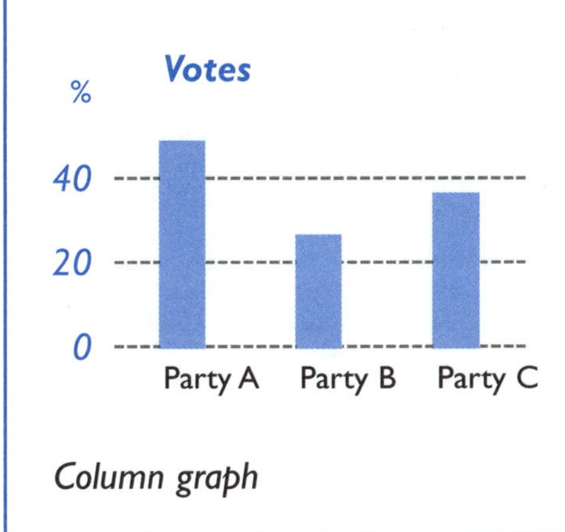

Column graph

See also **bar graph • column graph • line graph**

grapheme

The smallest unit of a written word that can change the word's meaning. Each grapheme is the written form of a ***phoneme***. Graphemes may be single letters or two or more letters.

By changing the letters **bad** to **pad**, **bad** to **bed**, or **bad** to **bat**, we change the meaning of these words. Therefore the letters ***b***, ***p***, ***a***, ***e***, ***d*** and ***t*** are all shown to be graphemes. We can also do this with two or more letters: **bad** to **bird**, or **bat** to **bath** or **batch**. So ***ir***, ***th*** and ***tch*** are also graphemes.

In the following words the letters in **bold** are all different forms (***allographs***) of the same grapheme, as they stand for the same sound (or phoneme) /k/:

clock **quest** **school** **Kim**

See also **morpheme • phoneme**

graphic

In a visual text, such as a diagram, the pictorial part could be called the ***graphic***. The graphic + the labels form a complete ***visual text***.

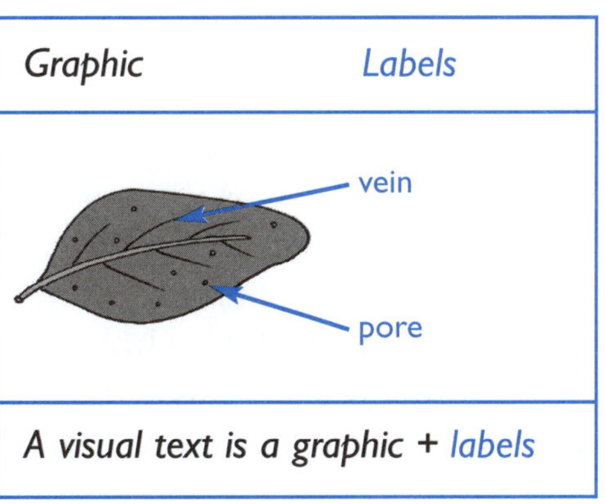

A visual text is a graphic + labels

See also **visual text**

G

graphic design

The arrangement of paragraphs, headings, graphics, captions and other elements to help the reader interpret a printed or electronic text.

Heading

The main text is arranged in paragraphs and sometimes in two or more columns. Cross-references can refer to a visual text (see *map*) or another page (see *page* 999).

A visual text could be a photograph, diagram, map, table or graph etc.

A caption relates the graphic (above) to the main text on the left.

A graphic designer organises the information on a printed page or a web page using layout and typography.

Layout is the positioning of text elements on the page. ***Typography*** is the choice of typeface (or font) and type size.

Graphic design helps the reader to understand connections between different parts of a text, and offers the reader a choice of entry points (or ***gateways***) into the text.

Typical gateways include chapter headings, tables of contents and indexes.

Graphic design also provides ***signposts*** that signal to the reader either entry points or connections between different parts of the text.

Signposts include cross-references, page numbers and footnote numbers.

Some common signposts

Main heading
Subheading
• bullet
.... leaders
☞ printer's hand
→ arrow
asterisk*

See also **font • gateway • integrated text • signpost**

graphic organiser

A visual text that helps a writer to plan a written text. For example, a writer may use a time line to organise events when planning to write a biography:

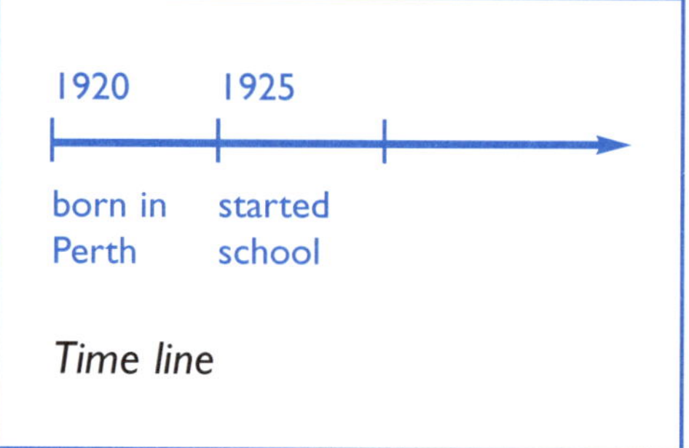

Time line

A table is another kind of graphic organiser. It can be used to compare views in a discussion:

Should voting be compulsory?	
For	**Against**
Reason 1:	Reason 1:
Reason 2:	Reason 2:

Table

The following ***graphic organisers*** may be useful when planning certain written texts (or non-fiction genres):

Graphic organiser	*Genre*
time line	recount
storyboard	procedure
tree diagram	information report
flow chart	explanation, argument
Venn diagram	discussion

More information about genres can be found under **text and context**.

See also **flow chart • graphic • storyboard • table • time line • tree diagram • Venn diagram**

Greek plurals

Words borrowed from ancient Greek that have plurals other than **-s**. Greek plurals include:

-a	as in	phenomen***a***
-es	as in	synops***es***

The singular and plural forms are:

Singular	*Plural*
criteri***on***	criteri***a***
phenomen***on***	phenomen***a***
ax***is***	ax***es***
synops***is***	synops***es***

See also **plural nouns**

grid

The network of lines on a map that divide it into cells each of which has a label, such as ***A4***:

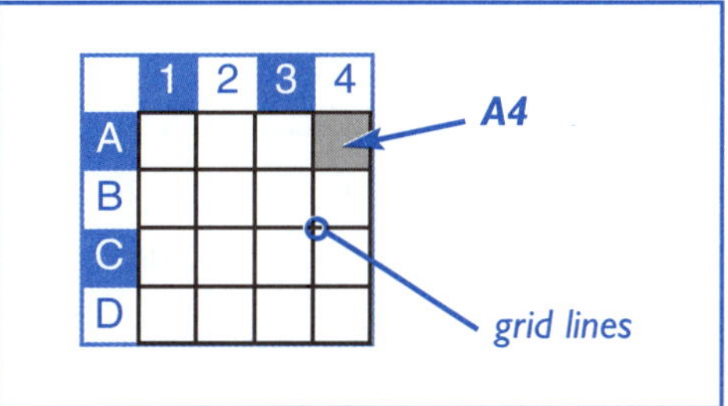

Each cell is labelled with both a number and a letter. Grid lines and labels help readers to locate features on the map.

See also **coordinates** (in maps) • **map**

half-title page

See **title page**

harbour or *harbor*?

The spelling **harbour** is the most common in Australia, but **harbor** is also used in Victoria and South Australia. Elsewhere in Australia, New Zealand, Canada, Ireland and the UK the spelling **harbour** is preferred. **Harbor** is also the American spelling.

The spelling of geographical names varies from place to place:

Sydney Harb**ou**r, NSW
Victor Harb**o**r, South Australia
Otago Harb**ou**r, New Zealand
Cork Harb**ou**r, Ireland
Charlotte Harb**o**r, Florida, USA

See also ***labour*** *or* ***labor?***

hard copy

Printed copy of a text that was composed digitally (such as with a word processing program).

You could email an attachment or print out a ***hard copy***.

See also **attachment • text**

have or *of*?

See ***could have, could've*** *or* ***could of?***

header and footer

In a word processing document the text at the top of the page is called the header and the text at the foot of the page is the footer.

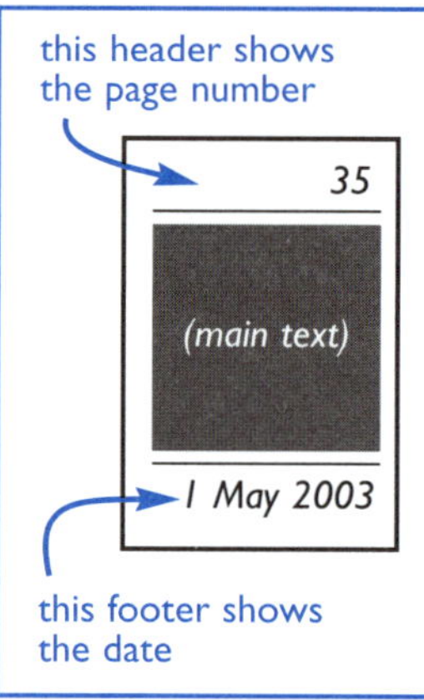

heading

A word or phrase that indicates the topic of the paragraphs that follow. A heading acts as a ***signpost*** helping the reader to find a particular topic.

Headings are often set in **bold** type, CAPITALS or *italics*.

Headings and capitals

Traditionally headings are written with a capital at the start of each main word. However, many books, newspapers and websites now use a capital only for the very first letter and for the initial letter in proper nouns:

Traditional style

Planning for Your Future

Blizzards Cause Blackouts in Canada and the USA

Modern style

Planning for your future

Blizzards cause blackouts in Canada and the USA

Heading levels

Headings can be of different levels, indicating different degrees of importance. The main heading in a chapter is usually described as a ***level 1 heading***. A level 2 heading would fall within the topic of a level 1 heading; similarly a *level 3 heading* would fall within the topic of a level 2 heading and so on:

Living and non-living

The world can be seen as made up of living and non-living things.

Living things

There are five main groups: animals, plants, fungi, bacteria and protists.

Animals are defined as …
Plants are …

Non-living things

The non-living world can be said to include solids, liquids and gases.

Solids are defined as …
Liquids are …

Heading levels are useful when classifying a topic (organising information into groups), as in an information report.

Heading levels can be planned using a tree diagram:

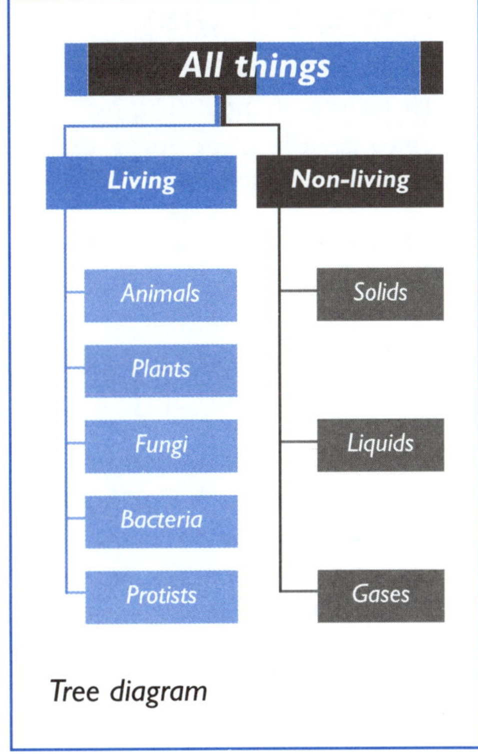

Tree diagram

See also **information report • nested list • signpost • subheading • tree diagram**

head noun

See **noun group**

headword

A word defined in a dictionary or explained in any alphabetic reference book. (The word ***headword*** at the start of this entry is this entry's headword.)

he or she + they?

In order to include all readers, many writers avoid using ***he*** to refer to people in general, and write ***he or she*** instead.

Each passenger should ensure that ***he or she*** has a ticket.

Where possible other parts of the sentence should agree:

Each passenger should ensure that ***he or she*** has ***his or her*** ticket with ***him or her***.

However, when this agreement rule produces a sentence congested with pronouns, some writers use the plural ***they*** instead, even though this results in a mixture of singular and plural:

Each passenger should ensure that ***they*** have ***their*** ticket with ***them***.

It is often possible to make the *whole* sentence plural, avoiding ***he or she*** entirely:

Passenger<u>s</u> should ensure that ***they*** have ***their*** ticket<u>s</u> with ***them***.

The phrase ***he or she*** can also be written ***he/she*** or ***s/he***:

Each passenger should ensure that ***he/she*** has a ticket.

Each passenger should ensure that ***s/he*** has a ticket.

Some writers use ***she*** instead of ***he*** to draw attention to issues of gender:

Each passenger should ensure that ***she*** has a ticket.

See also **agreement** • ***each*** **+** ***is*** *or* ***are?*** • ***everybody/everyone*** **+** ***is*** *or* ***are?*** • ***s/he*** • ***one*** *or* ***you?***

highlighted word

A word that is set in a different font to make it stand out.

In keyboarded texts the highlighted words can be set in *italic* or **bold**.

When handwritten the highlighted words can be <u>underlined</u>.

See also **font** • **signpost** • **<u>underlining</u>** or ***italic?***

historic present

See **present tenses**

home page

The main or first-visited page of a website. A home page usually introduces the subject of the site and provides a series of hyperlinks to other key pages, as well as a search field, email link and the site owner's identity.

A site's ***home page*** is usually its web address up to the first forward slash (/):

aschool.edu.au/sports/results

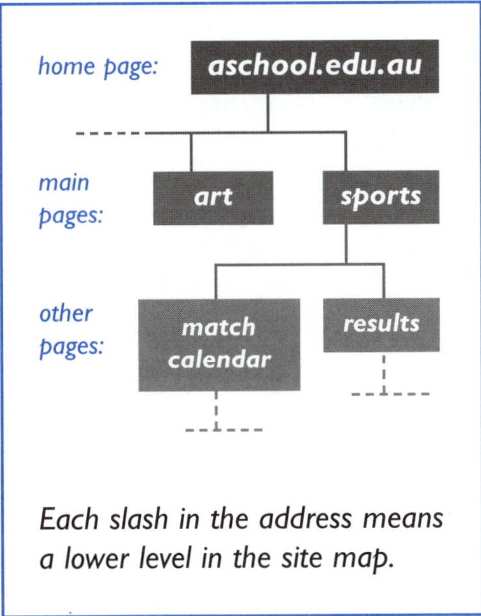

Each slash in the address means a lower level in the site map.

See *also* **hyperlink • search field • site map • slash [/] • website**

homonym, homograph or homophone?

These terms relate to pairs of words whose meanings are different but whose spelling or sound is the same.

Homonyms have the same sound and the same spelling, but different meanings:

It's not fair that we can't go to the fair.

Homographs have the same spelling, different meanings and a different sound:

Don't make a row [noise] when you row the boat.

Homophones have the same sound, different meanings and different spelling:

It's not fair that he didn't pay his fare.

The following table summarises the differences.

	Meaning	Sound	Spelling
homonym	different	same	same
homograph	different	different	same
homophone	different	same	different

however + comma?

When **However** starts a sentence:
• **However** (by itself) means "In whatever way …"
• **However,** (with a comma) means "On the other hand …" (= *However that may be*)

However you feel about it, you have to leave.

You may not agree. **However,** there are others who do.

See also **but** *ending a sentence* • **But** *starting a sentence*

html

(**h**yper**t**ext **m**arkup **l**anguage) The coding used to construct websites.

A URL that ends with either ***html*** (or ***htm***) is likely to be a text file (not a picture file).

See also **URL**

http

(**h**yper**t**ext **t**ransfer **p**rotocol) The rules used to exchange files on the world wide web.

All URLs that start with ***http://*** are websites. It is not necessary to type ***http://*** when keyboarding a web address.

URLs that start with ***https*** are "**s**ecure" websites. These sites are encrypted and require a membership number and password.

See also **URL** • ***internet*** *or* ***world wide web?***

hyperbole

An exaggeration, not to be taken literally.

We have ***a mountain*** of books to read.

hypercorrection

(Also called *overcorrection*) Hypercorrection is trying to "correct" a sentence that is already correct. The result is a sentence that is *not* correct.

In the following two examples the hypercorrection is followed by the **correct form**:

HYPERCORRECT between you and I
CORRECT **between you and me**

Why is **me** *correct here?*
Prepositions like **between** are always followed by an indirect object (**me**) not a subject (***I***).

HYPERCORRECT He's the one whom I thought lived there.
CORRECT He's the one **who** I thought lived there.

*Why is **who** correct here?*
In the sentence

He's the one ***who*** I thought lived there

who is the subject of the verb lived. It is not the object of the verb thought.

See also ***between you and me*** *or* ***between you and I?*** • ***I*** *or* ***me*** *(after* ***is****)?* • **object** (of a sentence) • ***who*** *or* ***whom?***

hyperlink

An internet term for a word, phrase or image on a web page that links to another part of the page or another website.

Hyperlinks were originally always blue and underlined, but this rule is becoming less strict. Many hyperlinks are images (also called ***interactive icons***).

See also **hypertext** • **icon** (2) • **web page** • **website**

hyper- or *hypo-?*

See ***hypo-*** *or* ***hyper-?***

hypertext

A text in which the parts are connected by interactive hyperlinks. An example of a hypertext is a web page.

Hypertexts can include words or images, sound or other files so long as they "link to" other parts of the text or to other texts.

The world wide web is made up of hypertexts in the form of web pages. Users navigate between web pages that are connected by their interactive links.

See also **hyperlink** • **web page**

hyphen [-]

A punctuation mark that is used either to *join two words* to make one, or to *break a word* at the end of a line.

Joining hyphen
A hyphen is used to join some (but not all) compound adjectives:

We overtook a ***slow-moving*** truck.

But** no hyphen after* ***-ly:

We overtook a ***slowly moving*** truck.

A hyphen is also used to join two words that are usually not joined, or have been recently joined. As the newly joined word becomes more familiar, the hyphen is often omitted:

☞

e-mail = ***email***
web-site = ***website***

Modern style tends to leave out hyphens (resulting in either one word or two):

Traditional style
story-book
reference-book

Modern style
storybook
reference book

Breaking hyphen
A hyphen is inserted at the end of a line to indicate that the word continues on the next line:

Word pro-
cessors can
be set to hy-
phenate
words auto-
matically.

See *also* **dash** • **hyphenation** • **syllable**

hyphenation

Hyphenation is the breaking of a word at the end of line.

The main conventions are:
- break a word between syllables
- do not break a one-syllable word
- avoid breaking a long word after the first syllable

The long word ***international*** can be broken at any of these places: ***inter-na-tion-al***

NOT *in-ternational*

Where a syllable ends with a double consonant, a hyphen is placed between the consonants:

syllable is broken at ***syl-lable***

NOT *syll-able*

See *also* **hyphen** • **syllable**

hyponym

See **cohesion**

hypo- or *hyper-*?

- ***hypo-*** means "under-" or "not enough"
- ***hyper-*** means "over-" or "more than" or "too much"

hypodermic = under the skin
hypothermia = not enough heat

hyperactive = overactive
hypertext = more than text

icon

(1) A symbol that has a meaning just as a word or clause has a meaning.

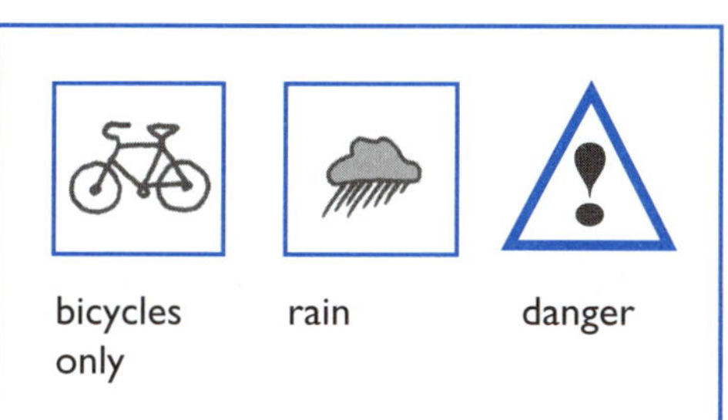

(2) On a website, a hyperlink symbol which, when clicked, is linked to another page or site.

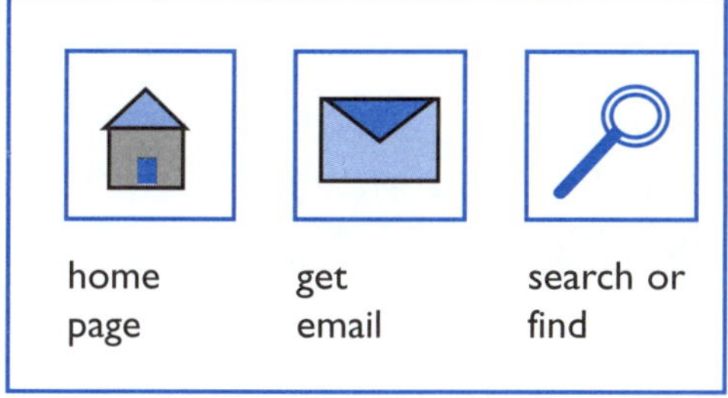

See also **hyperlink**

identifying name

A kind of post-modifier which identifies the name of someone. An ***identifying name*** comes after the noun to which it refers.

my cat ***Milo***

See also **noun group • post-modifier**

idiom

A frequently used expression that does not mean what it appears to say. An idiom's meaning is usually different from its literal meaning.

I'm ***up to my neck*** in homework.
They were ***over the Moon***.
She is ***under the weather***.

See also ***literally***, ***virtually*** *or* ***metaphorically****?*

i.e. or e.g.?

See ***e.g.*** *or* ***i.e.****?*

illustrations, list of

A list of all illustrations (such as photographs, diagrams or maps) with page numbers, usually placed at the front of a reference book.

The list arranges the illustrations in the order in which they appear in the book.

See also **front matter** and **end matter**

immigrate or emigrate?

See ***emigrate*** *or* ***immigrate****?*

imperative mood

See **mood** (of a verb)

imply or *infer*?

• ***to imply*** means "to *hint at* a logical conclusion"
• ***to infer*** means "to *arrive at* a logical conclusion"

The sign said "BICYCLES ONLY" which ***implied*** that we could not take the car.

When we saw the sign "BICYCLES ONLY" we ***inferred*** that we could not take the car.

Speakers and writers ***imply***; listeners and readers ***infer***.

indefinite adjective

See **adjective**

indefinite article

See **article**

indefinite pronoun

(1) A pronoun that is less definite than other pronouns. They include:

everyone	***everybody***
someone	***somebody***
anyone	***anybody***
no one	***nobody***

(2) The pronoun ***one*** when it is used to stand for people in general.

He thinks that ***one*** should always be on ***one's*** guard.

See also ***one or you?*** • **pronoun**

indented quotation

Text is *indented* when it is arranged with:

space on the left side of it, but *not* on the right side of it

space on the left side of it and *also* the right side of it

A quotation which is longer than two or three lines is often indented and sometimes set in smaller type:

According to Singh and Michaels in *Introduction to Biology*:

> Two parts of your body that feel no pain are your hair and nails. Both are made of dead cells. This is why it does not hurt when you cut your hair or nails.

Indented quotations do not need quotation marks (" ").

See also **quotation marks**

index

An alphabetical list of the more important words in a reference book, with page numbers.

Japan 10, 84
jellyfish 49
Jupiter 19, 23, 26–8, 30, 42
Jurassic period, 16, 55–6, 98,

An index with subtopics is more useful to the reader than one which simply lists page numbers:

Jupiter 19, 42
  and comets 23
  moons of 26–8
  voyages to 30
Jurassic period
  and climate 98
  extinction in 16, 55–6

On a website a ***search field*** serves the purposes of an index.

See *also* **alphabetical order** • **front matter** and **end matter** • **search field**

indicative mood

See **mood** (of a verb)

indicator

A word or mark in a caption that indicates the graphic to which the caption refers.

Indicator words

The usual indicator words are ***above***, ***below***, ***top***, ***middle***, ***bottom*** or an expression like ***Clockwise from left***.

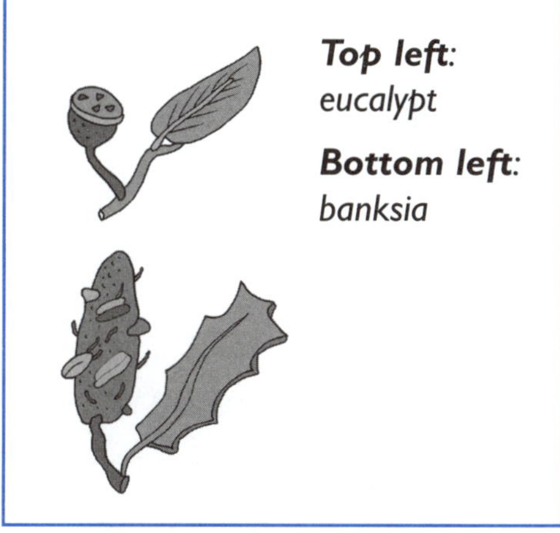

Top left: *eucalypt*

Bottom left: *banksia*

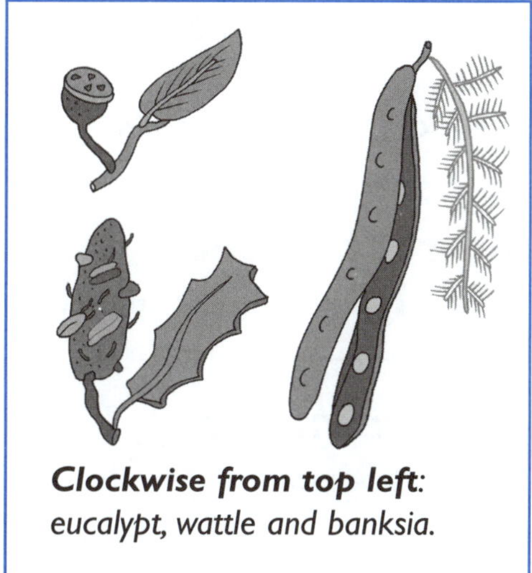

Clockwise from top left: *eucalypt, wattle and banksia.*

Indicator marks
Arrowheads (such as ▲ or ▼) can be used when the graphic is next to the caption.

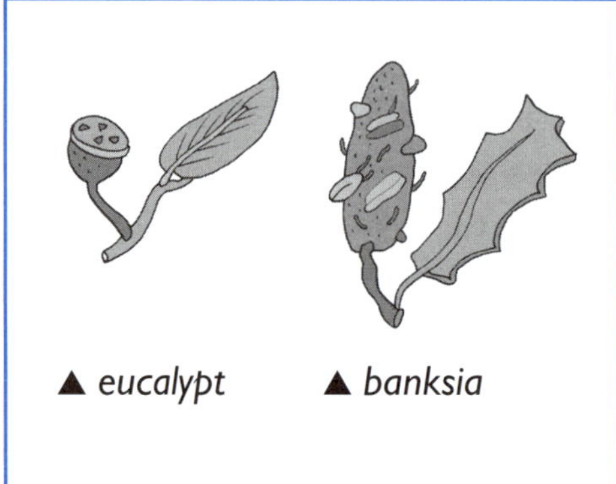

▲ *eucalypt* ▲ *banksia*

See *also* **caption** • **graphic**

indirect object

See **object** (of a sentence)

indirect questions and commands

See **direct** and **indirect questions** and **commands**

indirect speech

See **direct** and **indirect speech**

infer or *imply?*

See ***imply*** *or* ***infer?***

infinitive

See **finite verb** and **non-finite verb**

inflammable or *flammable?*

See ***flammable*** *or* ***inflammable?***

inflection

The alteration of a word that causes a change in the word's meaning. English has very few inflections; the main ones are:

-s, **-'s**, **-s'**	***-ing***
-ed, **-d**	**-en**, **-n**
-er, **-r**	**-est**, **-st**

Plural nouns (-s)
Most English plurals are inflected with the letter **s**, although some common plurals are inflected in other ways:

planet — planet**s** *foot* — *feet*

Possessive nouns (-'s and -s')
The inflection ***s*** + ***apostrophe*** is used in English to show ownership or belonging:

the moons of Jupiter
= Jupiter**'s** moons

the sizes of the moons
= the moon**s'** sizes

Singular 3rd person verbs (-s)
Regular verbs *add* **-s** in the third

person singular (present tense):

to write — she write***s***

Irregular verbs *include* ***-s*** in the third person singular:

to have — it ha***s***
to be — she i***s***

Gerunds and present participles (-ing)
These are also called the ***-ing*** form, used either as a noun or as a verb:

She likes swimm***ing***.
We were swimm***ing*** this morning.

Past forms (-ed** or **-d; -en** or **-n)
Many past forms of English verbs are formed with these endings:

She watch***ed*** the game.
He videotape***d*** the game.
Our team was beat***en***.
They were mistake***n***.

Many irregular verbs are inflected by changing a middle letter to show a past form:

beg*i*n — beg***a***n — beg***u***n

Comparatives and superlatives (-er** and **-est)
These adjective forms indicate "more" and "most":

Positive	*Comparative*	*Superlative*
fast	fast***er***	fast***est***
late	lat***er***	lat***est***

See *also* **apostrophe • gerund • person • plural nouns • regular** and **irregular verbs**

information text

See **factual text**

information report

(Also called a ***non-chronological report***) A kind of text in which the subject is defined and classified into groups. Facts about each group are organised in separate paragraphs.

An information report has:
- a ***main statement*** (usually a ***definition*** of the topic)
- a ***classification*** into groups
- a series of ***facts***, usually grouped in paragraphs

Vertebrates

Main statement (definition)
Animals with backbones are called vertebrates.

Classification
There are six main groups of vertebrates: fish, amphibians, reptiles, dinosaurs, birds and mammals.

Facts
Fish are vertebrates that have scales and gills.
Amphibians (such as frogs) begin life in water and move to land. Their gills change to lungs.

Reptiles have scales and lungs. All reptiles are cold-blooded.

Dinosaurs were warm-blooded and had scales, bare skin or feathers. Many could walk upright on their back legs.

Birds are descended from dinosaurs. All birds walk on their back legs and most can fly with their front legs (wings).

Mammals, like birds, are warm-blooded. Mammals can provide milk for their young. Most mammals have fur or hair.

A report can be planned using a tree diagram or a table.

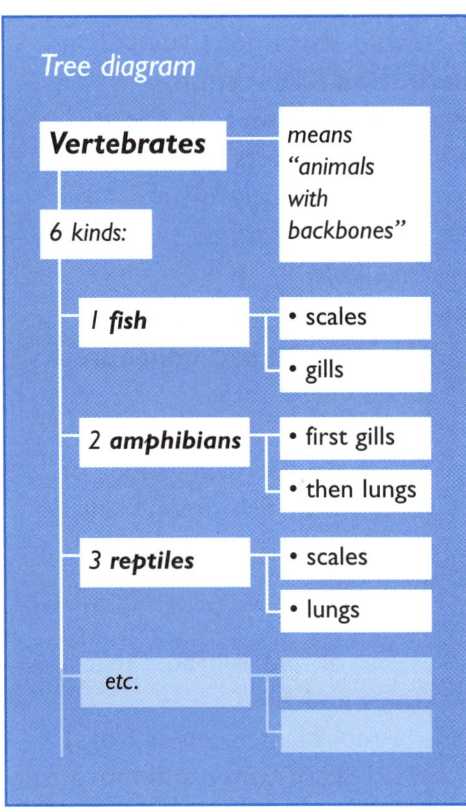

An information report is not to be confused with a ***news report***, which is usually a ***factual recount*** of events.

See also **description • factual recount • table • tree diagram**

inquire or ***enquire***? ***inquiry*** or ***enquiry***?

• both ***inquire*** and ***enquire*** mean "to ask" and both are accepted
• both ***inquiry*** and ***enquiry*** mean a "request for information", but in Australia an ***inquiry*** is often an official investigation, while an ***enquiry*** is a more personal request

"Can I help?" she ***inquired***.
= "Can I help?" she ***enquired***.
The Senate's ***inquiry*** is adjourned.

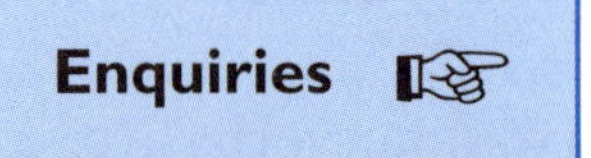

insofar or ***in so far***?

Both ***insofar as*** and ***in so far as*** mean "to the extent that" and both are accepted. The full expression is usually:

insofar as . . . is concerned

I agree with your plan ***insofar as*** the first part ***is concerned***.

In conversation some people

omit the phrase ***is concerned***. Use the full expression in formal writing.

See *also* ***as far as* + *is concerned*?**

instructional text

See **procedure**

insure or *ensure*?

See ***assure*, *ensure*** or ***insure*?**

integrated text

A text in which paragraphs, headings, visual texts and captions are linked, using the principles of graphic design. Professionally designed printed and electronic texts use graphic design to integrate these text elements.

In a typical page in an illustrated reference book or a web page:

- the heading unites all the information under it
- the caption links the graphic to the main paragraph
- the cross-references link the main paragraph to the graphic and caption
- the graphic helps to explain information in the main paragraph

Each of these features helps to integrate the text.

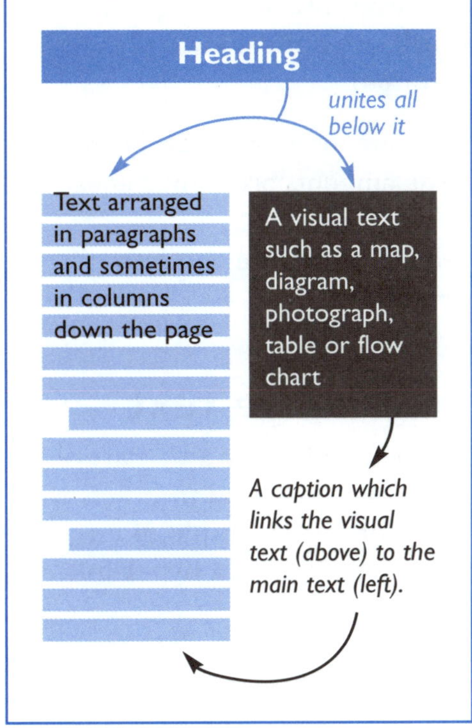

See *also* **graphic design**

intensifier

A word that increases or weakens the strength of another word or phrase (often an **adjective** or <u>adverb</u>).

very hot	***bitterly*** cold
extremely <u>slowly</u>	***slightly*** worn
hardly moving	***too*** <u>roughly</u>

Non-gradable adjectives and adverbs are said to be unable to take an intensifier:

The amounts are equal.
NOT ***very*** equal *or* ***slightly*** equal

However, lists of non-gradable words are almost always disputed:

The amounts are ***exactly*** equal?
The amounts are ***about*** equal?

See *also* **gradable and non-gradable**

---

interactive text

(Also called ***active text***) Part of an electronic text that interacts with the user. An example of an interactive text is a hyperlink.

See *also* **hyperlink**

---

interjection

A word that expresses emotion, but has little if any syntactical connection with the rest of the sentence. Often used in dialogue.

"Here's the boot: ***ugh***, it's dirty!"
"***Sh***, don't move!"
"Did you, ***um***, say something?"

Where strong feelings are expressed, an interjection takes an exclamation mark and stands alone:

Mmm! That's delicious.

See *also* **exclamation mark**

---

internet or *Internet*? *net, Net* or *'net*?

As with any fairly new word, there are many variants, all of which are accepted.

internet or *Internet?*

Some writers say that, because there is only one internet, it is a proper name and should have a capital: ***Internet*** (or **Net**). Others argue that the internet is just another information medium like television and radio, so it needs no capital: ***internet*** (or ***net***).

net or *'net?*

Abbreviations often take an apostrophe to show that something is missing, as in ***'net*** = inter<u>net</u>. However, some abbreviations (called ***clippings***) have become words in their own right (such as ***bus*** = omni<u>bus</u>). Clippings usually have no apostrophe. It could be argued that **net** has already become a clipping.

The simplest solutions are:

You can find us on the ***internet***.
= You can find us on the ***net***.

See *also* **abbreviation • apostrophe • *internet* or *world wide web?***

---

internet or ***world wide web***?

The ***internet*** is not the ***world wide web***:

• The ***internet*** is an international network of computers supporting many services, such as email, chat, data transfer and streaming, among others. *One* of the services which the internet supports is the world wide web.

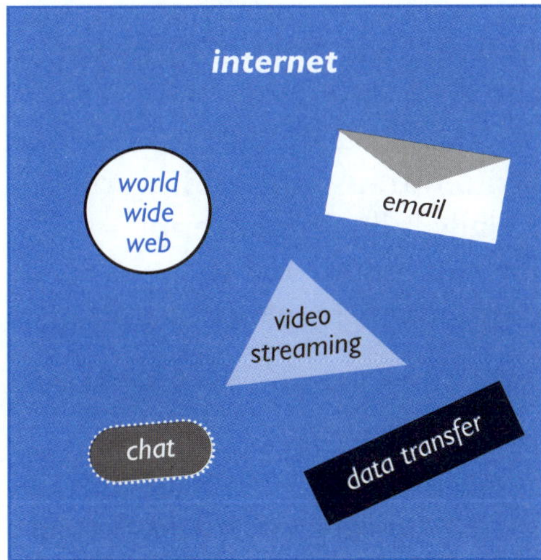

• The ***world wide web*** is a collective name for all websites that are connected by hyperlinks. The web uses the net as its communication platform.

Shortened forms include:

the internet = the ***net***
the world wide web = the ***web***

See also **hypertext** • ***world wide web*** *or* ***World Wide Web***?

inter- or ***intra-***?

• ***inter-*** means "between" (two or more things)
• ***intra-*** means "within" (only one thing)

inter*state* = between states
intra*state* = within one state

inter*net* = network connecting computers in all countries
intra*net* = network connecting computers in one building or organisation

interrogative mood

See **mood (of a verb)**

interrogative sentence

See **question**

interrogative words

Words that are used to ask a question. These are the so-called ***wh-*** words and ***how***.

How did you get here?
Where did he go?
When did he arrive?
What became of him?
Which bike can I use?
Who phoned you?
Whose bike is that?
To ***whom*** does this belong?
Why did he leave?

These words have different names depending on how they are used.

Interrogative adverbs
Where these words are used to ask a question about time, place, manner or cause, they are called interrogative adverbs:

How did you get here?
Where did he go?
Wherever did he go?
When did he arrive?
Why did he leave?

Interrogative pronouns
Where these words stand for a noun, they are called interrogative pronouns:

Which can I use?
Who phoned you?
Whose is that?
To ***whom*** does this belong?

Interrogative determiners (or adjectives)
Where these words precede a noun and modify it, they are called interrogative determiners (or interrogative adjectives):

Which bike can I use?
Whose bike is that?
What kind of bike is that?

See also **adjective • adverb • determiner • pronoun**

in the or *under the circumstances?*

See ***circumstances***: ***in*** or ***under***?

interview

An information text in which two or more people participate, one asking questions and the other replying.

Interviews are usually unscripted spoken texts that are recorded as audio or video.

Written transcripts of interviews usually follow a playscript format, identifying the participants by name or initials:

AK: I think you arrived in Australia in 1990?
BG: Yes, I came with my parents and my older sister.
AK: What were your first impressions?
BG: Well, I was only six and I didn't have much English …

into or *in to?*

- Use ***in to*** where ***in*** belongs with the verb that comes before it.
- Use ***into*** in all other cases.

In the following sentence ***in*** belongs with the verb call:

Don't call ***in*** **to** see me tomorrow.

In the following sentences ***into*** is a preposition:

> Try not to fall ***into*** the water.
> You may get ***into*** difficulties.

intranet or ***internet***?

See ***inter-*** *or* ***intra-****?*

intransitive verb

See **transitive verb** and **intransitive verb**

I *or* ***me*** *(after* ***is****)?*

Both ***It is I*** and ***It's me*** are accepted.

It's me occurs often in conversation but more rarely in written English. All of the following examples are accepted:

It's me.	***It's you.***
It's him.	***It's her.***
It's us.	***It's them.***

The following are formally correct but may sound stilted:

It is I.	***It is you.***
It is he.	***It is she.***
It is we.	***It is they.***

See also ***between you and me*** *or* ***between you and I****?* • ***It is + plural****?*

irony or ***sarcasm***?

Both irony and sarcasm are figures of speech in which the real meaning is the opposite of its apparent meaning. Often the purpose is to ridicule.

The difference lies in the speaker's attitude:
• ***irony*** can be understated and playful
• ***sarcasm*** is often overstated and hostile

Irony

> A to B (*who has just missed the ball*): Good one.

Sarcasm

> A to B (*who has just missed the ball*): Oh, *great*. I suppose you think that's a *really* good shot. I'm *so glad* you're on our team.

See also **figure of speech** • **parody**

irregular noun

See **regular** and **irregular nouns**

irregular verb

See **regular** and **irregular verbs**

-ise or -ize? -isation or -ization?

Both **s** and **z** are accepted in these endings:

organ***ise*** = organ***ize***
organ***isation*** = organ***ization***

In Australia the endings ***-ise*** and ***-isation*** are preferred, while in the USA the endings ***-ize*** and ***-ization*** are preferred.

Some words *always* end in ***-ise***:

surpr***ise***
franch***ise***
gu***ise***
r***ise***

Some words *always* end in ***-ize***:

s***ize***
pr***ize*** (= an award)
caps***ize***
seize

is or *are* after *anyone*, *everyone*, *someone*, *no one*, *none*?

See ***everybody/everyone*** + ***is*** or ***are***?

italic type

A style of type used for the names of books and foreign words or to emphasise a key word or phrase. Italic can be used when keyboarding a text.

Names of books
I've read *The Forests of Silence* but not *The Lake of Tears*.

Foreign words
In French *salut!* means "hi!"
Ciao is Italian for both "hello" and "goodbye".

Emphasis
I haven't *really* been to Japan.

See *also* **font** • **underlining** or ***italic***?

It is me or *It is I*?

See ***I*** or ***me*** (after ***is***)?

it is + plural?

Although ***it is*** (or ***it's***) is singular, it is sometimes followed by a plural complement. This construction is common in quoted speech.

"Look, ***it's*** the Smiths."

This construction also occurs in formal writing, usually to give emphasis to the complement:

It was the mammals and birds that replaced the dinosaurs.

Writers who find this apparent disagreement awkward can use an alternative emphatic phrase:

In fact the mammals and birds replaced the dinosaurs.

See also **agreement** • **complement** • ***I* or *me* (after *is*)?**

its or *it's*?

- ***its*** means "of it"
- ***it's*** means "it is" or "it has"

The possessive ***its*** belongs with ***my***, ***your***, ***his***, ***her***, ***our*** and ***their***, none of which has an apostrophe (**'**):

> the tiger and ***its*** environment
> = the tiger and the environment
> ***of the tiger***

The contraction ***it's*** belongs with ***I'm***, ***you're***, ***he's***, ***she's***, ***we're*** and ***they're***, all of which use an apostrophe to show that letters are missing:

> ***I'm*** = I am
> ***you're*** = you are
> ***he's*** = he is
> ***she's*** = she is
> ***it's*** = it is
> ***we're*** = we are
> ***they're*** = they are

In conversation ***it's*** has two possible meanings:

> ***it's*** going = ***it is*** going
> ***it's*** gone = ***it has*** gone

Similar contractions (used in quoted speech) include:

> ***it'll*** be easy = ***it will*** be easy
> ***it'd*** be easy = ***it would*** be easy
> ***it'd*** been easy = ***it had*** been easy

People have difficulty choosing between ***its*** and ***it's*** because nouns form the possessive with the apostrophe:

> this shirt's collar = ***its*** collar
> the sun's rays = ***its*** rays

See also **apostrophe** • **contraction** • ***I* or *me* (after *is*)?** • **possessive case**

-ize or *-ise*?

See ***-ise* or *-ize*?**

jargon

The technical language that is used by a particular art or science.

The bee's ***antennae*** (or feelers) are not to be confused with the ***tarsi*** (or feet).

journey line

A line on a map that shows a route. Journey lines are used on maps that show migration routes or voyages of discovery. They are also used to show a narrative in a story map.

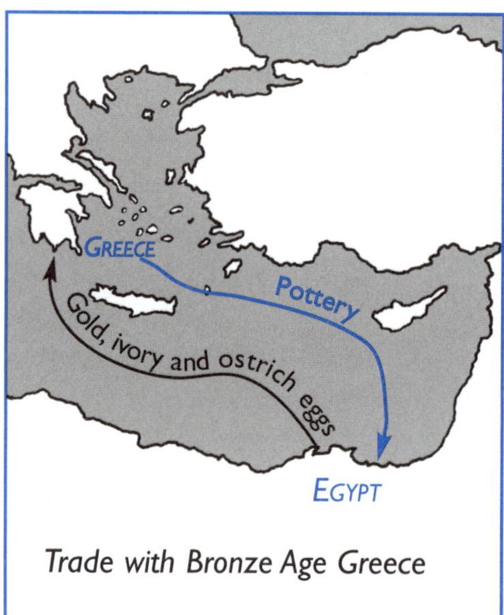

Trade with Bronze Age Greece

See *also* **story map**

jpeg

(***j****oint* ***p****hotographic* ***e****xperts* ***g****roup*) The coding used to compress a picture file, usually a photograph.

A URL that ends with ***jpeg*** or ***jpg*** is likely to be a photographic file.

See *also* **URL**

jump cut

See ***cut*** *or* ***fade****?*

justified text

See **alignment** (of text)

key

(1) Part of a computer keyboard.

(2) **IN VISUAL GRAMMAR**
(Also called a ***legend***) The explanation of symbols or colours in a map, graph or diagram. The key is often arranged inside a box which separates its contents from the rest of the diagram or graph.

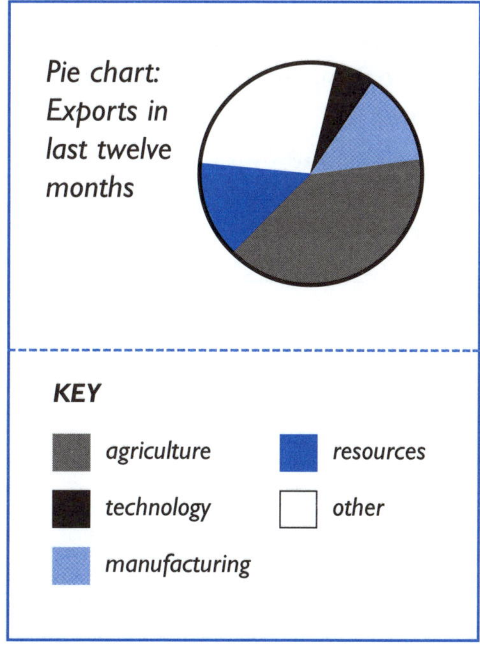

See *also* **keyboard**

keyboard

The set of keys attached to a computer that are used to write text or operate other programs.

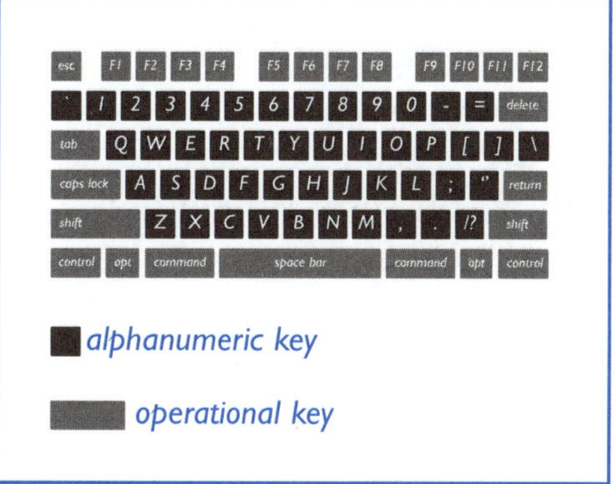

There are two kinds of key on a computer keyboard: ***alphanumeric*** and ***operational***.

Alphanumeric keys

These keys include:

- the letters of the alphabet
- punctuation symbols such as comma, full stop and brackets
- the numbers 0–9

Operational keys

These keys include:

TAB	RETURN
SHIFT	CAPS LOCK
OPTION	COMMAND
CONTROL	

TAB *key*

Moves the next word to the right by a fixed amount. This is called ***indenting*** the text.

RETURN *key*
Moves the next word to a new line below the preceding text. This creates a new paragraph.

SHIFT *key*
Changes the next letter or word from lower case to UPPER CASE (or CAPITALS). This key works only as long as it is held down. It is used to capitalise a single letter or word.

CAPS LOCK *key*
Changes the next word(s) from lower case to CAPITALS. This key works without being held, so that it can be used to capitalise longer passages. ***Caps*** is short for CAPITALS.

OPTION *key*
Changes the letter to a special character:

Option key + semicolon (;) = …
Option key + left bracket ([) = "
Option key + e + e = é

The option key is sometimes called the alternate (or ALT) key.

COMMAND *and* **CONTROL** *keys*
These are used in combination with other keys and do not produce any letters on screen. They are used for commands such as:

To copy text (on a Mac):
press the COMMAND key + C

To paste text (on a PC):
press the CONTROL key + V

See also **lower case** and **upper case**

kinds of + plural?

Writers disagree about whether ***kinds of*** always takes a plural. Some writers treat all cases as plural.

There are many ***kinds of*** rocks.

Other writers believe that sometimes ***kinds of*** can take a *singular*:

There are many ***kinds of*** *rock*.

The expressions ***sorts of*** and ***types of*** follow the same pattern as ***kinds of***.

See also **collective noun • plural nouns**

label

The name of a detail in a map or diagram, usually connected to the detail with an arrow or leader line.

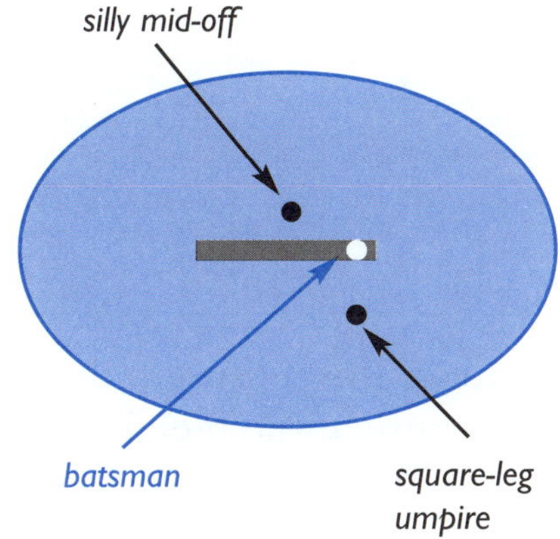

The label names the detail in the diagram, while the detail defines the meaning of the label.

See also **leader line** • **picture glossary**

labour or *labor*?

In Australia the spelling **labour** is the most common, but **labor** is sometimes used. In Canada, Ireland and the UK the spelling **labour** is preferred. **Labor** is the American spelling.

The **Australian Labor Party** is always spelt without the ***u***.

See also ***harbour*** *or* ***harbor?***

laid, lain or *lied?*

See ***lie*** *or* ***lay?***

Latin plurals

Words borrowed from Latin which have plurals other than ***-s***. Latin plurals include:

-i as in ***radii***.
-ae as in ***antennae***.
-a as in ***media***.

See **plural nouns**

lay or *lie?*

See ***lie*** *or* ***lay?***

layout

See **graphic design**

leader line

A line that connects two parts of a diagram, usually a label to a detail in the diagram.

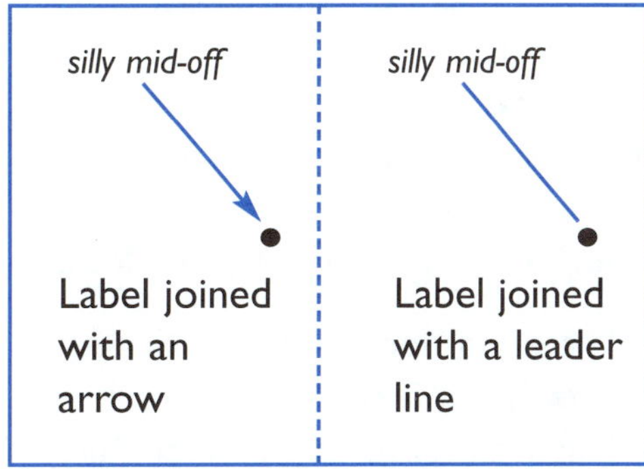

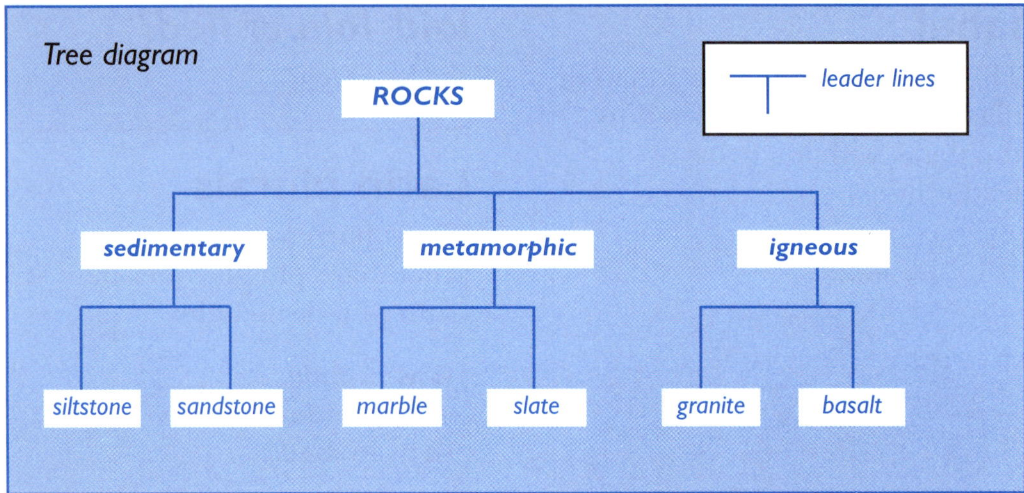

Leader lines are also used in tree diagrams (above).

Leader lines do not have arrowheads (➤).

See also **arrow • label • tree diagram**

lead or ***led***?

- ***lead*** (rhymes with ***head***) is a heavy, soft metal sometimes used to add weight to a fishing line
- ***lead*** (rhymes with ***bead***) can be a dog's leash or an electrical cable or wire
- ***to lead*** (rhymes with ***bead***) means "to draw along" or "to show the way"
- ***led*** is the past form of ***to lead***

The metal ***lead*** is easily melted.
Attach the ***lead*** to the TV set.
This trail ***leads*** to Perisher Valley.
Her dog ***led*** us to her house.

Because of the confusion in sound between the metal ***lead*** and the verb ***led***, people sometimes mistakenly write ***lead*** instead of ***led***:

Her dog ***led*** us to her house.
NOT Her dog ***lead*** us to her house.

leaders [................]

A row of small dots connecting two elements of a text. Leaders are used in some contents pages to connect chapter headings with the page numbers on which chapters begin.

Chapter 1 6
Chapter 2 11
Chapter 3 23
Chapter 4 30
Chapter 5 46
Chapter 6 55

legend

(1) A narrative based at least partly on actual events, or thought to be about people who once lived.

(2) A list on a map or diagram which defines the meanings of colours or symbols. Also called a ***key***.

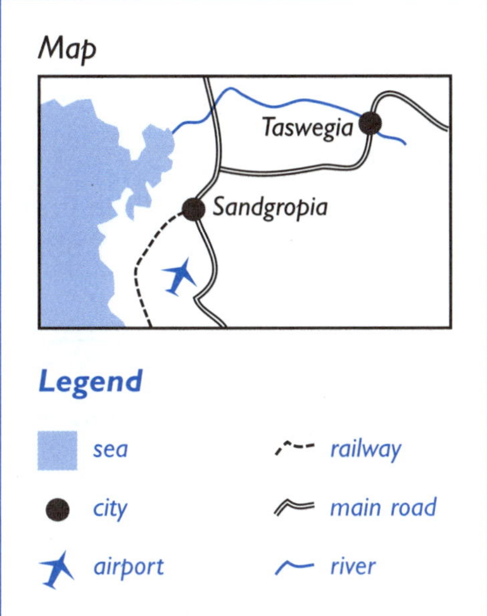

See *also* **key** • ***myth*** *or* ***legend?***

lend or *loan?*

• ***to lend*** means "to let someone borrow" (it is a verb)
• ***loan*** means "something borrowed" (it is a noun)

> Can you ***lend*** me a pencil?
> This video is on overnight ***loan***.

In formal writing avoid "to loan":

> Can you ***lend*** me a pencil?
> NOT Can you ***loan*** me a pencil?

less or *fewer?*

See ***fewer*** *or* ***less?***

lexical cohesion

See **cohesion**

lexical text

A text made of words in sentences (such as an email or a novel), as distinct from a ***visual text*** (such as a diagram or an atlas).

See *also* **text** • **visual text**

lexical verb

Most verbs are lexical verbs. They include all verbs *other than* the auxiliaries.

Auxiliary verbs usually support ***lexical*** verbs:

> We ***played*** tennis.
> We will ***play*** tennis.
> We should ***play*** tennis.
> We might ***play*** tennis.
> We are ***playing*** tennis.

See *also* **auxiliary verb** • **verb**

L

lie or *lay*? *lied*, *lain* or *laid*?

- ***to lie*** can mean:
  (1) "to say something false"
  (2) "to rest or lie down"
- ***to lay*** means "to put down" something

"Please don't ***lie*** to me."
After our swim we could ***lie*** on the beach.
We could ***lay*** the towels on the sand.

- ***to lie*** is an intransitive verb; you cannot "lie something"
- ***to lay*** is a transitive verb; you always "lay something"

"Don't ***lie***!"
"***Lie*** still."
"***Lay*** that plate on the table."

NOT "***Lay*** still."
NOT "***Lie*** that plate on the table."

Lied, *lain* or *laid*?

- ***lied*** is a past form of ***to lie*** (= to say something false)
- ***lain*** is a past form of ***to lie*** (= to rest or lie down)
- ***laid*** is a past form of ***to lay*** (= "to put down" something)

He has ***lied*** about his age.
Some logs have ***lain*** on the forest floor for a thousand years.
They have ***laid*** our new carpet.

These words are also confusing because ***lay*** is sometimes a past form of ***to lie***:

Yesterday we ***lay*** on the beach.

The three different forms are set out in this table:

	Past tense	*Past participle*
to lie (1)	lied	have lied
to lie (2)	lay	have lain
to lay	laid	have laid

(1) = to say something false
(2) = to rest or lie down

life line

One line in a multiple time line that represents the lifetime of a person or thing.

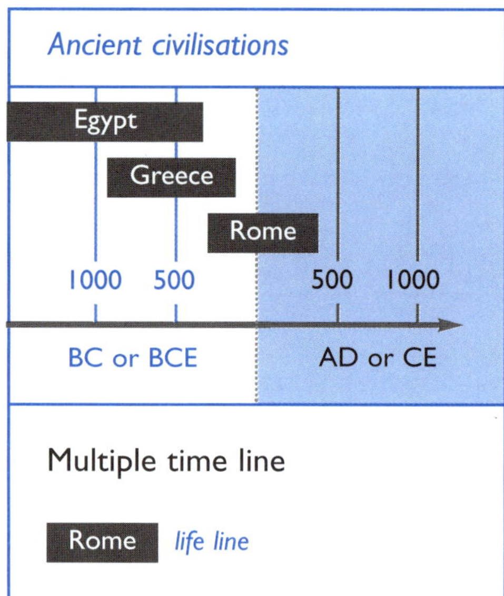

See also ***AD or BC?*** • **multiple time line**

lightening or *lightning*?

• ***lightening*** means "becoming lighter"
• ***lightning*** means "a flash of light in an electrical storm"

lighting (in film or TV)

Lighting can be used to establish mood and to influence the viewer's feelings towards the characters. Lighting effects include colour, brightness and contrast.

Colour

Some film directors have used colour filters (or processing) to convey mood such as:

• ***blue*** light for coldness or fear
• ***orange or pink*** light for warmth, security, homeliness or past times
• ***black and white*** for suggesting "realism" or "documentary" truth

Brightness and contrast

Dim or bright lighting has been used for various effects:

• ***dim*** lighting for uncertainty and danger
• ***harsh lighting with black shadows*** for grim "reality", as in detective movies of the 1940s known as *film noir* (= "black film")
• ***grainy*** texture (as if filmed on low-grade film stock) to suggest the eyewitness "reality" of "amateur video"

light or *lite*?

See **advertese**

like, as, as if or *such as*?

IN FORMAL WRITING

• ***like*** (in comparisons) is used in front of a single word or phrase (a group of words without a verb):

My backpack looks ***like*** yours.

My backpack looks ***like*** that green one.

• ***as*** (in comparisons) is used in front of a *clause* (a group of words that include a verb):

My backpack looks ***as*** *it did when I bought it.*

Their packs were *exactly* ***as*** *he had described them.*

• ***as if*** is used to make a comparison doubtful:

My backpack looks ***as if*** *a truck ran over it.*

• ***such as*** is used when giving an example:

Our backpacks, ***such as*** day packs and overnight packs, are half price.

☞

IN INFORMAL WRITING

In narrative dialogue or informal conversation, ***like*** is used in most situations:

> My backpack looks ***like*** it did when I bought it.
>
> Their packs were *exactly* ***like*** *he had described them.*
>
> My backpack looks ***like*** *a truck ran over it.*
>
> All backpacks, ***like*** day packs and overnight packs, are half price.

Some people suggest that

> I am just ***as*** *he is*

is "more correct" than

> I am just ***like*** him.

Both are accepted and the second may sound less stilted in many situations than the first.

line graph

A graph in which the amount of something is shown to go up or down over time.

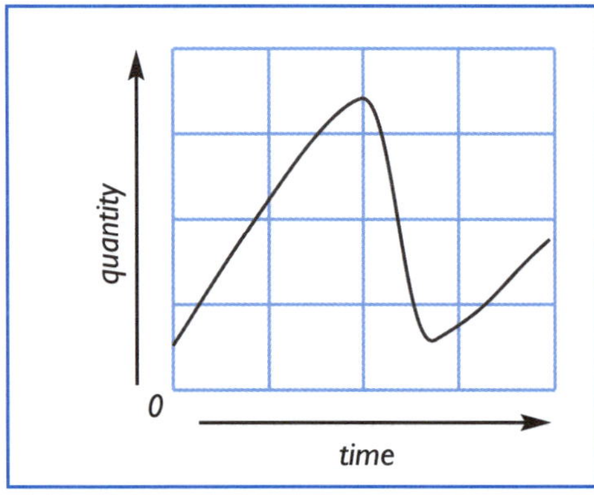

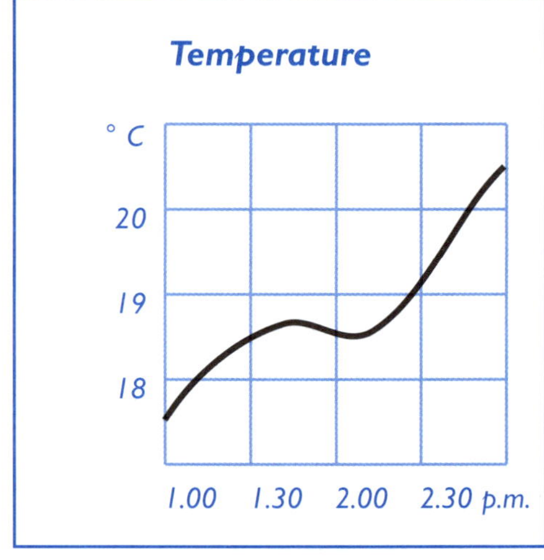

link (on a website)

See **hyperlink**

list

An arrangement of items or topics in which each new item is placed on a new line.

> *Parts of a flower*
> petals
> sepals
> anthers
> style

Lists are used in procedures to itemise materials. Lists arranged in columns with headings are called ***tables***.

There are two main kinds of list: ***simple lists*** and ***nested lists***. Lists can also be arranged as conventional sentences.

Simple list

Simple lists usually have no commas or full stops at the ends of the lines. Each new item can be introduced with a bullet (•):

Parts of a flower
- petals
- sepals
- anthers
- style

Nested list

Lists can be organised as a hierarchy in which each topic falls within the previous topic:

Identifying insects
```
|—with 2 wings
|—|—+ wings have scales
|—|—|—+ feelers are feathery
|—|—|—|—= moths
|—|—|—+ feelers are not feathery
|—|—|—|—= butterflies
|—|—+ wings have no scales ...
|—with 4 wings ...
|—with 0 wings ...
```

An example of a nested list is a ***site map*** on a website.

Sentence list

Sentences that list items usually separate the items with commas:

The parts of a flower include the petals, sepals, anthers and style.

See also **bullet • comma • nested list • site map • table**

literally, virtually or *metaphorically*?

- ***literally*** means "truly and without exaggerating"
- ***virtually*** means "almost but not quite"
- ***metaphorically*** means "not actually but with a similarity to"

It rained ***literally*** for twenty-two hours.
It rained ***virtually*** all day.
It was ***metaphorically*** a waterfall out there.

Metaphor is a figure of speech in which one thing (such as rain) is treated as if it were something else (such as a waterfall).

See also **figure of speech • rhetoric, rhetorical**

little or *few*?

See ***a few*** *or* ***a little****?*

loan or *lend*?

See ***lend*** *or* ***loan****?*

logbook

A form of factual recount in which facts and observations are arranged in the order in which they happened.

4 May
Planted six rows of beans.

12 May
The first shoots have appeared.

16 May
The bean shoots are 25 mm high.

23 *June*
Two plants have started to flower.

Logbooks, unlike diaries, usually avoid personal comments.

See also **diary entry • factual recount**

lose or ***loose***?

• ***to lose*** is the opposite of "to keep"
• ***loose*** is the opposite of "tight"

Your bike could ***lose*** its back wheel if the bolts are too ***loose***.

lots of or ***a great deal of***?

These phrases mean the same.

lots of = a great deal of

IN FORMAL WRITING

A great deal of is sometimes preferred to ***lots of***. Similarly:

a lot of = plenty of

lower case and **upper case**

These phrases refer to the style of alphabet letters.

• ***lower case letters*** = minuscules or "small letters"
• ***upper case letters*** = majuscules, capitals, capital letters or "block letters"

This sentence is in lower case.
THIS SENTENCE IS IN UPPER CASE.

Why ***case***? Until last century a printer's capital letters were kept in a wooden case (or box) *above* the case that held the "small" letters.

In word processing, ***upper case*** letters are formed by using the **SHIFT** or **CAPS LOCK** keys on the keyboard.

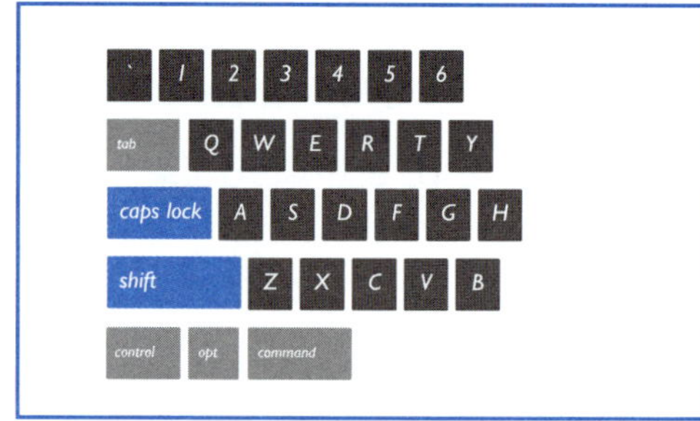

See also **keyboard**

malapropism

Using the wrong word that sounds similar to the word you want but has a very different meaning. The effect is supposed to be ridiculous.

> She's as headstrong as an ***allegory*** on the banks of the Nile.

Malapropisms are named after Mrs Malaprop (a character in Sheridan's play *The Rivals*) who meant to say:

> She's as headstrong as an ***alligator*** on the banks of the Nile.

Sometimes whole phrases can be confused in a similar way:

> I won't change my decision. It is ***cast in stone***.

To cast something is to pour it out and wait for it to set hard like concrete. It is not possible to do this with stone. The writer has confused ***cast in concrete*** and ***carved in stone*** (and possibly ***cast the first stone*** where *cast* means *throw*).

In French *mal à propos* means "inappropriately" or "improperly".

See also **spoonerism**

main clause

See **clause**

map

A visual text that usually reduces objects to a flat plane and shows the locations of places and the distances between them.

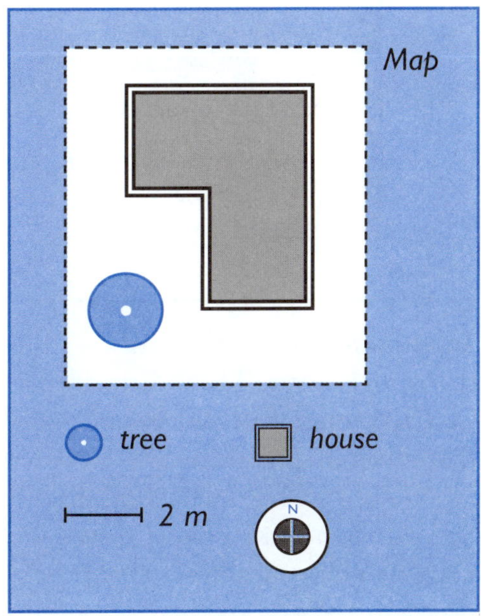

A map leaves out many details (such as the dog and the bird in the map on page 111) but adds other information (such as the scale and the compass rose).

Maps are useful when writing instructions and explanations. Features of a map can include a scale, a compass rose and a grid.

Map or flow chart?

Some maps show a sequence of places, but they show neither their true locations nor the true distances between them. One example of this kind of map is a ***transport map***, which is perhaps more like a flow chart than a true map.

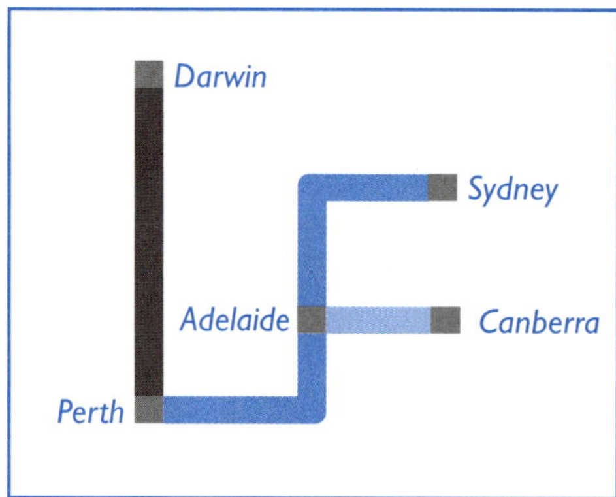

Story maps are similar to transport maps. They show items in a sequence but not exact distances or positions.

See *also* **compass rose** • **flow chart** • **grid** • **scale** (in a map or diagram) • **story map**

masculine

See **gender**

mass noun

See **count noun** and **mass noun**

matching

Checking that a list includes grammatically similar elements. The following list mixes *verbs* (actions) and nouns (things):

> You can *swim*, *play* basketball, *go* fishing or soccer.

The sentence could be rewritten so that the elements match:

> You can *swim*, *play* basketball, *go* fishing or *play* soccer. [all verbs]

Or:

> You can choose between swimming, basketball, fishing or soccer. [all nouns]

See *also* **nouns** • **verbs**

material process

See **process**

materials list

The list of items needed to carry out a procedure.

> *How to make pancakes*
> ***You will need:***
> - ***flour***
> - ***eggs***
> - ***milk …***

See also **procedure**

may or *can?*

See ***can*** *or* ***may****?*

medium or *media* + *is* or *are*?

- ***a medium*** is a substance or system through which something passes or is sent
- ***media*** is the plural form of ***medium***

> Water is a ***medium*** through which waves pass.
> Air and water are ***media*** through which waves pass.

- ***medium*** is singular and takes *is*
- ***media*** is plural and takes *are*

> Water *is* a ***medium*** …
> Air and water *are* ***media*** …

Media is a Latin plural.

The media can also mean "all systems of communication" including newspapers, TV, radio, film and the internet. Some writers think of ***the media*** as plural (kinds of information media). Others see ***the media*** as a single entity or a collective noun. Both are accepted:

Plural noun

> ***The media*** include all means of communication.

Singular collective noun

> ***The media*** includes all means of communication.

See also **multimedia text • plural nouns**

mega- or *giga-*?

- ***mega-*** means 10^6 or 1 000 000
- ***giga-*** means 10^9 or 1 000 000 000
- ***mega-*** can also mean "large"

> 10 ***megawatts*** = 10 million watts
> 10 ***gigabytes*** = 10 billion bytes
> The ***megalosaurs*** were large dinosaurs.

Computer memory is measured in ***megabytes*** or ***gigabytes***, often shortened to ***meg*** (or MB) and ***gig*** (or GB).

> This software takes up 20 ***meg***.
> = This software takes up 20 MB.

mental process

See **process**

M

menu

An interactive list from which a viewer can select a topic. Menus are found in computer programs, DVDs and websites.

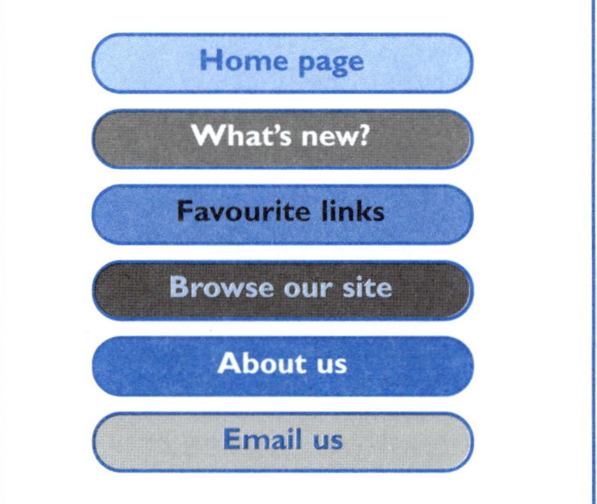

A menu works like a table of contents in a reference book, but without page numbers. Instead, a hyperlink sends the user to the selected topic.

A ***menu bar*** is a row of headings (such as ***File***, ***Edit*** and ***Help***), forming a menu across the top of a computer screen.

See also **hyperlink**

me *or* I *(after* is*)?*

See ***I*** *or* ***me*** *(after* ***is****)?*

me *or* my + -ing*?*

See **fused participle**

me *or* myself*?*

Some writers prefer ***myself*** to ***me*** in a sentence such as:

> This play is by Gina and **me**.
> This play is by Gina and ***myself***.

Other writers find this use of ***myself*** pompous and self-conscious.

meronym

See **chain • cohesion**

metaphor

See **figure of speech**

metaphorically, literally or virtually?

See ***literally, virtually*** *or* ***metaphorically****?*

meter or metre?

- ***a meter*** is a machine that measures water or gas, etc.
- ***a metre*** equals 100 millimetres

> Our gas **meter** is 5 **metres** from the front gate.

The American spelling of ***metre*** is ***meter***.

See also **metre** (in poetry)

method

IN FUNCTIONAL GRAMMAR

The sequence of steps needed to carry out a procedure.

How to make pancakes
First beat the eggs ...
Then add the milk ...
Next add the flour ...
Finally ...

See also **procedure**

method or *methodology*?

• ***method*** means "a way of doing something"
• ***methodology*** means "the study of different methods" such as teaching methods

What's the best ***method*** for catching tadpoles?

NOT What's the best ***methodology*** for catching tadpoles?

metre (in poetry)

The rhythm of a line of poetry that repeats a pattern of stressed and unstressed syllables.

The metre of a poem can be shown using ¯ above a stressed syllable and ˘ above an unstressed one.

Algy **met** a **bear**.

A **bear met Al**gy.

The **bear was bul**gy.

The **bulge was Al**gy.

— Anon.

Metre refers also to the number of beats in a line. For example, a line of five beats is a pentameter.

Note the different spellings:
metre ***pentameter***

See also **pentameter**

middle voice

A verb whose object is treated as a subject (or *IN FUNCTIONAL GRAMMAR* whose effect is treated as an agent).

Active voice
The sun melted the ice.

Passive voice
The ice was melted by the sun.

Middle voice
The ice melted.
Or:
The ice was melting.

See also **active voice • passive voice • voice**

M

might or ***could?***

See **can** or **may**?

mixed metaphors

Some writers try to avoid two or more metaphors in the same sentence if they suggest conflicting pictures of what is being described. It is felt that the result can be ridiculous or confusing.

> Blown by the winds of change our ship of state is led by a man who is full of hot air. We need a pilot who is steady as a rock and who can steer us away from the reefs.

However, many writers do mix metaphors successfully.

> *The hearts*
> *That spaniel'd me at heels, to whom I gave*
> *Their wishes, do discandy, melt their sweets*
> *On blossoming Caesar ...*
> — Shakespeare

See *also* **figure of speech**

mobile shorthand

An abbreviated writing of text on a mobile phone, usually in an informal style.

CU b4 5.30
= See you before five-thirty.

Y R U so L8 ? :,-(
= Why are you so late? I'm sad.

The same applies to email shorthand.

See *also* **email shorthand**

modal auxiliary

An ***auxiliary*** is a verb that supports a lexical verb.

> They ***can*** repair their bikes.
> They ***should*** repair their bikes.

The modal auxiliaries (or ***modals***) include:

can	***could***
may	***might***
will	***would***
shall	***should***
must	***ought*** *(to)*

Most ***modals*** express degrees of certainty or doubt:

> They ***should*** be arriving soon.
> He ***could*** be coming by train.
> She ***must*** have caught the bus.
> We ***might*** have been able to stay.

The ***non-modal auxiliaries*** are sometimes called ***primary verbs***. These are the verbs to be, to do and to have.

See *also* **auxiliary • lexical verb • primary verb • verb**

modality

The expression of doubt or certainty, usually by using ***modal auxiliaries*** such as **could**, **might** or **should**.

See *also* **modal auxiliary**

mode

See **text and context**

modifier

IN FUNCTIONAL GRAMMAR

A ***word or phrase*** that defines or limits a head noun in a noun group.

that tall, thin girl
the girl ***wearing the cap***

• a modifier that comes *before* the head noun is a ***pre-modifier***
• a modifier that comes *after* the head noun is a ***post-modifier***

Pre-modifier	*Head noun*	*Post-modifier*
that tall, thin	girl	wearing the cap

See *also* **noun group • post-modifier • pre-modifier**

modulation

The use of various words or phrases by a speaker (or writer) to influence the listener (or reader) to act in a certain way.

The speaker might choose any of the following ways to say "be quiet". The strongest expressions are at the top of the list, and the weakest ones are at the bottom:

Silence!
Be quiet.
You ought to be quiet.
I'd like you to stop talking.
Can you stop talking?
Try to be a bit quieter.
You could be quiet.
I wish you wouldn't talk.

mood and residue

IN FUNCTIONAL GRAMMAR

A sentence can be divided into two parts: its ***mood*** and ***residue***. The part called the mood shows whether the speaker (or writer) claims to state a fact, asks a question or makes a command.

The mood is made up of the ***subject*** and the ***finite***. The rest of the sentence is the residue.

Declarative mood

The speaker (or writer) claims to state a fact. The subject comes first:

Mood		***Residue***
Subject	*Finite*	
They	have	gone away.

☞

Interrogative mood

The speaker asks a question. The finite comes first:

Mood		Residue
Finite	Subject	
Have	they	gone away?

Imperative mood

The speaker makes a command. There is no subject:

Mood		Residue
Subject	Finite	
	Go	away!

See *also* **mood** (of a verb)

mood (of a verb)

A way of grouping verbs, depending on whether they express a fact, a question, a command or a possibility.

There are two ways of grouping verbs:

- Do they form a statement, a question or a command?
- Do they express a fact or a possibility?

Statement, question or command?

A verb that claims to state a fact is said to be "in the ***declarative*** mood":

They ***bought*** some oranges.

A verb that puts a question is said to be "in the ***interrogative*** mood":

Did they ***buy*** some oranges?

A verb that expresses a command is said to be "in the ***imperative*** mood":

Buy some oranges.

Fact or possibility?

A verb that claims to express a fact is also said to be "in the ***indicative*** mood":

He ***stayed*** at home.

A verb that expresses a possibility (which may or may not be true) is said to be "in the ***subjunctive*** mood":

If she ***were*** to stay, I***'d stay*** too.
I am asking that he ***be taken*** home.

The subjunctive mood is "disappearing" as fewer people are using it. Many would now write:

If I ***was*** you I'd give it back.

See *also* **mood and residue**

morpheme

The smallest part of a word that has meaning. If it is made any shorter, it ceases to mean something (in English).

For example, in the word *impossible*:

-possible means "likely" and *im-* means "opposite of" or "not".

If *-possible* is shortened (for example to *-ossible* or *-possi*), then it no longer has a meaning (in English). Therefore *-possible* is a morpheme.

If *im-* is shortened (for example to *m-* or *i-*), then it no longer means "opposite of". Therefore *im-* is a morpheme.

Free and bound morphemes

Morphemes can be called ***free*** or bound. A free morpheme still has a meaning when it stands alone, but a bound morpheme makes sense only when it is attached to another word.

For example, in the word *impossible*:

-possible can stand alone, so it is a ***free morpheme***.

im- makes sense only when it is attached to another word, so it is a bound morpheme.

Allomorphs

Where different morphemes all have the same meaning, they are said to be ***allomorphs***.

For example, these allomorphs all mean "opposite of" or "not":

im- ***un-*** ***in-***
dis- ***ig-*** ***il-***

im*possible* ***un****friendly*
in*frequent* ***dis****qualify*
ig*noble* ***il****literate*

See *also* **base • prefix** and **suffix**

morphology

The study of word formation. Morphology includes the study of how words are inflected (***inflection***).

See *also* **inflection**

multimedia text

A text which combines different media. The media used might include film, video, words, still images, sound, hypertext, etc.

A multimedia text might be:
- a ***website*** that includes text, video files, audio files and still images
- a ***DVD*** that includes a movie with actors and animated characters, a menu for finding different scenes, digital music or interviews with the film-makers

See *also* ***medium*** *or* ***media*** **+** ***is*** *or* ***are****?*

M

multiple line graph

A line graph that has two or more lines, each recording data for a different item.

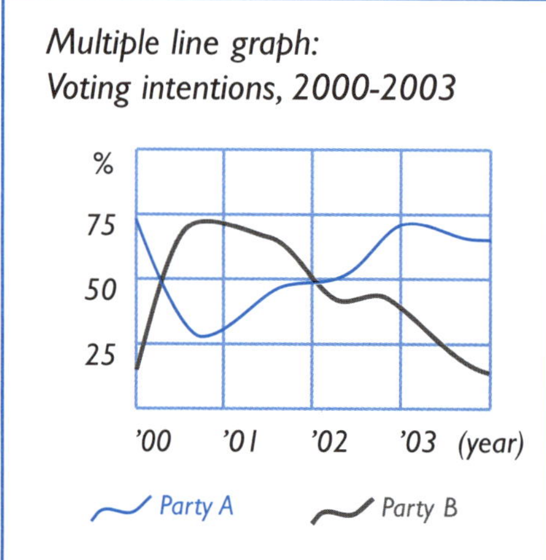

Multiple line graphs help the reader to compare data. They may be found in information reports and explanations.

See *also* **line graph**

multiple time line

A time line that has two or more ***life lines***.

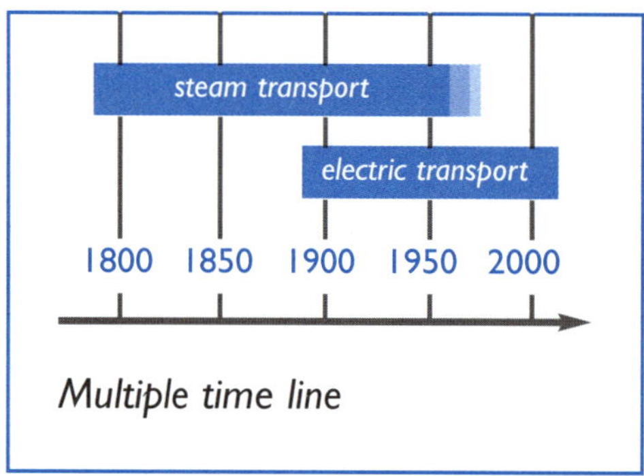

Multiple time line

Multiple time lines are used in recounts and explanations.

See *also* **life line • time line**

myself or *me*?

See ***me*** *or* ***myself***?

myth or *legend*?

- a ***myth*** is a narrative that includes characters, some or all of whom are superhuman or imaginary
- a ***legend*** is a narrative based at least partly on actual events, or thought to be about people who once lived

The Greek ***myths*** include gods who could change shape and monsters that were half-human and half-animal.

The ***legend*** of King Arthur is about a king who *may* have ruled Britain in the sixth century AD.

- a ***myth*** can also mean something that is untrue or "made up"
- a ***legend*** can also mean "a famous or outstanding person"

Some people have claimed that extraterrestrials are among us. That's just a ***myth***.

Mike kicked six goals in the last quarter. He's a ***legend***.

names

Names are written or keyboarded differently, depending on the person or thing to which they refer.

Names of people and places

All names have an initial capital as they are proper nouns:

> My friend **L**isa is from **N**ew **Z**ealand.

Names of books, plays, films, CDs, newspapers and magazines

The names of published works are keyboarded in *italic* or handwritten with an underline:

> They said they liked *The Hobbit* more than *The Lord of the Rings*.

> They said they liked The Hobbit more than The Lord of the Rings.

Names of poems, short stories and songs

The names of shorter works are usually written in quotation marks:

> Do you know the second stanza of "Waltzing Matilda"?

Names of websites

Websites can be written:

Site name.<URL>

Jokes Online.<www.hahaha.org.au>

Names in bibliographies

In bibliographies the names of books, websites, films and so on are keyboarded in the same way.

See also **bibliography** • **underlining** or ***italic?*** • **URL**

narrative

(1) The sequence of events in a work of fiction. Also called the ***plot*** or ***storyline***.

(2) A kind of text in which a story is told. A narrative is similar to a recount but is wholly or partly fictional.

A narrative text may have:

- an ***orientation*** that establishes the narrative's main characters, setting, atmosphere or themes
- a ***plot*** or sequence of events (and sometimes a less important ***subplot***) including ***complications***
- a ***climax*** or ***crisis***
- a ***resolution*** or ***dénouement*** that may "solve" the crisis or "disentangle" the complications (***dénouement*** is French for "untying" a knot)

Into the Pit

Orientation

> We were minding our own business—just drifting about and taking the air—when a great wind blew us past jagged white rocks into a cave near by.

Plot and complications

The cave echoed and even seemed to roar as we were swept into an even darker tunnel deep inside it. Some of my companions were trapped in the long tendrils that hung from the walls and roof of that tunnel. We never saw our friends again. Meanwhile those of us who survived were dumped at the bottom of a great pit, the walls of which were wet, sticky and in constant movement.

Crisis

Now we could not move. We were afraid we would never escape this trap. Even if a search party found us, we were too puny to climb out.

Resolution

Suddenly we heard a roaring wind which this time seemed to pull us upwards. Back into the tunnel we all flew, only to be hurled once more across the cave and into the open air again. We had survived! Relieved, we drifted among specks of dust much greater than ourselves. It was then that we decided never to go near that snoring dog's mouth again.

Narratives can take many forms other than this traditional structure. For example, a narrative may include ***flashbacks***, tell the story in reverse or retell the story several times from different points of view.

A narrative can be planned using a story map or a flow chart.

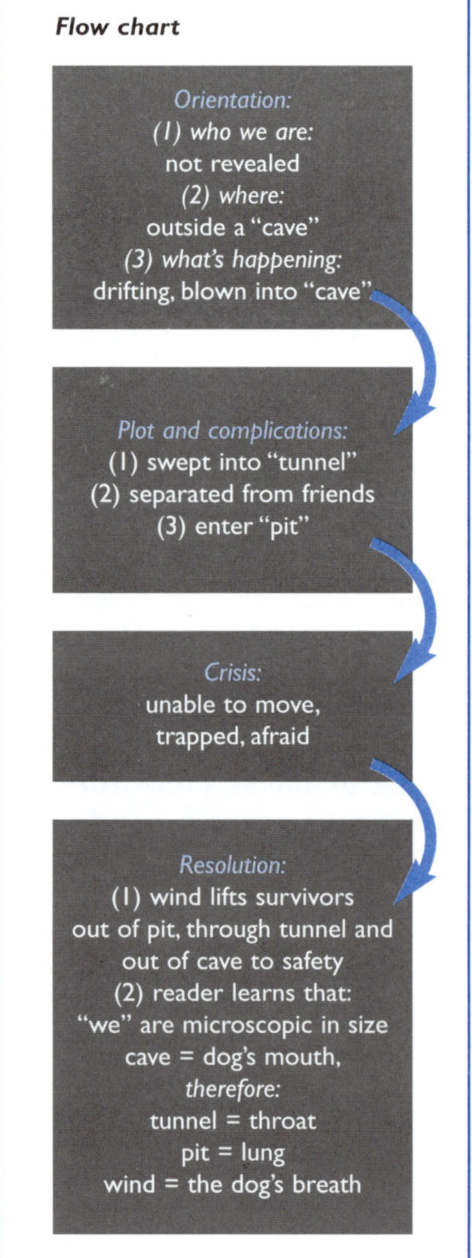

See *also* **character • crisis** (in a narrative) **• flashback • flow chart • line graph • recount • resolution** (in a narrative) **• setting** (in a narrative) **• storyboard**

narrative present

Another term for ***historic present*** tense.

See **present tenses**

narrator

The character in a novel, poem or movie who narrates (tells the story) by "speaking" to the reader or viewer. The narrator can be seen as a separate character and is often not the same as the author.

In some narrative movies and documentary films the narrator takes the form of a voice-over.

See *also* **documentary • voice-over**

nearby or *near by?*

- ***nearby*** can be used as an adjective or an adverb
- ***near by*** can be used *only* as an adverb

Used as an adverb

Our grandparents live ***near by***.
= Our grandparents live ***nearby***.

Used as an adjective

Our grandparents live in a ***nearby*** apartment.
NOT Our grandparents live in a ***near by*** apartment.

negative

Changing the meaning of a sentence to its opposite.

I'm going.
I'm ***not*** going.

A negative is usually formed with the word ***not***. **Not** (or ***n't***) is sometimes called a ***negative adverb*** or a ***negative particle***.

There are several ways to make a negative using forms of ***not***:

I have***n't*** any.
I do ***not*** have any.
I do***n't*** have any.
I have***n't*** got any.
I've ***not*** got any.

Other words can be used to form negatives:

I always go.	I ***never*** go.
I have more.	I have ***no*** more.
I have one.	I have ***none***.

either here or there
neither here ***n***or there

See *also* ***negative adverb*** *or* ***negative particle?***

negative adverb or *negative particle*?

Both are grammatical terms for the word **not**. If you think that **not** *modifies* the verb, then it is an adverb. If you think that **not** is *part of* the verb, then it is a particle.

See *also* **adverb** • **negative** • **particle**

neither + *is* or *are*?

See ***each* + *is*** or ***are***?

nested diagram

A diagram that shows magnified details in a sequence, each magnification being greater than the one before.

Magnification can be shown by this symbol:

Nested diagrams are useful in explanations that show:

- how parts fit together
- how a system or process works

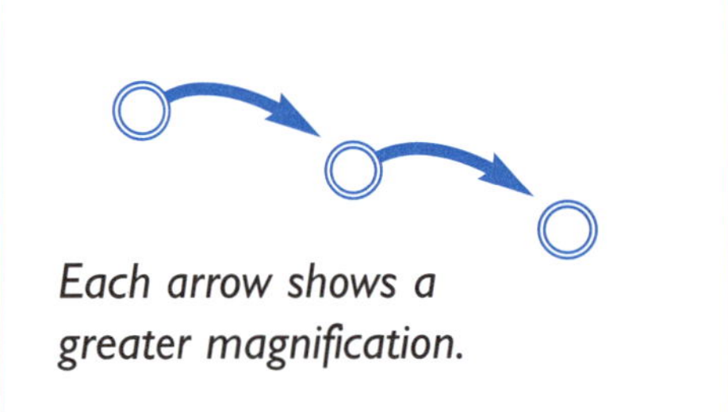

Each arrow shows a greater magnification.

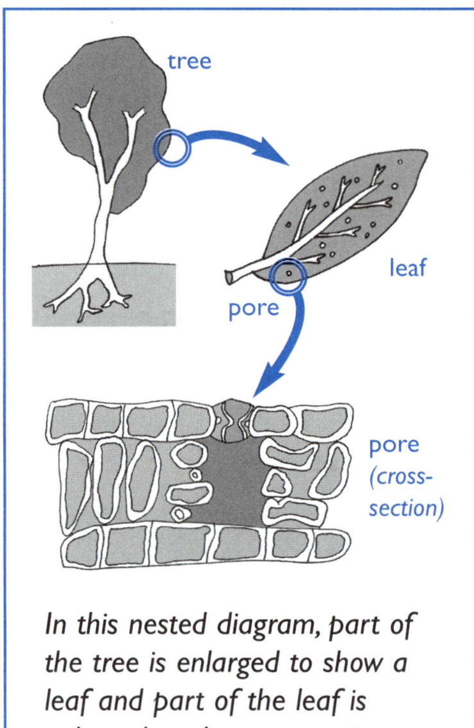

In this nested diagram, part of the tree is enlarged to show a leaf and part of the leaf is enlarged to show a pore in cross-section.

nested list

A list that is arranged to show topics divided into subtopics.

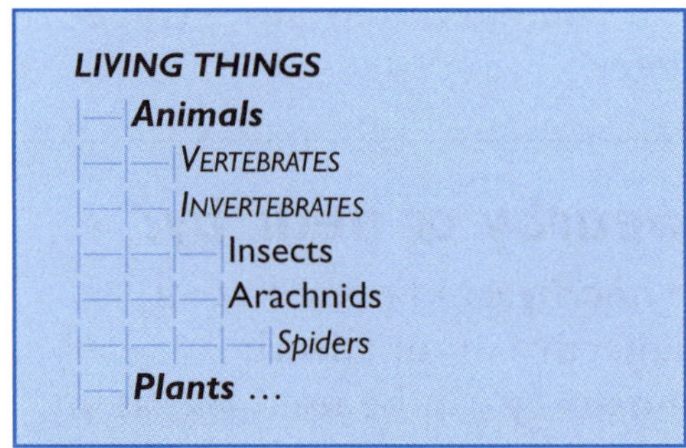

In a nested list a line is indented (moved to the right) to show that it belongs to the topic above it. In the example on page 124 ***Animals*** belong under ***LIVING THINGS***; *VERTEBRATES* and *INVERTEBRATES* are two kinds of ***Animal***; an Insect is an *INVERTEBRATE*; and so on.

Some writers use a numbering system to show this nesting arrangement:

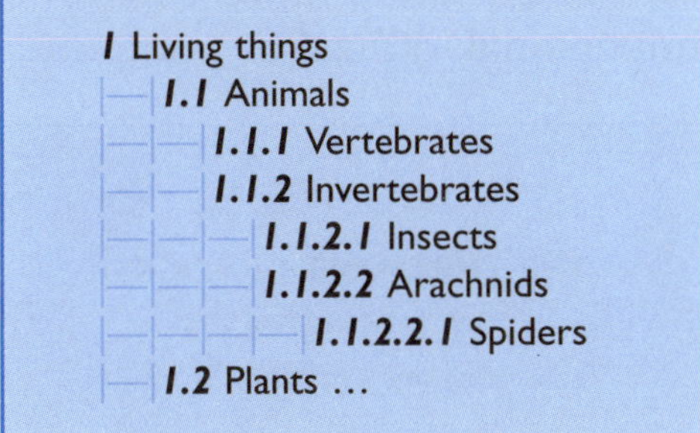

A nested list is useful when writing or editing a text which has many headings. Each heading that belongs within the previous topic is then set in a less prominent font:

A heading

LIVING THINGS

B heading

Animals

C heading

VERTEBRATES

A ***site map*** is an example of a nested list. A ***tree diagram*** serves a similar purpose.

See *also* **font** • **list** • **site map** • **tree diagram**

net, Net or 'net?

See ***internet*** *or* ***Internet?*** ...

net or web?

See ***internet*** *or* ***world wide web?***

neuter

See **gender**

new

See **given** and **new**

news report

A ***factual recount*** in which recent information is printed (in a newspaper), broadcast (on radio or TV), updated (on a website), downloaded (as a file) or posted (on an internet bulletin board).

A news report is *not* a kind of information report.

News report (factual recount)
- is in the past tense
- organises the facts in the order in which they happened

Information report
- is in the timeless present tense
- groups facts by topic

See *also* **factual recount** • **information report** • **tense** (of a verb)

N

nice

The word ***nice*** is used for anything you like or are comfortable with. It can mean "good", "kind", "OK", "likable" or "pleasant".

no more Mr ***Nice*** Guy

Another meaning of ***nice*** is "exact", "subtle" or "fine-tuned":

a ***nice*** distinction

Some writers try to avoid using ***nice*** when it means "something I like". They substitute other words to avoid repetition:

We had a ***nice*** day at her dad's place. He was really ***nice*** and gave us a ***nice*** ride on his boat.

This can be be re-phrased in many ways to avoid a crowd of ***nice***s, such as:

We had a ***fun*** day at her dad's place. He was really ***kind*** and gave us a ***great*** ride on his boat.

night or nite?

See **advertese**

nobody + is or are?

See ***everybody/everyone* + *is*** *or* ***are?***

nominalisation

Turning a verb into a ***noun***, often by adding ***-ing***.

Do not swim = No ***swimming***
Do not enter = No ***entry***

Nominalisation can have the effect of making an explanation or an instruction more impersonal, official or pompous:

NOTICE
THE ***THROWING*** OF ROCKS
AT THIS NOTICE
IS PROHIBITED.

There are many ways to form a noun from a verb. For example, the endings ***-tion*** (or ***-ation*** or ***-ition***) can also be used:

I don't intend to go.
= I have no ***intention*** of ***going***.

Nominalisation can be used to make the generalisations found in explanations and reports.

See *also* **explanation • generalisation • generalised participant • gerund • information report**

nominative case

See **case • subject** (of a sentence)

non-countable

See **count noun** and **mass noun**

non-chronological report

See **information report**

none + *is* or *are*?

See ***everybody/everyone*** + ***is*** or ***are***?

non-fiction

See **factual text**

non-finite clause

See **clause**

non-finite verb

See **finite verb** and **non-finite verb**

non-gradable

See **gradable** and **non-gradable**

non or ***non-***?

Both these prefixes mean "not" and both spellings are accepted.

She prefers ***non-fiction***.
= She prefers ***nonfiction***.

no-one or ***no one***?

Both mean "not anybody" and both spellings are accepted.

No-one is home.
= ***No one*** is home.

BUT NOT
Noone is home.

no-one + *is* or *are*?

See ***everybody/everyone*** + ***is*** or ***are***?

not and ***-n't***

See **negative**

noun

The name of a thing, place or person.

Sue has ***relatives*** in ***China***.

Nouns can be grouped into alternate pairs:

- *common* and *proper* nouns
- *abstract* and *concrete* nouns
- *count* and *mass* nouns

Common and proper nouns

A ***proper*** noun names a person or a unique thing (there is only one of them). All other nouns are common nouns:

Sue has relatives in ***China***.

Abstract and concrete nouns

A ***concrete*** noun names something you can normally see or touch. An abstract noun stands for something that you cannot see, such as an idea:

Put the ***pen*** on the ***table***.
He won by luck as well as skill.

Count and mass nouns

A ***count*** noun can be singular or plural, but a mass noun can only be singular:

Put these **biscuits** on a ***plate***.

Ice melts to form water, which evaporates to form steam.

See also **abstract noun • common noun • concrete noun • count noun** and **mass noun • proper noun**

noun clause

A clause that does the job of a noun. Noun clauses can be the ***subject***, *object* or complement of a sentence.

The stolen bag has been found.
Who stole it is still unclear.

He denies *that he stole it.*

The question is who stole it.

See also **complement • noun • object** (of a sentence) **• subject** (of a sentence)

noun group

IN FUNCTIONAL GRAMMAR

A group of words based on a noun (called the ***head noun*** of its noun group).

Some small red ***crabs*** were in the ***pool*** where we were swimming.

The head noun is modified by the other words in its group. The words that come *before* the head noun are ***pre-modifiers***, while those that come *after* it are called ***post-modifiers***.

Pre-modifier

Some small red …

Post-modifier

… where we were swimming.

See also **modifier • pre-modifier • post-modifier**

noun phrase

A phrase that does the job of a noun.

The ***trees*** on the edge of the park have new green ***leaves***.

In this sentence ***trees*** and ***leaves*** are nouns and the underlined words are noun phrases.

See also **noun group • phrase**

noun–pronoun agreement

See **agreement**

number

The grouping of words according to whether they are ***singular*** or plural. These words are said to "have number".

> ***He says*** that all our books are overdue.
> They say that ***each book is*** overdue.

Singular number	*Plural number*
He	They
says	say
each	all
book	books
is	are

Nouns, pronouns, determiners and verbs can have number.

Nouns

Nouns usually form plurals by adding ***-s***. Some nouns form plurals in other ways:

Singular number	*Plural number*
book	books
woman	women
sheep	sheep
fish	fish *or* fishes

Pronouns

Pronouns that have number include:

Singular number	*Plural number*
I, me, my	we, us, our
she, her, her	they, them, their
he, him, his	they, them, their
this, that	these, those

Determiners

Words that determine or limit a noun (such as ***each***, ***all***, ***some*** and ***a***) can have number:

Singular number	*Plural number*
each	both
a, an	some

Verbs

Some verb forms show number, especially third person (he/she/it/they) and first person (I/we):

Singular number	*Plural number*
I ***am***	we are
he ***says***	they say
she ***has***	they have

See also **determiner • noun • plural nouns • pronoun • verb**

number adjective

An adjective that defines the amount (how many?) or order (which one in a sequence?) of the following noun.

> She invited ***twelve*** friends to her ***sixteenth*** birthday.

N

Number adjectives are of two kinds: ***cardinal*** and ***ordinal***.

Cardinal number adjective

A cardinal adjective states "how many":

> ***twelve*** friends
> ***365*** days

Ordinal number adjective

An ordinal adjective states "which one in a sequence":

> ***first***, ***second*** and ***third*** person
> ***1st***, ***2nd***, ***3rd*** and ***4th*** place
> the ***365th*** day
> the ***second-last*** page

See also **adjective**

number adverb

An adverb that defines the ***frequency*** (how often?) or ***order*** (which one in a sequence?) of a verb.

> She swam in the relay ***once*** and came ***second***.

See also **adverb**

number label

A label in a diagram that links part of the diagram to a key. The key defines the meaning of each ***number***.

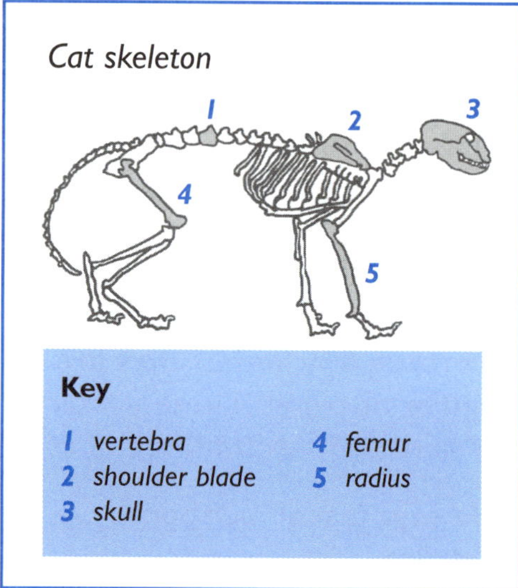

Number labels can also serve as signposts that lead the reader through a text, as in the ***numbered*** boxes in a storyboard.

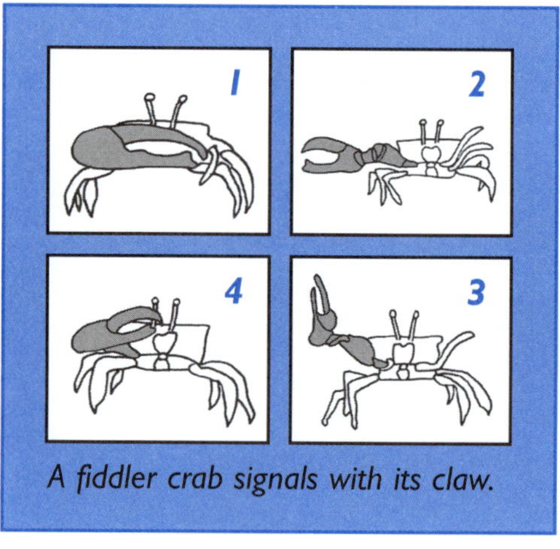

A fiddler crab signals with its claw.

See also **diagram • label • signpost • storyboard**

numerative

See **pre-modifier**

object (of a sentence)

Part of a sentence affected by or receiving the action of a verb. Objects can be ***direct*** or ***indirect***.

Direct object

The part of the sentence directly affected by the action of a verb:

> First break ***two eggs*** into a bowl.
> Add ***the rest of the milk***.
> Could you give her ***this parcel***?

A direct object is said to be "in the ***objective case***".

Some people argue that verbs like *to be* and *to remain* cannot have an object, since they describe a relationship, not a change that affects anything. These verbs are said to have a ***complement*** instead of an object.

Indirect object

The part of a sentence that receives the action of the verb:

> Give this to ***them***.
> Give ***them*** this.
> Could you give ***her*** this parcel?

See also **complement • objective case**

objective case

The case of the direct object in a sentence.

> The car hit ***the tree***.

In this sentence ***the tree*** is affected by the action of the verb hit, so ***the tree*** is the object of the verb and it is said to be "in the objective case".

See also **case • object** (of a sentence)

octopi or ***octopuses***?

Both spellings are accepted. The first is a Latin plural and the second is an English plural.

See also **plural nouns**

offline

See ***online*** *and* ***offline***

off, off of or ***from***?

In conversation people sometimes say:

> I bought it ***off*** my brother.
> I bought it ***off of*** my brother.
> I bought it ***from*** my brother.

IN FORMAL WRITING only the last is accepted:

> I bought it ***from*** my brother.

of or ***have***?

See ***could have*** *or* ***could've*** *or* ***could of?***

of or *off*?

- ***of*** means "belonging to"
- ***off*** means "away from"

One of the moons ***of*** Jupiter is made of ice.
The ball rolled ***off*** the table.

See also **off, off of** or **from**?

older or elder?

See **elder** or **older**?

one or you?

Both of these words are used as *indefinite pronouns*.

What should **one** do in an emergency?

What should **you** do in an emergency?

They are called "indefinite" pronouns because they refer to people in general, not to one particular person.

Whichever word you prefer, use it consistently:

Where can **you** walk **your** dog?
= Where can **one** walk **one's** dog?

NOT
Where can **one** walk **your** dog?
Where can **you** walk **one's** dog?

Where can **one** walk ***his or her*** dog?

See also **agreement • indefinite pronoun**

one another or each other?

See **each other** or **one another**?

online and offline

- ***online*** means "while connected to the internet"
- ***offline*** means "while disconnected from the internet"

To *send* an email you need to go ***online***.
You can *type* an email when you are ***offline***.

Before the internet became a public medium, ***online*** meant only "while connected to another computer". It can still have this meaning as well.

only

The word ***only*** can apply either to the words that follow it or to the words that go before it.

That game is ***only*** for children.
That game is for children ***only***.

However, this can cause confusion in some sentences:

Entry is free for children ***only*** this Saturday.

In this sentence ***only*** could apply either to children or to this Saturday. This confusion can be solved by always placing ***only*** so that it refers to only one noun:

Only children can enter for free this Saturday. [not adults]

Children can enter for free this Saturday ***only***. [not next Saturday]

See *also* **word order**

onomatopoeia

See **figure of speech**

on or upon?

See ***upon, on*** *or* ***up on?***

open question

See **question**

opinion

See **persuasion**

or + comma?

See **comma**

oral or ***aural?***

See ***aural*** *or* ***oral?***

ordinal

See **number adjective**

orientation (in a recount or narrative)

The part of a text that sets the context for (and precedes) a sequence of events.

Orientation in a recount

In a recount the orientation may answer some or all of the questions: who or what is involved, where did it happen and when?

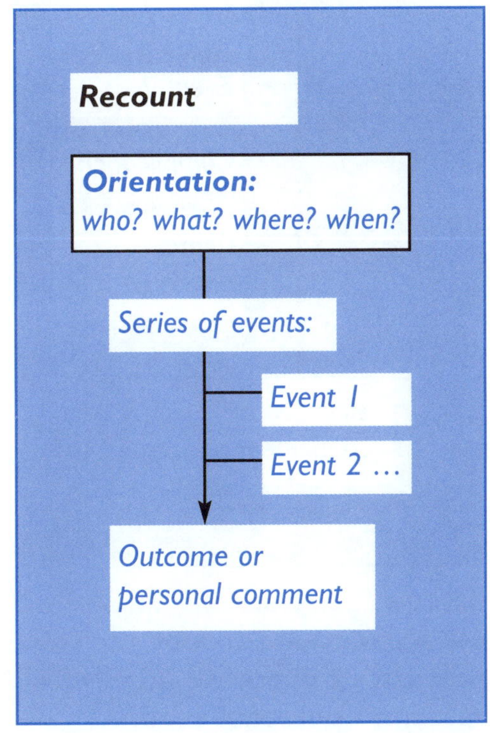

Orientation in a narrative

The orientation of a narrative may establish some of the story's main characters, its setting, the atmosphere or its themes.

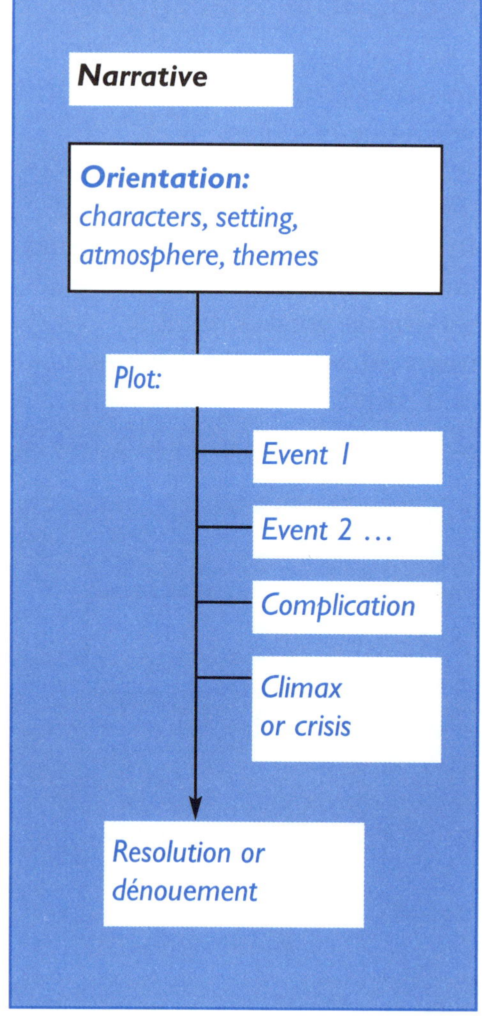

See *also* **factual recount** • **narrative** • **outcome** (in a factual recount) • **personal recount** • **setting** (in a narrative)

-our or -or?

Many English words ending in ***-our*** are sometimes spelt ***-or***:

col**our** = col**or**
harb**our** = harb**or**
Lab**our** = Lab**or**

The usual spelling in Australia is ***-our***, and the usual American spelling is ***-or***. However ***harbor*** and ***Labor*** are preferred in some Australian phrases and place names:

The Australian ***Labor*** Party
Franklin ***Harbor***, SA

See *also* **harbour** or **harbor?** • **labour** or **labor?**

outcome (in a factual recount)

The final part of a text that states the outcome or results of a series of actual events.

See *also* **factual recount**

overcorrection

See **hypercorrection**

owing to or *due to*?

See ***due to*** or ***owing to?***

packaging

Product packaging can be thought of as a kind of text that has the features of ***persuasion*** (or persuasive text). Like advertising, commercial packaging is designed to excite, reassure or flatter buyers.

Packaging also includes mandatory information such as a list of contents or ingredients.

See also **persuasion**

page layout

See **graphic design**

page number

(Also called a ***folio***) Each page in a printed book is usually numbered.

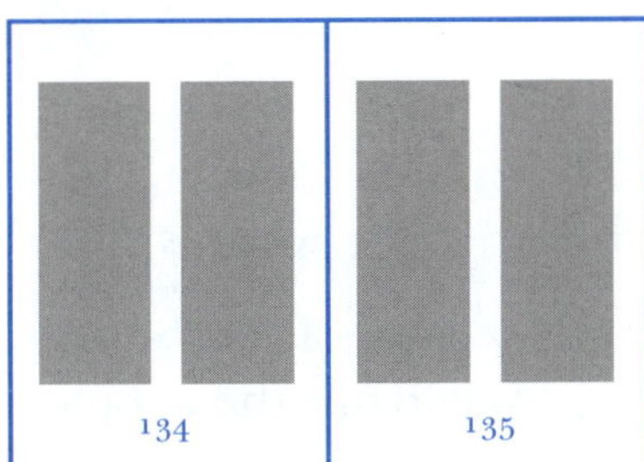

In an information book these numbers are used in tables of contents, indexes and cross-references to guide the reader to a page which mentions related information.

There is no need for page numbers on a website, because hyperlinks and search fields automatically locate related topics and can be thought of as interactive tables of contents, indexes and cross-references.

See also **cross-reference** • **hyperlink** • **index** • **table of contents** • **website**

paired conjunction

A conjunction is a word used to join two words, phrases or clauses. Paired conjunctions are two conjunctions that work together to link two words, phrases or clauses.

I speak ***both*** English ***and*** Chinese.

In this sentence the words ***both*** and ***and*** are paired conjunctions. Other paired conjunctions include:

He is ***either*** at home ***or*** at school.
I can ***neither*** phone ***nor*** email her.

See also **conjunction**

1 Wide shot: a city street.

2 The camera ***pans*** left, revealing a building on fire.

3 Then it ***zooms in*** on one window in the building.

pan or *zoom*?

Both are camera actions in film, TV and video production.

- ***pan*** means "to move the camera sideways"
- ***zoom*** means "to move the camera closer or further away"

- ***zoom in*** = camera seems to be moving towards the subject
- ***zoom out*** = camera seems to be moving away from the subject

Another phrase for ***zoom out*** is ***pull back***.

Zoom effects are usually produced by turning a zoom (or telescopic) lens; the camera itself does not have to move.

The same effects can be produced digitally without the use of a lens or even a camera. Computer programs and internet sites may have a **zoom** tool for enlarging or reducing an image on the screen.

Pan and ***zoom*** are different from ***dolly shots*** and ***tracking shots***.

See *also* **tracking shot**

paragraph

A section of text, of one or more sentences, all of which are usually on the same topic.

The first paragraph of a text is usually aligned at left, as shown here by the pale blue lines.
The first line of each of the following paragraphs is often indented, which means it is moved to the right.

See *also* **alignment** (of text)

parallel clauses

See **coordinate clauses**

parenthesis

(1) A punctuation mark: a round bracket ( ).

(2) Part of a sentence (such as an explanation, remark or comment) interrupting the sentence's flow.

> All reptiles ***(such as snakes, lizards, tortoises and alligators)*** have scales.

A parenthesis can be punctuated with round brackets, dashes or commas:

> All reptiles ***(such as snakes, lizards, tortoises and alligators)*** have scales.
>
> All reptiles—***such as snakes, lizards and alligators***—have scales.
>
> All reptiles, ***such as snakes, lizards, tortoises and alligators,*** have scales.

Short parentheses do not need punctuation:

> Reptiles ***such as snakes*** have scales.

See *also* **brackets • comma • dash**

parody

A form of satire using imitation and irony. Parody may imitate and undermine a writer's style, a literary form, a speaker's tone of voice and so on. The purpose of parody is usually to criticise ideas and attitudes held by others.

Books, poems, movies, songs, magazines—indeed any form of expression—can employ parody.

See also ***irony*** *or* ***sarcasm?*** • **satire**

participant

IN FUNCTIONAL GRAMMAR

One of the three main parts of a sentence:

- ***participant***: refers to a *thing*
- ***process***: refers to *what happens*
- ***circumstance***: refers to the *context* in which things happen (usually a time or place)

Participant	*Process*	*Circumstance*
Fossils	are found	in rocks.
Circumstance	*Participant*	*Process*
In 1851	***gold***	was discovered.
Circumstance	*Process*	*Participant*
Next	pour	**the cement**.

There are three main kinds of participant: the ***agent*** of a process, or its ***effect*** or ***beneficiary***. Other participants are ***entities***.

Agent

The participant that causes or starts a process:

The rain soaked the spectators.

Effect

The participant that is affected by or is the result of a process:

The rain soaked ***the spectators***.
The rain led to ***major flooding***.

Beneficiary

The participant that benefits from a process:

Moisture is carried to ***the leaves***.
The leaves receive moisture.
Pass ***me*** the salt.

Entity

In some processes nothing is caused or changed. These are relational or existential processes. Participants in these processes are called ***entities***:

Kim is ***the one*** who found you.
Mars has ***two moons***.
There were ***two main groups of dinosaurs***.

See also **circumstance** • **process**

participial clause

A clause that includes a ***participle*** (a non-finite verb ending in ***-ing***, ***-ed*** or ***-en***).

Provided they have tickets they can come.
There lay the mirror ***broken*** in a thousand fragments.
Walking past the window I saw the car parked at the gates.

See also **clause** • **finite verb** and **non-finite verb** • **participle**

participle

A kind of verb usually ending in ***-ing***, ***-ed*** or ***-en***.

I am ***finishing*** my book.
They were ***dazed*** and ***shaken***.

Participles can be ***present*** or ***past***.

Present participle (*-ing*)

A participle that indicates that the action is happening *now*:

We are ***watching*** TV.
Open the packet, ***taking*** care not to spill the contents.

Past participle (*-ed* or *-en*)

A participle that indicates that the action happened *in the past*:

We were ***surprised***.
Morning has ***broken***.

Irregular past participles have forms other than ***-ed*** or ***-en***:

We had ***left***. She had ***gone***.
It was ***burnt***. I've ***bought*** one.

Participle or gerund?

Gerunds are also words that end in ***-ing***. However, gerunds are not verbs; instead they are the names of things ("verbal nouns"):

Participle
She was ***swimming*** and ***diving***.
Gerund
She prefers ***swimming*** to ***diving***.

See also **dangling participle** • **gerund** • **number** • **person** • **regular** and **irregular verbs** • **tense**

particle

A preposition or adverb that forms part of a compound verb.

He wants **to** come home.
He passed out, then he came **to**.

The **to** in **to** come is an ***infinitive particle***.

The **to** in came **to** is an ***adverb particle***.

Infinitive particle

The particle **to** is used to form infinitive verbs, such as the verbs **to** write and **to** have written. This particle always goes at the *front* of the verb:

I'd like **to** give this back.
Try not **to** give up.

P

Adverb particle

Many verbs include adverb particles. This kind of particle goes at the *end* of the verb:

He might fall ***over***.
Try not to give ***up***.
We looked ***forward*** to the game.

Particle or preposition?

Some words can be used as a particle or a proposition:

(*a*) They looked ***up*** the answer.
(*b*) They looked ***up*** the road.

In (*a*) the verb is "to look ***up***" and the particle ***up*** is part of the verb.

In (*b*) the verb is "to look" while ***up*** is a preposition that belongs with the phrase "***up*** the road".

See also **adverb • compound verb • finite verb** and **non-finite verb • preposition**

passive voice

A verb form in sentences in which the subject "receives" the action of the verb.

Subject (effect)	*Verb (process)*	*Object (agent)*
The traffic	was stopped	by the dog.

Agentless passive

Some passives do not have an agent. These are called ***agentless passives***:

Subject (effect)	*Verb (process)*	*Object (agent)*
The traffic	was stopped.	

Get-passive

The ***get***-passive is formed with **get** or **got**.

Subject (effect)	*Verb (process)*	*Object (agent)*
The traffic	**got** held up	by the dog.

See also **active voice • get** *and* **got • middle voice**

past participle

See **participle**

past tenses

Forms of a verb that refer to an event that happened in the past.

Past simple

(Also called ***preterite***) The most commonly used past tense. This tense can be formed by:

- adding **-ed** or **-d** to a regular verb
- changing the form of an irregular verb

Regular verbs *Present*	*Past*
They ***open***	They ***opened***
He ***looks***	He ***looked***
I ***like***	I ***liked***

Irregular verbs	
Present	*Past*
They **come**	They **came**
I **go**	I **went**
We **buy**	We **bought**
You **see**	You **saw**

Past continuous

This past tense is used for an event which continued over a period of time in the past:

I ***was sleeping*** when she phoned.

This continuous tense is formed from a past form of the verb **to be** + the present participle (a verb ending in ***-ing***):

They ***were*** planning their holiday for months.

Past perfect

Also called the ***pluperfect*** tense, this tense usually refers to a time *even earlier than* a past event in the same (or nearby) sentence:

Past event	*Earlier event*
By the time I arrived	he ***had escaped***.

This tense is formed using ***had*** + the past participle (a verb usually ending in ***-ed*** or ***-en***):

The phone rang just after I ***had*** closed the door.
I knew he ***had*** tripped and fallen.

Past perfect continuous

This past tense is used for an event that had been continuing over a period of time before a later event in the past:

They ***had been*** living in Brisbane for a year when I first met them.

This tense is formed by combining ***had been*** + the verb ending in ***-ing***:

I was injured after I ***had been*** running each day for two weeks.

Present perfect

This tense is for an event that has been happening in the past and continues right up to now. It can be seen as *both* a present tense *and* a past tense:

I ***have*** known her all my life.

This tense is formed from a past form of the verb ***to have*** + the past participle (a verb usually ending in ***-ed*** or ***-en***):

They ***have*** lived in Melbourne since February.

See also **participle • regular** and **irregular verbs • tense** (of a verb)

pathway (through a text)

The route we take when reading a text. In a line of ***lexical text*** (a text made of words in sentences) we read from left to right, and in a paragraph we usually start at the top line and read down.

However, when reading a ***visual text*** (such as a time line or a map), we may read the text using other pathways. These include reading from right to left or bottom to top.

Reading from right to left

To make sense of a time line we could read from left to right (to read events in chronological order) or from right to left (to see what happened a year ago).

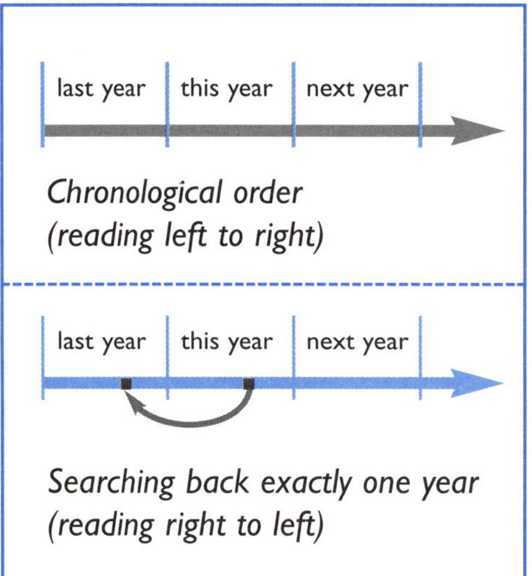

Chronological order (reading left to right)

Searching back exactly one year (reading right to left)

Reading from bottom to top

The same time line may be presented in a way that makes *narrative* sense only when read from bottom to top.

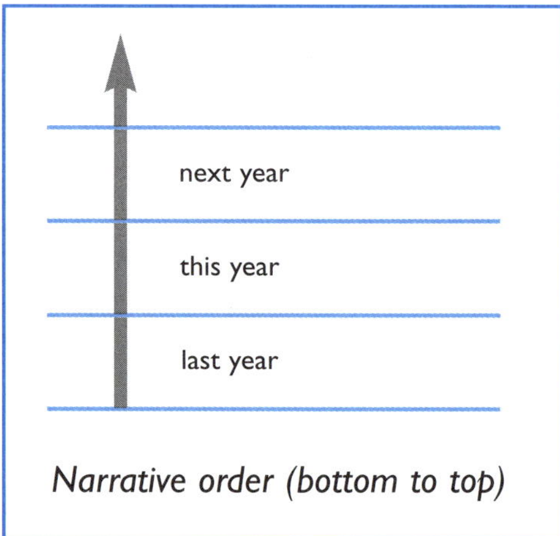

Narrative order (bottom to top)

Zigzags and other pathways

Maps can be read following many possible pathways, depending on the purpose of the reader.

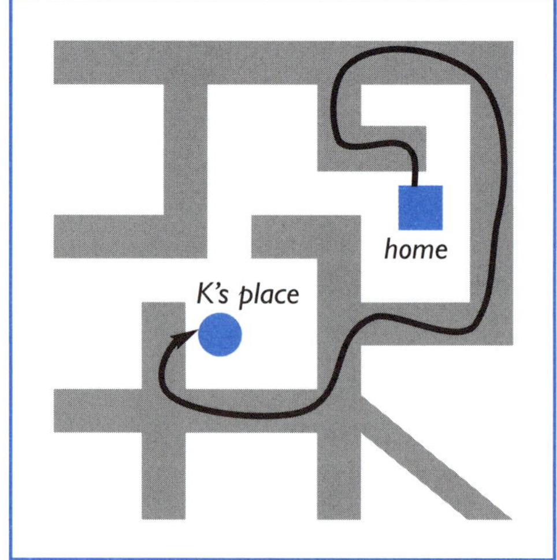

"Skim and scan"
When researching information the reader may use any of the above pathways to locate key words in a paragraph without reading every word or line.

Pathways and signposts
Signposts such as headings and highlighted words provide entry points into a text, allowing for many pathways other than starting at the first line.

See also **heading • highlighted word • lexical text • map • signpost • time line • visual text**

pdf

(**p**ortable **d**ocument **f**ormat)
A file that can be sent over the internet and can be printed out to resemble the pages of a book.

A URL that ends with ***pdf*** is likely to be a printable file.

See also **URL**

pentameter

A line of poetry with five beats.

1 2 3 4 5
˘ — ˘ — ˘ — ˘ — ˘ — ˘
Is **this** a **dag**ger **that** I **see** be**fore** me?

See also **metre** (in poetry)

perfect tense

See **past tenses**

person

Pronouns and verbs are said to have first, second or third person.

First person
Indicates the speaker or writer:

I am over here.
We have our results.

Second person
Indicates the listener or reader (the person being addressed):

Can I rely on ***you***?

Third person
Indicates any person or thing *other than* speaker or listener (writer or reader):

Do you think ***she has*** arrived?
I assure you that ***he is*** not here.
Your wallet? I think ***it's*** in the car.
Perhaps ***they're*** late.

Nouns are sometimes said to have person, but they do not inflect to indicate this.

See also **inflection • personal pronoun**

P

personal comment

A remark expressing the writer's feelings or attitudes.

> ***I was surprised*** to see them.
> It was an ***amazing*** day.

IN FUNCTIONAL GRAMMAR

Personal comments distinguish a personal recount from a factual recount.

See also **factual recount** • **personal recount**

personal pronoun

Pronouns that indicate person, number, gender and case.

The personal pronouns are:

	Singular Subject	Singular Object	Plural Subject	Plural Object
1st person	**I**	**me**	**we**	**us**
2nd person	**you**	**you**	**you**	**you**
3rd person				
masculine	**he**	**him**	**they**	**them**
feminine	**she**	**her**	**they**	**them**
neuter	**it**	**it**	**they**	**them**

Related forms are the ***possessive determiners***, ***possessive pronouns*** and ***reflexive pronouns***.

Possessive determiners

(Also called ***possessive adjectives***) A determiner precedes a noun and limits its meaning. They *cannot* stand alone:

> Is that ***her*** house or ***your*** house?

The possessive determiners are:

	Singular	Plural
1st person	**my**	**our**
2nd person	**your**	**your**
3rd person		
masculine	**his**	**their**
feminine	**her**	**their**
neuter	**its**	**their**

Possessive pronouns

The possessive pronouns stand for things that belong. Unlike determiners, they *can* stand alone:

> Is that house ***hers*** or ***yours***?

The possessive pronouns are:

	Singular	Plural
1st person	**mine**	**ours**
2nd person	**yours**	**yours**
3rd person		
masculine	**his**	**theirs**
feminine	**hers**	**theirs**
neuter	**its**	**theirs**

Reflexive pronouns

Pronouns ending in ***-self*** or ***-selves***. These pronouns are used when the agent does something to her/himself:

> I hurt ***myself***.

The reflexive pronouns are:

	Singular	Plural
1st person	**myself**	**ourselves**
2nd person	**yourself**	**yourselves**
3rd person		
masculine	**himself**	**themselves**
feminine	**herself**	**themselves**
neuter	**itself**	**themselves**

Pronouns that are used to emphasise another word or phrase are called ***emphatic pronouns***:

I ***myself*** was not hurt.
The children ***themselves*** are safe.

See also **case • determiner • gender • number • person • possessive case • *s/he***

personal recount

A kind of text in which events are recalled, with personal comments from the writer. Examples of personal recounts include letters and diaries.

A factual recount usually has:

- an ***orientation*** answering the questions: What is the subject? When and where did the events take place?
- a ***series of events*** arranged in chronological order
- a ***personal comment*** that sums up the writer's feelings about the events recounted

Overnight in the Valley

Orientation

Last weekend my friends and I hiked to Blue Forest.

Series of events

We started early on Saturday and reached the Pylon for lunch. The view was amazing. Then we descended into the valley and camped by the river in Blue Forest. I'd not been there before. On Sunday we returned by Hammer Rock to Redheath railway station.

Personal comment

The climb out of the valley was hard but it was worth it.

A personal recount can be planned using a storyboard, story map or time line.

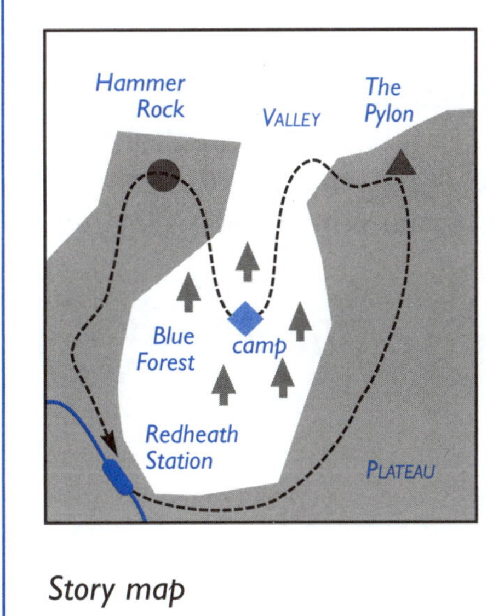

Story map

Saturday morning	afternoon	**Sunday** morning	afternoon
hiked to Pylon, had lunch	walked to valley, set up camp	hiked to Hammer Rock	returned to Redheath Station

Time line

☞

P

A ***personal recount*** is different from a ***factual recount***.

Personal recount

A personal recount includes the personal responses of the writer, and may have a more intimate or conversational tone:

The view was amazing …
I'd not been there before …

Factual recount

A factual recount attempts an impersonal tone and is limited to statements of what happened.

See also **factual recount • personal comment • story map**

personification

See **figure of speech**

persuasion

(Also called ***persuasive text***)
Persuasion may take the form of a logical ***argument*** and is sometimes referred to as ***exposition*** or ***expository text***. Examples are often found in newspaper opinion pieces, editorials and letters.

Persuasion also includes advertising and other texts that seek to persuade the reader to a point of view or an action.

In the case of more formal ***arguments***, a persuasive text usually has:

- a ***statement of opinion***
- a ***series of reasons*** for that opinion
- a ***conclusion*** which is supported by the series of reasons
- an (optional) ***call for action*** that follows from agreement with the writer's opinion

Children Should Be Given the Vote

Statement of opinion

In a democracy it is said that "everyone has a vote". Surely "everyone" includes children.

Series of reasons

Many government decisions affect children. Children go to school, get sick and ride on public transport. It's outrageous that they cannot vote on how these services affect them.

Once it was said that women did not deserve to vote because they weren't smart enough. The case against the vote for children is just as unfair.

Conclusion

Therefore there is only one choice: voting rights should be given to children.

Call for action

Sign our petition asking for a referendum to amend the constitution on voting rights.

A persuasive text can be planned using a flow chart.

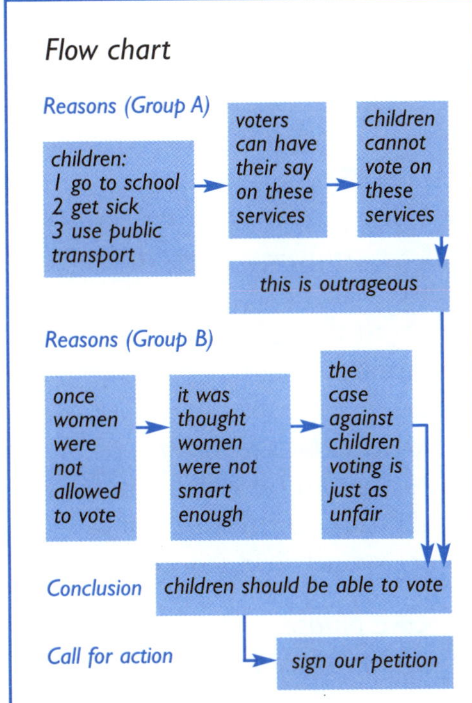

Persuasion is different from ***discussion***.

Persuasion
Persuasion puts *one* side of an argument and defends it. A persuasive text sometimes expresses personal feeling (It's outrageous) and bias (there is only one choice).

Discussion
A discussion attempts to put two or more sides of an argument. Discussions claim to avoid personal feeling and bias.

See *also* **call for action** • **conclusion** (in an argument or discussion) • **discussion**

phenomenon

See **explanation**

phenomenon or *phenomena*?

See **Greek plurals**

phoneme

The smallest speech sound that can change the meaning of a word. For example, the sound /**s**/ added to the spoken word /***boat***/ changes its meaning from singular to plural.

By changing the sounds

/**b**ad/ to /**p**ad/
/b**a**d/ to /b**ir**d/
/ba**d**/ to /ba**tch**/

we change the meaning of these words. Therefore the sounds /**b**/, /**p**/, /**a**/, /**ir**/, /**d**/ and /**tch**/ are all shown to alter meaning.

There are said to be forty-four phonemes in English. However, there are many ways we can pronounce the "same" phoneme. Each different form of the same phoneme is called an ***allophone***.

The written form of a phoneme is a grapheme.

See also **grapheme • morpheme**

photograph

A visual text that records only a particular surface appearance. Photographs differ from diagrams in that they do not analyse, generalise or explain their subject.

Photographic images can be manipulated by computer programs to add or remove details or to change colours, textures and shapes. These changes can create different moods or attitudes towards the subject of the photograph.

Image of the photographer's shadow (while running)

Software can alter the photograph to suggest a night scene

phrase

Two or more words that do not make a complete sentence or clause. This term means different things in different grammars.

IN TRADITIONAL GRAMMAR

A phrase can be two or more words that do the work of an adjective, adverb, noun or verb:

Adjective phrase

The bugs were ***hard to see***.

Adverb phrase

We saw his dad ***last week***.

Noun phrase

She met ***the owner of that dog***.

Verb phrase

They ***have been talking*** to her.

Phrases that start with a ***preposition*** are called prepositional phrases. Usually they function as adverb phrases:

There are some fruit ***on*** that tree.

See also **adjective phrase • adverb phrase • clause • noun phrase • prepositional phrase**

IN FUNCTIONAL GRAMMAR
A phrase is a reduced clause.

There are some fruit on that tree.

The phrase on that tree can be seen as a reduction of the clause that are on that tree.

However, the following examples would be seen *not* as phrases but as ***groups***, since they "cannot" be expanded into clauses:

Adjective group
The bugs were ***hard to see***.

Adverb group
We met them ***last week***.

Noun group
She knows ***that man in the bus***.

Verb group
They ***have been talking*** to me.

See also **adjective group • adverb group • noun group • verb group**

picture glossary

A diagram which names parts of its subject. The graphic helps to define the meaning of the labels. In the picture glossary (above right):
• each label, such as cumulus cloud, names a different kind of cloud
• the graphic helps to define what the label means

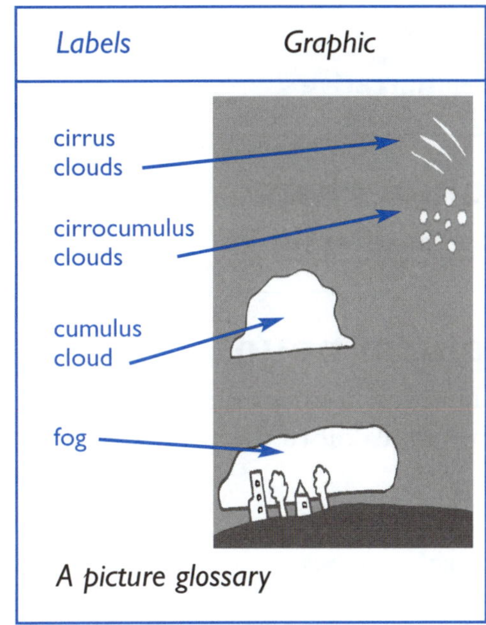

A picture glossary

See also **diagram • label**

pie chart

A visual text that shows fractions or percentages of a topic.

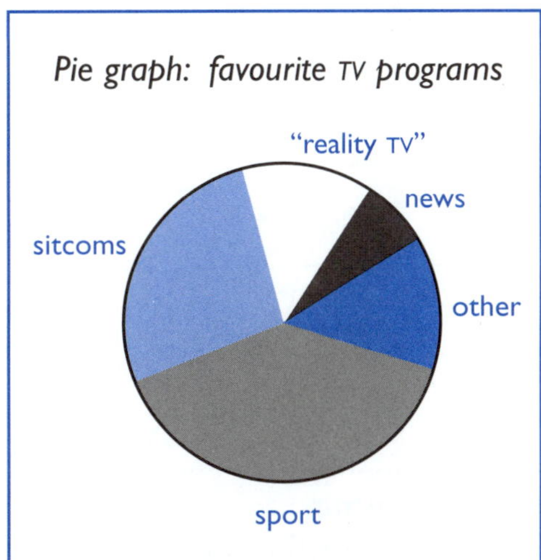

Pie charts are used in reports, discussions and explanations.

P

plot

See **narrative**

pluperfect

See **past tenses**

plural nouns

The plural form of a noun indicates more than one.

Singular	Plural
boat	boat**s**

Most plurals are formed with **-s** but some are formed in other ways. These include old English plurals and foreign plurals.

Old English plurals

Some words that have been part of English for many hundreds of years form plurals in ways other than adding **-s**:

Singular	Plural
child	child**ren**
foot	feet
woman	women
sheep	***sheep***
ox	ox**en**
cow	***cattle***
person	***people***

Foreign plurals

Foreign words that have become part of English often form their plurals as they would in their original language:

Singular	Plural	Language
plateau	plateau**x**	*French*
index	ind**ices**	*Latin*
syllabus	syllab**i**	*Latin*
antenna	antenn**ae**	*Latin*
datum	dat**a**	*Latin*
medium	medi**a**	*Latin*
curriculum	curricul**a**	*Latin*
phenomenon	phenomen**a**	*Greek*
criterion	criteri**a**	*Greek*

Many of these foreign plurals are becoming *standardised*. This means that the foreign plural is replaced with the standard **-s** ending. Standardised plurals seem to be accepted for some but not (yet) all foreign words:

Singular	Standardised plural
plateau	plateau**s**
index	index**es**
syllabus	syllabus**es**
antenna	antenna**s**

BUT

Singular	Plural
datum	dat**a**
medium	medium**s** *or* medi**a**
phenomenon	phenomen**a**

See *also* **number**

pointer

See **pre-modifier**

portmanteau word

A word formed by combining *parts* of two other words.

motel** = **mot**or + **hotel
brunch** = **br**eakfast + l**unch

See *also* **compound word**

positive degree

See **degree**

possessive adjective

See **personal pronoun**

possessive case

(Also called ***genitive case***)
The form of a word that indicates possession or ownership.

Lin's brother	***her*** brother
the ***trees'*** leaves	***their*** leaves
this is ***Mark's***	this is ***his***

Nouns, determiners and pronouns can all take the possessive case.

Possessive nouns

Nouns form the possessive case by adding ***-'s***, ***-s'***, ***of***, or ***'***:

this ***dog's*** collar
those ***dogs'*** collars
the streets ***of Paris***
Paris' streets

The form ***dog's*** indicates one dog; ***dogs'*** indicates more than one dog.

An apostrophe (***'***) can be used without the ***s*** if the word already ends in ***s***, as in ***Paris'*** streets.

Possessive determiners

These determiners limit the nouns that follow them:

My bike is the same as ***their*** bikes.

The possessive determiners are:

	Singular	*Plural*
1st person	***my***	***our***
2nd person	***your***	***your***
3rd person		
masculine	***his***	***their***
feminine	***her***	***their***
neuter	***its***	***their***

Possessive ***determiners*** are sometimes grouped with the possessive ***pronouns***.

Possessive pronouns

The possessive pronouns stand for things that belong:

Mine is the same as ***theirs***.

The possessive pronouns are:

	Singular	*Plural*
1st person	***mine***	***ours***
2nd person	***yours***	***yours***
3rd person		
masculine	***his***	***theirs***
feminine	***hers***	***theirs***
neuter	***its***	***theirs***

See *also* **apostrophe • case • personal pronoun**

P

possessive determiner
See **possessive case**

possessive pronoun
See **possessive case**

post-modifier
One or more words that define the head noun preceding them.

the road ***that leads to the sea***

A post-modifier can be a single word, a phrase or a clause:

my sister ***Kristin***
the horse ***in that paddock***
the place ***where I was born***

See *also* **clause** • **modifier** • **noun group** • **phrase** • **pre-modifier**

practice or *practise*?
• ***practice*** is a noun (or thing)
• ***practise*** is a verb (or action)

I need time for guitar ***practice***.
I have to ***practise*** the guitar.

The American spelling for both noun and verb is ***practice***.

precede or *proceed*?
• ***precede*** means "to go before"
• ***proceed*** means "to continue"

Explorers ***preceded*** the squatters. They ***proceeded*** slowly on foot.

• ***precede*** is transitive (it needs a direct object to follow it)
• ***proceed*** is intransitive (it does not have a direct object)

Subject	*Verb or verb phrase*	*Direct object*
Explorers	***preceded***	the squatters.
They	***proceeded*** slowly on foot.	

See *also* **object** (of a sentence) • **transitive verb** and **intransitive verb**

predicate
All that part of the sentence which is not the subject.

Any sensible person ***would agree***.
I***'m the one you want***.
The subject of this sentence ***is not its predicate***.

See *also* **sentence** • **subject** (of a sentence)

prefix and suffix
Part of a word that has been added either before or after a base. For example, the prefix ***un-*** and the suffix ***-able*** have been added to the base ***break*** to form the word ***un**break**able***.

Prefix	*Base*	*Suffix*
un	break	able

Prefix
A prefix comes *before* the **base**:

unhappy **re**write
prefix **inter**net

Suffix
A suffix that comes *after* the base:

trust**ed** kind**ness**
hope**less** football**er**

Unlike prefixes, suffixes often change a word grammatically. For example the suffix ***-ness*** changes an adjective (sad) to a noun (sad***ness***). Other examples include:

Singular to plural:	bottle**s**
Adjective to adverb:	foolish**ly**
Noun to adjective:	mess**y**
Present tense to past:	escape**d**
Noun to verb:	length**en**
Verb to noun:	paint**er**

Prefixes and suffixes are affixes. The general term ***affix*** refers to any addition that is made to a base to form a new word.

See also **base**

pre-modifier
One or more words that define the head noun that follows them.

those two red sports cars

There are four main kinds of pre-modifiers: ***pointers***, ***numeratives***, ***epithets*** and ***classifiers***.

Pointer
A word that "points to" the **head noun** that follows it, indicating:
- whether it is a particular thing or "things in general"
- whether it is a nearby or distant thing

Particular	*General*
the referee	***a*** referee
these players	***some*** players
that ball	***any*** ball
the first card	***one of the*** cards

Near by	*Distant*
this tree	***that*** tree
these cars	***those*** cars

Numerative
A word or phrase that indicates an amount:

two cars
39 steps
plenty of ideas
both swimmers

A numerative can also indicate a position in a sequence:

the ***9th*** planet
the ***third*** man
the ***final*** chapter
the ***second-last*** runner

Epithet

A word that describes the head noun that follows it:

red cars
rusty, old wheels
a ***clever*** idea

Classifier

A word that classifies the following head noun (saying *what kind of* thing or person):

sports cars	***TV*** news
AFL coach	***diamond*** ring

These four kinds of pre-modifier are usually written in this order:

1 Pointer	2 Numerative	3 Epithet	4 Classifier	Noun
those	***two***	***red***	***sports***	*cars*

See also **classifier • epithet • post-modifier**

preposition

A word or phrase that links parts of a sentence and is said to "govern" the word or phrase that immediately follows it.

Sit ***with*** us ***in front of*** the band, or ***beside*** Mike's family ***at*** the long table.

Simple preposition

A one-word preposition is called a ***simple preposition.*** The most common ones include:

against	***around***	***among***	***at***
behind	***beside***	***between***	***by***
down	***from***	***in***	***into***
off	***on***	***over***	***under***
up	***through***	***to***	***with***

Complex preposition

Two or more words that work as a preposition are called a *complex preposition*:

away from	***by means of***
in addition to	***in front of***
out of	***with respect to***

Preposition and indirect object

Words that are "governed" by a preposition are said to be the indirect object of the preposition:

	Preposition	Indirect object
Sit	***with***	us
	in front of	the band.

See also **article • object** (of a sentence) **• prepositional phrase • preposition** *ending a sentence?* **• preposition group**

prepositional phrase

A ***preposition*** + the indirect object that follows it is said to be a prepositional phrase.

We're standing ***outside*** their new library building.

See also **object** (of a sentence) **• preposition • preposition group**

preposition *ending a sentence?*

Some writers object to ending a sentence with a preposition.

> "A preposition is a word you should never end a sentence ***with***."

The "reason" appears to be that the word ***preposition*** comes from the Latin words for "placed in front of" and in Latin a preposition rarely ends a sentence.

If you wish to avoid ending a sentence with a preposition, there is usually a way of re-phrasing the sentence:

> "A preposition is a word ***with which*** you should never end a sentence."

However, there are some cases where placing the preposition "correctly" sounds mannered and self-conscious:

> What are you looking at?
> = At what are you looking?

In some cases the "correct" form is ***hypercorrect***:

> She's fun to play tennis with.
> **NOT** She's fun with whom to play tennis.

In very formal writing it may sometimes be necessary to observe the rule more strictly, if you have a reason to avoid offending the reader's prejudices about "grammatical English".

See *also* **hypercorrection • snob grammar • *to whom*** *or* ***who . . . to****?*

preposition group

A ***preposition*** + its modifier.

> The Sun is just ***above*** the trees.
> That's right ***out of*** the question.
> Her story is slightly ***over*** the top.

A preposition usually shows a relationship between the subject of a sentence and the phrase that follows. The modifier adds precision to the preposition.

See *also* **modifier • preposition**

prescribe *or* ***proscribe****?*

- ***prescribe*** means "to order"
- ***proscribe*** means "to forbid"

> The doctor ***prescribed*** antibiotics and ***proscribed*** cigarettes.

present participle

See **participle**

P

present tenses

Various forms of a verb that refer to an event happening now.

Present simple

This is the simplest tense for events that happen now:

I ***am*** outside the main entrance but I ***have*** no ticket.

The present simple tense is the same as the base verb, except that ***she***, ***he*** and ***it*** add ***-s***:

I ***like*** netball but she ***likes*** football.

Present continuous

Also called ***present progressive*** tense. This tense is used for events that are continuing over a period of time and are "in progress" now:

I ***am*** waiting for my friends.

The present continuous tense is formed from the verbs ***am***, ***is*** or ***are*** + the present participle (a verb ending in ***-ing***):

He ***is*** learning Indonesian.
They ***are*** hoping to reach the finals.

Timeless present

This tense is used for facts that:

- are *always* true
- happen now *as well as* in the past and in the future

Birds and reptiles ***are*** vertebrates.
The Moon ***goes*** round the Earth.

The timeless present is formed in the same way as the present simple tense:

We ***go*** to the gym once a week.

Present perfect

This tense is for an event that has been happening in the past and continues right up to now. It can be seen as *both* a present tense *and* a past tense:

I ***have*** lived here all my life.

This tense is formed from a past form of the verb **to have** + the past participle (a verb usually ending in **-ed**, **-d** or **-en**):

She ***has*** practised the trumpet every day this year.

Historic present

(Also called ***narrative present***)
This tense is used to give immediacy to events that really happened in the past:

I ***walk*** in the front door. The TV ***is*** on but there ***are*** no people in the room. As I ***climb*** the stairs I ***begin*** to worry. Then I ***find*** my brother on the verandah. He ***has*** a pair of binoculars in his hand. "Don't say anything!" he ***whispers*** and ***points*** to a man in the street below us …

The historic present can be used for book, film or chapter titles:

"Flinders ***Sails*** around Australia"
Mr Smith ***Goes*** *to Washington*

The present used as a future tense

The present simple and present continuous tenses are sometimes understood by the listener to refer to the future:

The plane ***arrives*** in two hours.
I ***am seeing*** my friends tomorrow.

See also **base • future tenses • participle • past tenses • tense** (of a verb)

preterite tense

The same as ***past simple tense.***
See **past tenses**

primary verb

A verb that can work as a lexical verb or an auxiliary.

The ***primary verbs*** can identify the tense, number and person of lexical verbs. There are three primary verbs: ***to be***, ***to have*** and ***to do***.

To be

The snow ***is*** starting to fall.
Was she catching the bus?

To have

I ***have*** moved. = I***'ve*** moved.
Has someone seen the paper?

To do

I ***do*** swim.

Some writers see primary verbs as ***auxiliaries***, which must be used with other (lexical) verbs. However, primary verbs can be used as lexical verbs:

She was at the gate.
They have the answer.
He did his homework.

See also **auxiliary verb • lexical verb • verb**

principal clause

The same as a main clause.
See **clause**

principal or *principle*?

• ***principal*** means "most important"
• ***principal*** also means "head of a school"
• ***principle*** means "a belief" or "a rule"

Our ***principal*** said that her ***principal*** concern was the ***principle*** of fairness.

printed text

See **text**

procedure

(Also called a ***procedural text*** or ***instructions***) A kind of text in which the writer instructs the reader to carry out a task in a series of steps.

Examples of procedures include recipes, do-it-yourself manuals and instructions for assembling and using something (such as a new computer or DVD).

A procedure usually has:
- a ***goal***, stating what is to be made or done
- a ***list of materials*** arranged as bulleted items
- a ***method*** arranged as a series of steps (often numbered)

Goal

How to Make Burritos

List of materials (ingredients)
- tortillas
- fried chicken pieces
- cheese
- lettuce
- refried beans
- salsa

Method
1. Grate the cheese.
2. Shred the lettuce.
3. Put the salsa in a jug.
4. Reheat chicken and beans.
5. Heat the tortillas.
6. Put one tortilla on a plate.
7. Add the chicken, beans, cheese, lettuce and salsa.
8. Fold the tortilla into a parcel.

A procedure is different from an explanation.

A procedure uses commands:

1. Grate the cheese.
2. Shred the lettuce.

An explanation uses passive verbs:

1. The cheese is grated.
2. The lettuce is shredded.

A procedure can be planned using a flow chart (below) or a storyboard (above right).

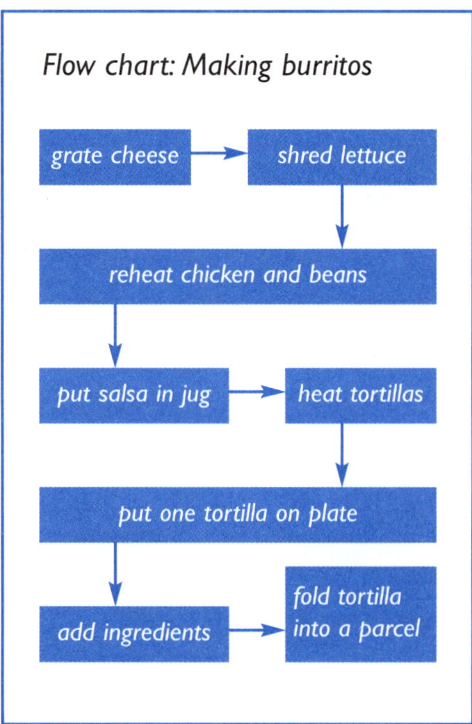

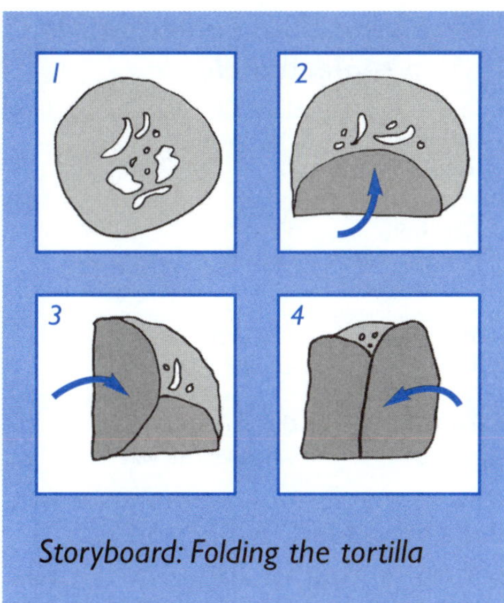

Storyboard: Folding the tortilla

See *also* **bullet • explanation**

proceed or precede?

See **precede** or **proceed?**

process

IN FUNCTIONAL GRAMMAR

One of the three main parts of a sentence:

- ***participant***: refers to a *thing*
- ***process***: refers to *what happens*
- ***circumstance***: refers to the *context* in which things happen (usually a time or place)

Participant	*Process*	*Circumstance*
Fossils	***are found***	in rocks.

Circumstance	*Participant*	*Process*
In 1851	gold	***was discovered.***

Process	*Participant*	*Circumstance*
Pour	the cement	before it sets.

There are six kinds of process: material, verbal, behavioural, mental, relational and existential.

Material process

An action or event in which something is "done":

My cat ***scratched*** me.
The money ***was stolen***.
She ***was walking*** away from him.

Verbal process

Any act of speaking or other communication:

She ***said***, "Come in."
They ***were asked*** to come in.

Behavioural process

An action over which a person usually has no control:

He ***was born*** in July.
She ***blinked***.

Mental process

Thinking or feeling, or any action of the senses (seeing, hearing, touch, smell, taste):

I ***know*** the poem but I don't ***understand*** it.
She ***loves*** chocolate.
We can ***hear*** a mouse but we can't ***see*** it.

Relational process

Shows how two participants are related, or connects a participant to its *attribute*:

This goldfish ***belongs to*** my sister.
All the photos ***are*** *blurry*.
Some dinosaurs ***had*** feathers.

Existential process
Asserts that something does or does not exist, usually in the form ***there is*** or ***there are***:

There's a chemist at the station.
There are no easy answers.

See also **circumstance** • **participant**

program or programme?

Both words mean the same thing. ***Programme*** is the original (French) spelling. Both spellings are accepted.

the TV ***programme***
= the TV ***program***

When referring to computers the spelling is usually ***program***.

progressive tenses

See **continuous tenses**

projection

IN FUNCTIONAL GRAMMAR
Using the words of someone else and including them in what we say or write. The quoted words form a ***projected clause***.

Projected clause	*Projecting clause*
"I'm ready,"	she said.
"Are you late?"	I asked.

Projecting clause	**Projected clause**
She said	that she was ready.
I asked	whether she was late.

An embedded projection is a sentence that includes the words of someone else as an ***embedded clause***:

The claim ***that she was at the crime scene*** has been disproved.

His warning ***to run*** was ignored.

See also **embedded clause** • **embedded phrase**

prolixity

See **redundancy**

pronoun

A ***word*** that is said to stand for a noun or noun phrase.

The whole family went to the beach. = ***They*** went ***there***.

There are many kinds of pronouns. The main ones are defined on the next two pages.

Demonstrative pronoun

Any of the words ***this***, ***that***, ***these*** or ***those*** when they are used instead of a noun or noun phrase:

I'd like the blue flowers over there. = I'd like ***those***.

Distributive pronoun

A pronoun that refers to the separate items in a group. The distributive pronouns are ***each***, ***either***, ***neither*** and ***none***:

Either can go but not both.
Neither can go.
None can go.

Emphatic pronoun

A pronoun which is used to give emphasis to a *noun* or pronoun:

The *driver* ***herself*** was unhurt.
They ***themselves*** were mistaken.

The emphatic pronouns look the same as the reflexive pronouns but are used differently:

myself	***ourselves***
yourself	***yourselves***
herself himself	
itself oneself	***themselves***

Indefinite pronoun

(1) A pronoun that is less definite than other pronouns:

everyone	***everybody***
someone	***somebody***
anyone	***anybody***
no one	***nobody***

(2) The pronoun **one** when it is used to stand for people in general:

He thinks that ***one*** should be always be on ***one's*** guard.

Interrogative pronoun

Pronouns that are used to ask a question. These are the so-called ***wh-*** words when they are used instead of a noun or noun phrase:

Which pair of shoes do you want?
= ***Which*** do you want?

Which person phoned you?
= ***Who*** phoned you?

Personal pronoun

Pronouns that are inflected to indicate person, number, gender and case:

Is that ***her*** house or ***your*** house?

The personal pronouns are:

	Singular Subject	Singular Object	Plural Subject	Plural Object
1st person	***I***	***me***	***we***	***us***
2nd person	***you***	***you***	***you***	***you***
3rd person				
masculine	***he***	***him***	***they***	***them***
feminine	***she***	***her***	***they***	***them***
neuter	***it***	***it***	***they***	***them***

Possessive pronoun

The possessive pronouns stand for things that belong:

Is that house ***hers*** or ***yours***?
That's your book; this is ***mine***.

P

The possessive pronouns are:

	Singular	Plural
1st person	**mine**	**ours**
2nd person	**yours**	**yours**
3rd person		
masculine	**his**	**theirs**
feminine	**hers**	**theirs**
neuter	**its**	**theirs**

Reference pronoun

IN FUNCTIONAL GRAMMAR

A pronoun that refers to someone or something *other than* the speaker/writer or the listener/reader:

"I assure you that ***she*** is coming."

In this sentence the ***reference pronoun* she** refers to someone *other than* the speaker or listener.

The reference pronouns are:

Base form	Objective	Possessive		Reflexive
he	**him**	**his**	**his**	***himself***
she	**her**	**her**	**hers**	***herself***
it	**it**	**its**	**its**	***itself***
they	**them**	**their**	**theirs**	**themselves**

Reflexive pronoun

Personal pronouns ending in ***-self*** or **-selves**. They direct the reader back to the pronoun subject in the same sentence:

Subject (a pronoun)	Verb	Reflexive pronoun
She	looked at	***herself***.
They	helped	**themselves**.

The reflexive pronouns look the same as the emphatic pronouns but are used differently:

myself **ourselves**
yourself **yourselves**
herself himself
itself **oneself** **themselves**

Relative pronoun

A pronoun that joins a relative clause to its *main clause*:

*The money **that** was in this box has disappeared.*

The relative pronouns are **who**, **whom**, **whose**, **which** and **that**.

Speech-role pronoun

IN FUNCTIONAL GRAMMAR

A pronoun that refers to the speaker/writer or the listener/reader:

"***I*** assure **you** that she is coming."

In this sentence ***I*** and **you** refer to the speaker and listener and are called ***speech-role pronouns***.

The speech-role pronouns are:

Base form	Objective	Possessive		Reflexive
I	**me**	***my***	**mine**	***myself***
you	**you**	**your**	**yours**	***yourself***

See also **relative clause**

proofreading

The re-reading of a text to check for keyboard mistakes, sometimes called typos.

Proofreading is often done letter-by-letter and is different from reading for meaning, which usually involves recognising word-size or phrase-size chunks of text.

Traditional proofreaders' marks include the following:

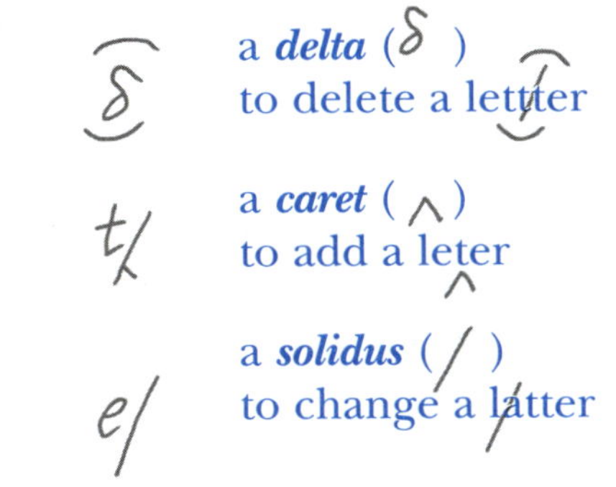

See *also* **typo**

proper noun

The name of a particular person, place or thing.

Dr Watson	Japan
Mt Kosciuszko	Christmas

Proper nouns start with a capital letter.

All other nouns are called common nouns. The following sentence includes ***proper nouns*** and common nouns:

My sister ***Alison*** arrived on a plane from ***Sydney***.

See *also* **common noun**

proscribe or prescribe?

See **prescribe** or **proscribe**?

provided that or providing that?

Both phrases mean "if".

I'll go ***if*** you go.
= I'll go ***provided that*** you go.

Some writers argue that ***provided that*** is more "correct" than ***providing that***, since it is a shortened form of *if it were provided that* ... However, both forms are widely used and accepted.

pull back

Another term for **zoom out**.
See **pan** or **zoom**?

pun

A joke that relies on the same word having two meanings, or two different words that have the same sound, for example:

☞

BOY (opening door): Yes?
SALESMAN: May I speak to your father?
BOY: He ain't home.
SALESMAN: "*Ain't*"! Where's your **grammar**?
BOY: She ain't home either.

Words that sound the same but have different meanings are ***homonyms*** or ***homophones***.

See also **homonym, homograph** *or* **homophone**?

punctuation mark

Punctuation is the division of a text into sentences, clauses or phrases, using punctuation marks.

.	full stop
,	comma
:	colon
;	semicolon
?	question mark
!	exclamation mark
—	dash
-	hyphen
( )	parentheses or brackets
" "	quotation marks

Each of these punctuation marks is discussed separately.

See separate entries for each mark

Some punctuation marks are used to *join* parts of a text, while others are used to *separate* them:

Joining

I have books**,** pens**,** pencils and paper.
It was a strange**-**looking animal.
Here's the plan**:** you open the door . . .

Separating

I have pens and paper**;** I need a book.
You go first**.** I'll follow later.
Mammals **(**such as dogs**)** have fur.

purpose

See **text and context**

purposely or *purposefully*?

• ***purposely*** means "deliberately" or "on purpose"
• ***purposefully*** means "resolutely" or "with determination"

I didn't drop it ***purposely***; it was an accident.
She strode ***purposefully*** into the room and demanded an apology.

question

A sentence that usually requests information or agreement. A question is sometimes called an ***interrogative sentence*** and is said to be in the ***interrogative mood.***

Most questions end with a question mark (**?**).

Yes/no or "closed" question

This kind of question allows very few ways to answer it, usually by a simple "yes" or "no":

Is there any water left?
Are you coming with us?
Is 9 a prime number?

Wh- or "open" question

These are questions that usually include one of the so-called **wh-** words (chiefly **who**, **what**, **where**, **when**) or **how**. These questions can be answered in many ways:

Where's Mark?
Who knew and **when** did they know it?
How many fish did you catch?

Tag question

This kind of question sometimes asks for agreement, rather than for information. A tag question includes a statement, followed by a tag:

You'll play on our team, OK?
He can come, can't he?

Alternative question

(Also called an ***or-question***)
This kind of question seeks information but gives the listener a limited choice of answers.

Do you want chicken **or** fish?

The questioner expects one of only two possible answers to this question.

Rhetorical question

This kind of sentence *looks* like a question (it has a question mark), but the speaker is telling, not asking.

What do I care?
= I don't care.

Will we ever escape?
= We will probably never escape.

Question-command

This kind of sentence *looks* like a question (it has a question mark), but the speaker is really giving an instruction.

Can you close that door?
= Close that door.

Statement-question

This kind of sentence looks like a statement (there is no question mark) but is really a question.

You've got to be joking.
= Are you really joking?

Direct and indirect questions

Quoted questions can be ***direct*** or <u>indirect</u>. Indirect questions do not have a question mark.

> ***"Who won?"*** I asked.
> I asked them <u>who had won</u>.

An indirect question shifts the event into the PAST TENSE:

> ***"Where* IS *my cat?"*** I asked.
> I asked them <u>where my cat WAS</u>.

See also **direct** and **indirect questions** and **commands** • **interrogative words** • **mood** (of a verb) • **rhetorical question** • **tag question**

question mark [?]

A mark placed at the end of a *direct question.*

> Do you have a dog**?**
> You have a dog, don't you**?**
> "Who has a dog**?**" he asked.

Question marks are not used with *indirect questions*:

> He asked whether anyone had a dog.

See also **direct** and **indirect questions** and **commands** • **question**

quit or close?

• ***to quit*** a computer application means "to close all documents plus the application itself"
• ***to close*** means "to remove only the current document but to leave the others open plus the application itself"

quotation marks [" " or ' ']

These punctuation marks are used to start and finish words copied (or quoted) by the writer from someone else:

> **"**Can I come too?**"** she asked.
> = **'**Can I come too?**'** she asked.

Single or double quotation marks?

Quotation marks can be either single (**' '**) or double (**" "**). Both are accepted, but writers should be consistent, whichever is used.

Embedded quotation

Sometimes a quotation occurs within another quotation. This is said to be an embedded quotation. In this case use a different mark for the embedded quotation:

> **"**I knocked on the door of her one-room flat, which she called her **'**studio apartment**'**, but there was no answer,**"** he explained.

or:

> 'I knocked on the door of her one-room flat, which she called her "studio apartment", but there was no answer,' he explained.

Distancing quotation

Quotation marks are also used to show that the writer may dislike, or disagree with, the words used:

> They now have a "smart" bomb that navigates to its target. Often it misses.

Quote-unquote

Punctuation marks such as quotation marks cannot be heard in spoken English. For this reason people sometimes say the words ***quote*** and ***unquote*** to indicate that the words they are speaking are someone else's:

> TV REPORTER: Today the Green Party described the government's new environment policy as ***quote*** utter garbage ***unquote***.

The same sentence, if written in a newspaper, would be:

> Today the Green Party described the government's new environment policy as "utter garbage".

The words ***quote*** and ***unquote*** are generally used only when speaking.

Quotation marks and other punctuation marks

These punctuation rules differ between countries.

Australian style

In Australia quotation marks usually include *only* the words *and punctuation marks* that were said or written by someone else:

> According to this dictionary, "Words such as 'Australia', 'Japan', 'United States' and 'France' are proper nouns".

American and Canadian style

However, in North America, other punctuation marks (such as commas and full stops) are included inside quotation marks, *even though they are not strictly quoted*:

> According to this dictionary, "Words such as 'Australia,' 'Japan,' 'United States,' and 'France' are proper nouns."

This is an example of "correct" style in one country being "incorrect" style in another.

Indirect quotation

Indirect quotations do *not* have quotation marks:

Direct quotation

> She asked him, "Who are you?"

Indirect quotation

> She asked him ***who he was***.

☞

Indented quotation

In a written text a quotation of more than three lines is sometimes indented. Indented quotations do *not* have quotation marks:

> In the book *Sharks* it is claimed that:
>
> > The whale shark stays on the surface of the ocean, but the great white shark can dive to more than a kilometre deep. The bull shark swims in rivers as well as the sea.

Names of poems and short stories

Quotation marks are used when referring to titles of poems and short stories.

"The Man from Snowy River" by A. B. Paterson

"The Drover's Wife" by Henry Lawson

Website and email addresses

Both website and email addresses are quoted using ***angular brackets*** [< >]:

Our home page is <xyx.net.au> and you can contact us at <mail@xyx.net.au>.

Quoted emails

When quoting a previous email, some programs insert angular brackets at the start of each line:

Hi Kay
It's on the piano.
Theo

Kay wrote:

\> Theo
\> Have just got home and
\> thought I'd take Grunge for a
\> walk. Where's his lead?
\> Kay

See also **comma • direct** and **indirect speech • indented quotation**

quoted speech

See **direct** and **indirect speech**

quoted writing

See **quotation marks**

RAM or ROM?

See **ROM** or **RAM**?

-re or -er?

A number of words can end in either **-re** or **-er**.

In the following words the usual Australian spelling is **-re** and the usual American spelling is **-er**:

Australian spelling	*American spelling*
cent**re**	cent**er**
theat**re**	theat**er**
kilomet**re**	kilomet**er**
lit**re**	lit**er**

Some words are *always* spelled **-re**:

genre
timb**re** = sound quality

Some words are *always* spelled **-er**:

splint**er**
paint**er**
timb**er** = wood

Words ending in **-re** are usually French in origin.

See also **meter** or **metre**?

reason is (because)?

Sometimes people say:

The ***reason*** I am late ***is because*** I missed the bus.

This is an example of redundancy (saying the same thing twice).

the reason* . . . *is = ***because***

The sentence can be rewritten in two ways:

The ***reason*** I am late ***is*** I missed the bus.

I am late ***because*** I missed the bus.

See also **redundancy**

recipe or receipt?

- a ***recipe*** is a set of instructions for cooking something
- a ***receipt*** is a record of payment for something that was bought

Here's a ***recipe*** for making pizza.
Here's a ***receipt*** for the TV repair.

recomposing

Rewriting information in a different format, usually to summarise the key facts.

To summarise a narrative you can ***recompose*** it as a storyboard or a time line.

R

Recomposing helps the reader to locate the key information in a text and to organise it in a visual format that shows the text's "shape" or structure.

All written genres can be recomposed as visual texts:

Written genre	*Visual text*
narrative	storyboard
recount	storyboard or time line
report	tree diagram or table
procedure	flow chart or storyboard
explanation	flow chart or web diagram
persuasion	flow chart
discussion	table or Venn diagram

For examples of how these genres can be recomposed as visual texts, *see individual entries for each genre*.

See also **genre • visual text**

recount

IN FUNCTIONAL GRAMMAR

A kind of text in which events are recalled, usually in the order in which they occurred.

Recounts are divided into ***factual recounts*** and ***personal recounts***, but in both cases the events described are said to be true.

Examples of recounts include news items (sometimes called "reports" or "stories"), as well as diaries, records of science experiments and biographies.

See also **factual recount • personal recount**

recto or verso?

- ***recto*** is any right-hand page of a book
- ***verso*** is any left-hand page of a book

The title page is always a ***recto*** page, and the copyright notice is usually on a ***verso*** page.

See also **front matter** and **end matter**

recur or re-occur?

- ***recur*** means "to happen again"
- ***re-occur*** is a misspelling

See your doctor if pain ***recurs***.

The ***r*** is doubled when adding ***-ed*** or ***-ing***:

recurred ***recurring***

redundancy

Using unnecessary words to say something.

> ***Finally*** and ***in completion*** let me ***finish*** and ***conclude*** by saying …

Two examples of redundancy are ***tautology*** and ***prolixity***.

Tautology

If exactly the same thing is said twice it is a tautology:

> I will ***repeat*** the question ***again***.

Since ***repeat*** means "say again" the speaker appears to be saying:

> I will ***say again*** the question ***again***.

To avoid this tautology the sentence could be rephrased in either of two ways:

> I will ***say*** the question ***again***.

> I will ***repeat*** the question.

Prolixity

If a speaker or writer uses many unnecessary words, without always repeating the meaning, the text is said to be prolix:

> In a word, and without beating about the bush, I would like to introduce our next speaker who needs no introduction from me and by the way I notice he's wearing the same tie as mine, and yellow is my favourite colour—which reminds me of the time when …

reference

See **cohesion**

reference pronoun

IN FUNCTIONAL GRAMMAR

A pronoun that refers to someone or something *other than* the speaker/writer or the listener/reader.

> I assure you that ***he*** is coming with ***them***.

In this sentence I and you refer to the speaker and listener, so they are called speech-role pronouns. The pronouns ***he*** and ***them*** refer to people *other than* the speaker and listener and are called ***reference pronouns***.

The reference pronouns are:

Base form	*Objective*	*Possessive*		*Reflexive*
he	***him***	***his***	***his***	***himself***
she	***her***	***her***	***hers***	***herself***
it	***it***	***its***	***its***	***itself***
they	***them***	***their***	***theirs***	***themselves***

Reference pronouns give cohesion to the text.

See *also* **cohesion • speech-role pronoun**

references

(Also called a ***reference list***)
A list of the books (or websites, etc.) that have been mentioned in a text.

In an information book the references are listed separately from the bibliography. A ***bibliography*** lists all recommended books on the topic, whereas ***references*** include only those books that have been mentioned in the text.

The references are usually listed at the end of the book, after the notes (or footnotes) and before the bibliography.

See also **bibliography • cross-reference • front matter** and **end matter**

---

reflexive pronoun

Personal pronouns ending in ***-self*** or ***-selves***. These pronouns are used when the agent does something to her/himself.

> I looked at ***myself*** in the window.
> She dressed ***herself***.

See also **personal pronoun**

---

register

See **text and context**

---

regular and irregular nouns

Nouns are said to be regular or irregular depending on how they form the plural.

Regular nouns

Most nouns form the plural by adding ***-s***:

Singular	*Plural*
computer	computer***s***
country	countr***ies***

Irregular nouns

Nouns that form the plural in other ways are said to be irregular:

Singular	*Plural*
child	child***ren***
sheep	***sheep***
foot	***feet***
sylla***bus***	sylla***bi***
person	***people***
medium	medi***a***

See also **plural nouns**

---

regular and irregular verbs

Verbs are said to be regular or irregular depending on how they form the past tense or past participle.

Regular verbs

Most verbs form the past tense

and the past participle by adding ***-ed*** or ***-d***:

Present	Past
bake	bake***d***
cook	cook***ed***

Irregular verbs

Verbs that form the past tense or past participle in other ways are said to be irregular:

Present tense	Past tense	Past participle
I see	I ***saw***	I have **seen**
I take	I ***took***	I have ***taken***
I put	I ***put***	I have ***put***
I go	I ***went***	I have ***gone***
I ring	I ***rang***	I have ***rung***
I am	I ***was***	I have **been**

See *also* **participle • past tenses**

relational process

See **process**

relative clause

(Also called an ***adjective clause***)
A clause that is related to another clause by a ***relative pronoun***.

The money ***that*** was in this box is gone.

The relative pronouns are ***who***, ***whom***, ***whose***, ***which*** and ***that***.

See *also* **clause**

relative pronoun

See **relative clause**

re-occur *or* recur?

See **recur** *or* **re-occur?**

report

A term used for two different kinds of information text: an ***information report*** or a ***news report***.

Information report

A kind of text in which the subject is defined and classified into groups.

See **information report**

News report

An article in which recent events are recounted, usually in a newspaper or a radio or TV news program.

See **factual recount**

reported speech

See **direct** and **indirect speech**

residue

See **mood** and **residue**

resolution (in a narrative)

The conclusion of a narrative or plot in which a crisis is resolved. Also called ***dénouement*** (which is French for "untying" a knot).

Crisis

Romeo decides to take poison. When Juliet finds Romeo dead she stabs herself.

Resolution

On hearing of their deaths and recognising that their families' rivalry has led to this crisis, the Montagues and Capulets are reconciled.

See also **complication** • **narrative**

---

rheme

See **theme and rheme**

---

rhetoric, rhetorical

Rhetoric originally meant the art of speaking and later the art of writing, especially prose. Students of rhetoric were taught ways of persuading an audience.

Rhetoric now usually means the use of exaggerated expressions:

My backpack has ***a ton*** of books in it. I'll ***never*** be able to lift it.

Rhetorical question

A rhetorical question is not intended to be answered. It is a persuasive device:

What does he know about art?
= He knows nothing about art.

See also ***literally, virtually** or **metaphorically?*** • **question**

---

rhyme or *rhythm?*

• ***rhyme*** means "a word whose ending sounds the same as another word"
• ***rhythm*** means "the pattern of beats in a poem or song"

"Mistake" ***rhymes*** with "cake" and "opaque".
That track is in 4/4 ***rhythm***.

See also **metre** (in poetry)

ROM or *RAM?*

• ***ROM*** means "**r**ead-**o**nly **m**emory"
• ***RAM*** means "**r**andom-**a**ccess **m**emory"

Both are computer terms. ***ROM*** holds information that can be read but not altered. ***RAM*** contains information that can be altered or deleted.

roman type

See **font**

row (in a table)

Part of a table of information that is read *across* the table, usually from left to right. The cell at the left is usually the **ROW HEADING**.

	Reptiles	Birds
LEGS	4	2
COVERING	**scales**	**feathers**
WARM BLOOD	✗	✓

See also **cell** (in a table) • **column** (in a table) • **table**

rule

A printer's term for a ruled line, such as those that divide the entries in this dictionary.

Solid rule: ________________

Dotted rule: ....

Dashed rule: ------------------------

Rules can be solid, dotted or dashed. Main topics might be separated by solid rules. Dotted or dashed rules would then separate subtopics.

Rules are also used to connect information in diagrams. These are also called ***leader lines***.

See also **leader lines**

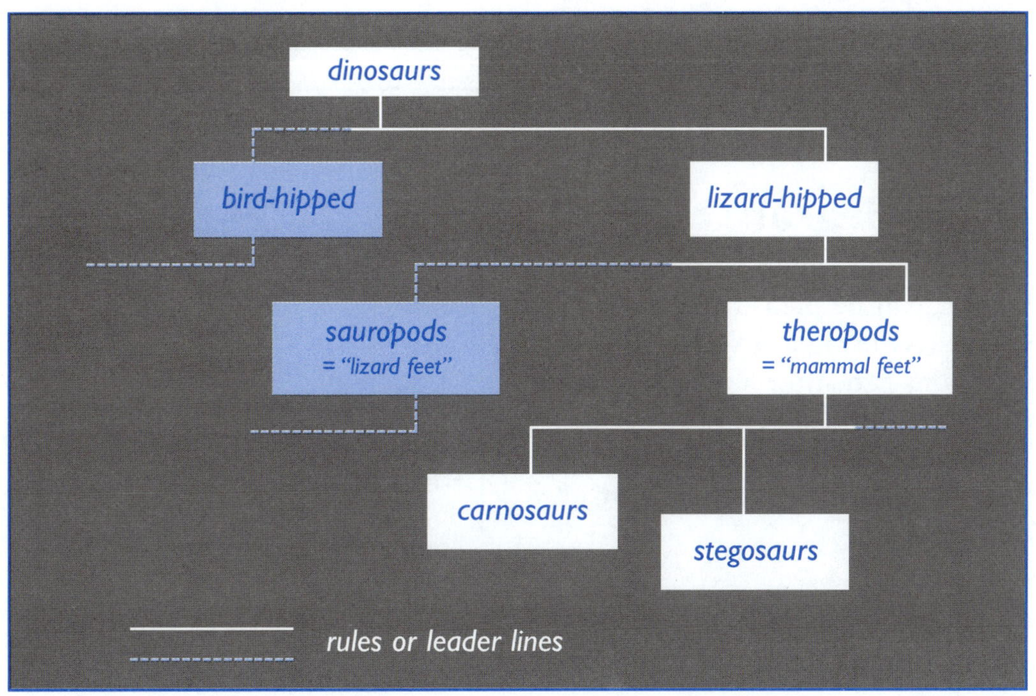

S

sans serif font

See **font**

sarcasm or *irony*?

See ***irony*** *or* ***sarcasm***?

satire

A piece of writing or a performance that uses irony or parody to mock someone else's beliefs or attitudes. Such a piece of writing ***satirises*** its subject.

Hypocrisy (saying one thing but really believing its opposite) is a frequent subject of satire.

Satire that imitates a writer's style or a speaker's tone of voice is called a ***parody***.

See *also* ***irony*** *or* ***sarcasm***? • **parody**

scale diagram

A diagram in which parts of the subject can be measured accurately using a scale. Scale diagrams can show length, height, weight, speed or area.

See *also* **diagram** • **scale** (in a map or diagram)

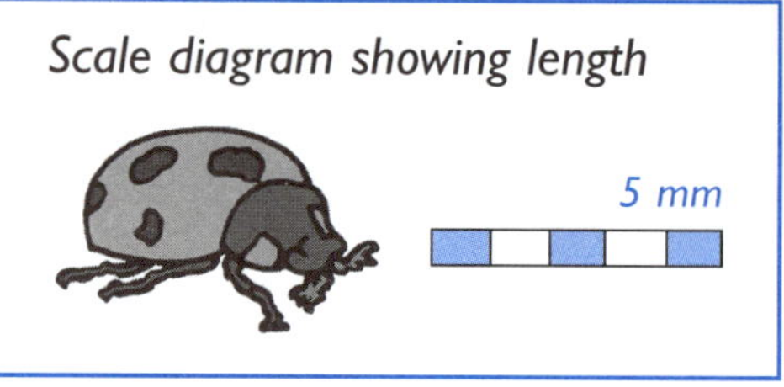

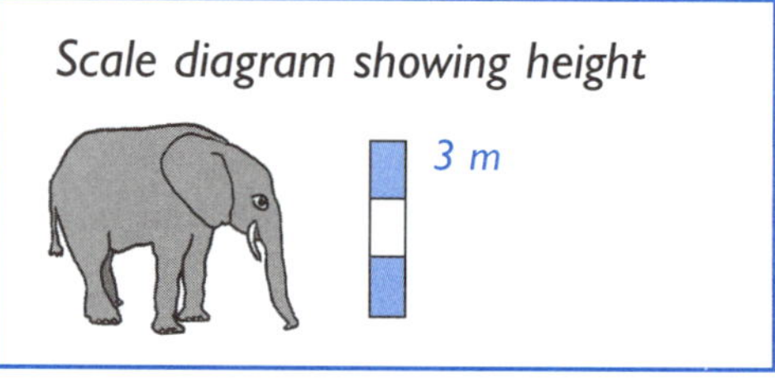

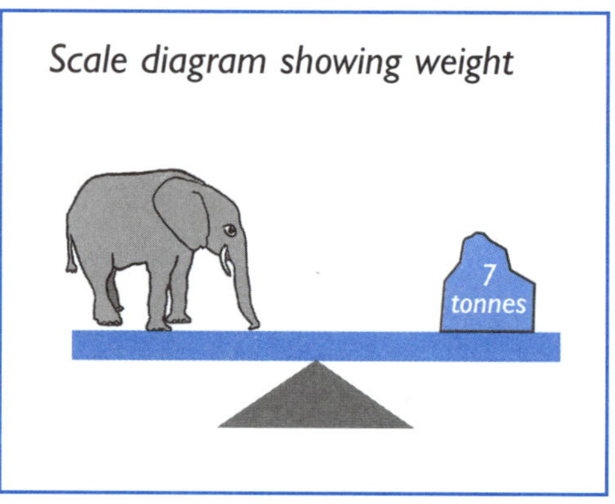

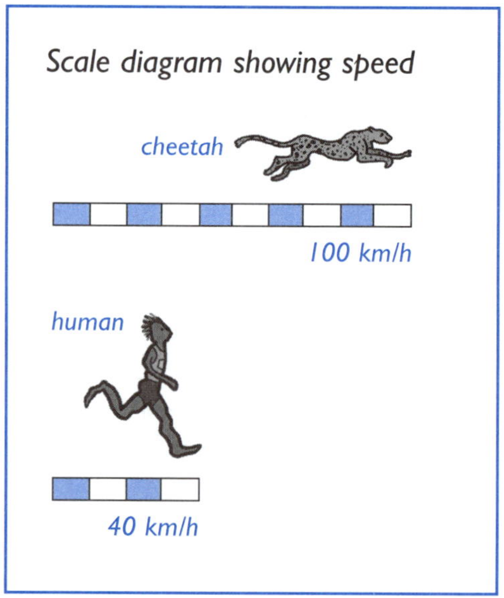

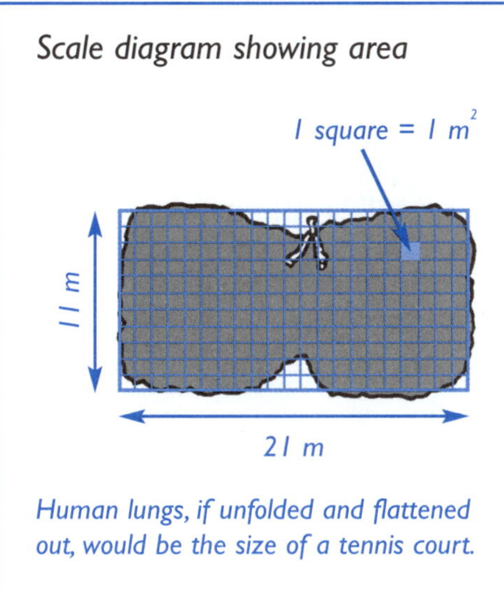

Human lungs, if unfolded and flattened out, would be the size of a tennis court.

scale (in a map or diagram)

A graduated symbol (usually including numbers) that shows the relative size or distance in a diagram or map.

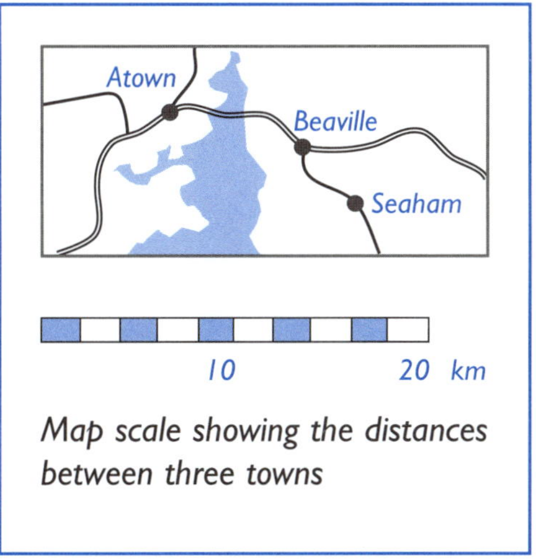

Map scale showing the distances between three towns

See also **map • scale diagram**

scan and skim

See **skim and scan**

script, synopsis or *treatment*?

In film or TV there are three stages in the writing process:

- a ***synopsis*** or one-page outline of the whole story
- a ***treatment***, which is a more detailed telling of the story, making no mention of technical details such as camera angles or special effects
- a ***script*** (or ***shooting script***) that provides a scene-by-scene account of the movie with all dialogue, camera work, sound effects and so on

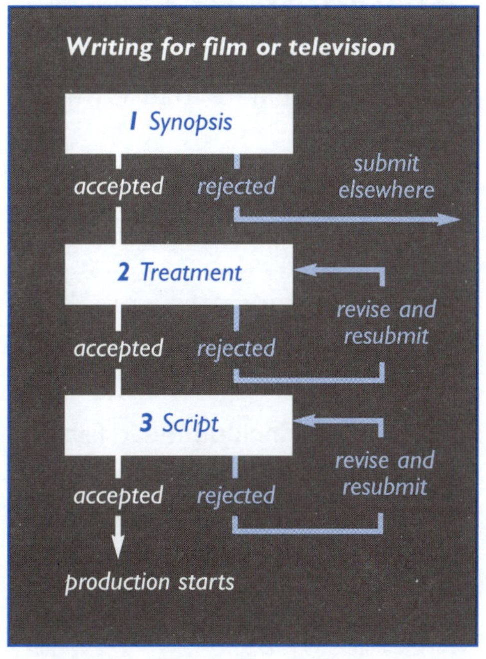

search field

An active part of a web page where the user types a word that can be found in the text. Once the **SEARCH** button is clicked, all instances of the *word or phrase* on the website are listed.

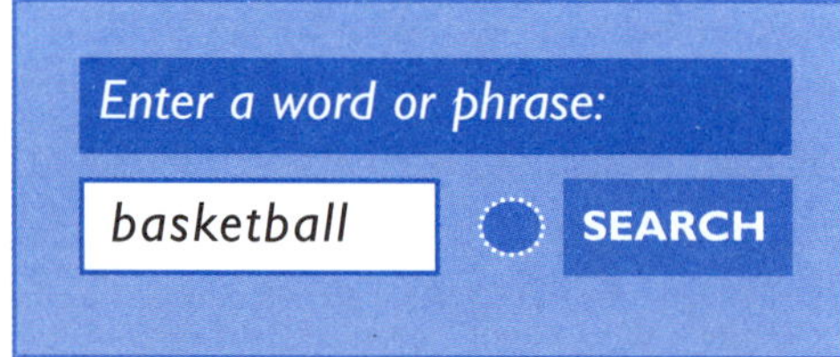

See *also* **browse**, **find** or **search**?

second person

See **person**

semicolon [;]

A punctuation mark that indicates a break or pause within a sentence.

The car rolled to a stop**;** the train swept past.

A semicolon indicates a break that is stronger than a comma but weaker than a full stop:

Food groups include meat, fish and eggs**;** green and yellow vegetables**;** fruit, such as oranges and apples**;** and cereals.

See *also* **comma** • **full stop**

sentence

A clause (or group of clauses) usually including a verb, starting with a **C**apital **L**etter and ending with a full stop, question mark or exclamation mark (**. ? !**).

Dad made lunch for us**.**
Diamonds are made of carbon**.**

Most (but not all) sentences can be divided into a subject and a predicate:

Subject	*Predicate*
She	poured the milk into the bowl.
The milk	was poured into the bowl.

Some sentences have no subject:

Subject	*Predicate*
	Pour the milk into the bowl.

Sentences can be statements, questions, commands or exclamations:

Statement
He stayed at home.
Question
Did he stay at home?
Command
Stay at home!
Exclamation
He *really* stayed at home!

Sentences can also be grouped as simple, complex or compound.

Simple sentence
A sentence that contains only one clause:

This sentence has just one clause.

Complex sentence
A sentence that includes at least one ***subordinate clause*** as well as a main clause. A subordinate clause sounds "incomplete" without its main clause:

This main clause, ***which has this subordinate clause***, is part of a complex sentence.

Subordinate clauses are said to "depend on" the main clause and "do not make complete sense by themselves". They are often joined by one of the following conjunctions:

which ***that***
who ***what***
because

A ***complex*** sentence contains subordinate clauses, whereas a ***compound*** sentence contains coordinate clauses.

Compound sentence
A sentence that includes two or more coordinate clauses:

This a coordinate clause ***and this is one as well.***

Coordinate clauses are said to "make sense" when they stand alone. They are usually joined by one of the following conjunctions:

and
but
or
either … ***or***
neither … ***nor***

See *also* **clause** • **coordinate clause** • **predicate** • **subject** (of a sentence) • **verb**

sentences starting with **And** *or* **But***?*

See ***And*** *starting a sentence?* • ***But*** *starting a sentence?*

sequence of events (in a recount)

See **factual recount** • **personal recount**

serif font

See **font**

setting (in a narrative)

The context in which a narrative takes place.

Once upon a time ***in a dark wood where it always rained*** there lived a …

Setting can include descriptions

☞

of place, time of day and ***atmosphere*** (the general "feeling" or mood of a place).

See *also* **narrative**

shall or ***will***?

IN TRADITIONAL USAGE
Shall is used differently from ***will***. A writer makes a distinction between:

I *or* we ***shall***
he, she, it, one, you, *or* they ***will***

To convey *strong feeling* traditional usage is to reverse the pattern:

I or we ***will***
he, she, it, one, you, or they ***shall***

Few Australians now follow traditional usage.

IN CURRENT USAGE
Most writers now use ***will*** in *all* situations:

I *or* we ***will***
he, she, it, one, you, *or* they ***will***

When speaking most people use the contraction ***'ll***:

"***Who'll*** help me?"
"***We'll*** help you."

When speaking we also use ***will*** when it stands for another verb:

"***Who'll*** help me?"
"We ***will***."

s/he

This contraction, invented in the 1960s, is short for ***she or he*** or ***she/he***. It is used to include female as well male subjects.

The reader may omit the next chapter if ***s/he*** wishes.

Here ***s/he*** refers to the reader who could be male or female.

See *also* ***he or she*** + ***they***?

should have, ***should've*** or ***should of***?

See ***could have***, ***could've*** or ***could of***?

sidebar

A text element separated from the main text and placed to one side of it. Sidebars are used in websites, where they function like a table of contents or an index. They are also similar to ***breakouts*** in printed texts.

A sidebar like this one can be used to:
- *explain a key detail in the main text*
- *give examples*
- *serve as a table of contents or an index*

See *also* **breakout** • **hyperlink**

signpost

In an information text a signpost indicates an entry point into the text, allowing for a unique pathway through the text.

Signposts include ***headings*** and *highlighted words*:

> ***The highest mountain***
> Measured from sea level the highest mountain on earth is *Mt Everest*. However, if we measure all mountains from their base, the highest mountain on Earth is *Mauna Kea* on Hawaii.

In this example ***The highest mountain*** is a heading and the mountain names (*Mt Everest* and *Mauna Kea*) are highlighted words. All are signposts that allow the reader to locate a topic quickly when "skimming or scanning" an information text.

There are many kinds of signposts, all serving to alert or redirect the reader. The most common signposts include:

- headings
- subheadings
- bullets
- highlighted words
- asterisks and footnotes
- cross-references
- page numbers
- number labels

In electronic texts some signposts (such as cross-references and page numbers) are replaced with hyperlinks, which serve the same purpose.

See *also* **asterisk** • **bullet** • **cross-reference** • **footnote** • **heading** • **highlighted words** • **hyperlink** • **number label** • **page number** • **pathway** (through a text) • **subheading**

simile

See **figure of speech**

simple sentence

See **sentence**

singular

See **number**

site map

A ***nested list*** or ***tree diagram*** that represents all the pages on a website. Although a site "map" is not a true map, it does help the user to "navigate" around the site. The two kinds of site maps serve different purposes for different users.

Site map (nested list)

A site map in the form of a ***nested list*** often appears as a page on a website. Visitors to the site use this list to locate the topic or group of topics that they want:

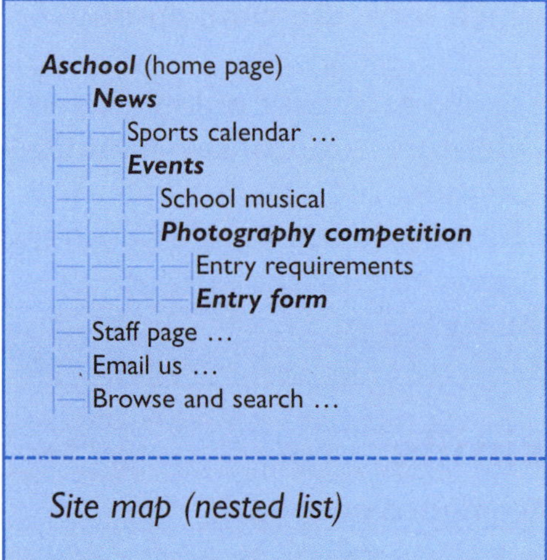

Site map (nested list)

In this site list of pages on a website, the names are indented (moved to the right) to show that they are linked to the page above it. This is shown in the site's URL as a forward slash (/):

aschool/news/events/photocomp/entryform

Site map (tree diagram)

A site map that is in the form of a ***tree diagram*** (*top right*) is used by a web designer when planning or altering a website. A tree diagram helps the designer to see:

- where each page "fits"
- which pages are connected by hyperlinks

See also **nested list • tree diagram • list • map • URL**

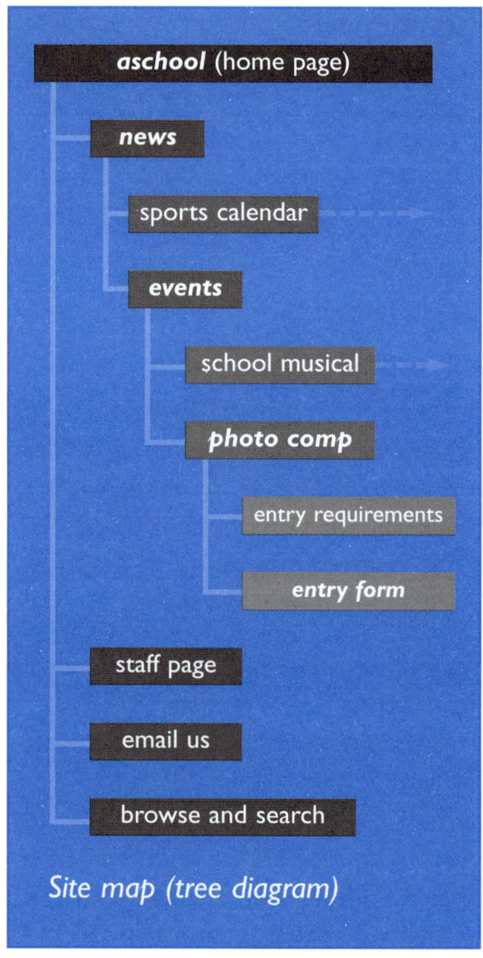

Site map (tree diagram)

skim and scan

A reading strategy suited to information texts, in which the reader looks for one or two key words and overlooks the rest.

When using this strategy the reader might take a zigzag ***pathway*** through the text, not reading every word.

See also **pathway** (through a text)

slash [/]

(Also called a ***solidus***, ***virgule***, ***slant*** or ***diagonal***) A punctuation mark with several meanings or uses.

"Or" slash

When used with words the slash often means "or":

Please bring to the picnic:
1 steak/vegieburgers
2 bread rolls/pitta/focaccia
3 salads

= Please bring to the picnic:
1 steak **or** vegieburgers
2 bread rolls **or** pitta **or** focaccia
3 salads

The expression ***and/or*** means "either ***and*** or ***or***":

We had steak ***and/or*** vegieburgers

= Some of us had both steak and vegieburgers; some had only steak; and some had only vegieburgers.

"Over" slash

When used with numerals the slash can mean "divided by" or "over":

2/3 = two-thirds or
two divided by three
two over three

Abbreviating slash

Some writers use a slash to indicate missing letters in abbreviations (usually when writing by hand):

steak & v/burgers w/ salad
= steak and vegieburgers with salad

URL forward slash

In a website address the forward slash (/) indicates a new folder or page. Websites are designed as a tree diagram with some topics (or folders) placed within other topics (or folders):

www.sportznewz/soccer/UK/results

Forward or backward slash?

In web design a forward slash (/) is different from a backward slash or ***backslash*** (\ ). Backslashes have different functions in different programs, such as:

- to cancel a forward slash
- to mean "instruction continues on the next line"

Other meanings and uses

A slash can be used to mean "per" or to separate parts of the date:

km/h = kilometres ***per*** hour
2/2/10 = 2 February 2010

In language studies a slash before and after a letter indicates the sound it makes, not the letter itself:

☞

You don't hear the sound /k/ in the word *knight*.

See *also* **abbreviation • site map • URL**

snob grammar

Grammar that identifies the user as "correct" rather than clarifies the meaning of the language.

One example of snob grammar is to insist that

I am better than ***he***

is "correct", whereas

I am better than ***him***

is "incorrect".

In fact both expressions are clear in meaning. The main difference is that the expression I am better than ***he*** identifies the speaker as a believer in snob grammar.

Snob grammar often involves "correcting" an expression that is already correct (that is, clear in meaning and widely accepted in use). This is also called ***hypercorrection***.

Other examples of snob grammar include:

- always avoiding ***split infinitives*** even when this sounds clumsy and mannered
- always making sentences agree in number or gender *regardless of meaning or clarity*

See *also* ***he or she + they?*** • **hypercorrection • split infinitive** • ***than me*** *or* ***than I?***

sociogram

A kind of ***web diagram*** in which the participants are people or organisations. The relationships between the participants can be written along each arrow.

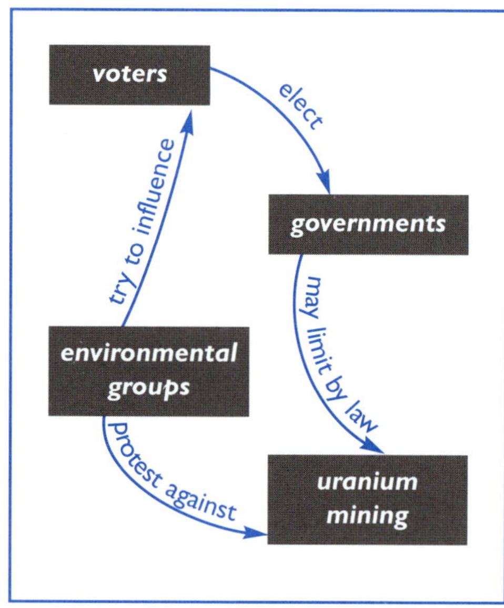

Sociograms are useful when planning explanations or information reports. Typical topics are government, the media and conflict resolution.

See *also* **web diagram**

solidus

See **slash** [/]

somebody/someone + ***is*** or ***are***?

See ***everybody/everyone*** + ***is*** *or* ***are****?*

some time, sometime or ***sometimes***?

• ***some time*** means "an unknown time"
• ***sometime*** means "*at* an unknown time"
• ***sometimes*** means "occasionally"

> We may communicate with aliens at ***some time*** in the future.

> We may communicate with aliens ***sometime*** in the future.

> My aunt writes to me ***sometimes***.

sorts of + plural?

See ***kinds of*** + plural?

speech-role pronoun

IN FUNCTIONAL GRAMMAR

A pronoun that refers to the speaker or the listener.

> ***I*** assure ***you*** that he is coming with them.

In this sentence ***I*** and ***you*** refer to the speaker and listener and are called ***speech-role pronouns***. The pronouns he and them refer to people *other than* the speaker and listener and are called reference pronouns.

The speech-role pronouns are:

Base form	Objective	Possessive		Reflexive
I	***me***	***my***	***mine***	***myself***
you	***you***	***your***	***yours***	***yourself***

See *also* **reference pronoun**

spelling checker

A utility within a word processing program that checks all the words in a document against the program's dictionary. If a word is not found, the spelling checker provides a list of alternative spellings. The user is asked to select one or to add the "new" word to the dictionary.

Two problems can occur with spelling checkers:
• The checker may replace a correct word with another word (correctly spelt but with the wrong meaning) because it does not recognise the original word:

> Upload your ftp now.

A checker may change this to:

> Unload your foot now.

☞

• The checker may ignore a word with the wrong meaning because it is correctly spelt:

We visited Hungry and Whales.

Checker may *not* change this to:

We visited Hungary and Wales.

In either case the user cannot rely on the spelling checker.

See also **ftp • grammar checker**

spelt or ***spelled***?

Both ***spelt*** and ***spelled*** are the past form of ***to spell*** and both spellings are accepted.

that's ***spelt*** correctly
= that's ***spelled*** correctly

split infinitive

A ***to-infinitive*** that is split by another word or phrase.

to rather foolishly ***chatter***
= ***to chatter*** rather foolishly

Some writers try to avoid putting any other word between the two parts of a ***to-infinitive***:

Split infinitive

The truck began ***to*** slowly ***move***.

Infinitives not split

The truck began ***to move*** slowly.
Slowly the truck began ***to move***.

Other writers believe that in some situations the split infinitive is useful, and may have a unique meaning. This is especially where the infinitive is split to emphasise the adverb:

He refused ***to*** completely ***agree***
(= He was willing to agree partly)

has a different emphasis from

He completely refused ***to agree***
(= He would not agree at all).

In the following sentences, completely could refer to either refused or ***to agree***, and the reader does not know whether the person agrees partly or not at all:

He refused ***to agree*** completely.
He refused completely ***to agree***.

The rule that we "must always" avoid splitting the infinitive began when grammarians wanted English grammar to behave like Latin grammar. In Latin all infinitives are single words and therefore cannot be split; but in English the ***to-infinitives*** are always two words.

See also **finite verb** and **non-finite verb**

spoonerism

Mispronouncing two words in the same sentence by swapping the first letters of each.

Spoonerisms are named after the Reverend William Spooner, who is supposed to have said

You have **h**issed my **m**ystery classes

instead of

You have **m**issed by **h**istory classes.

Spoonerisms can be unintended or they can be used as a deliberate stylistic device or word play.

square brackets [ ]

See **brackets** ( ) and [ ]

statement

A sentence that states something. Sentences can be grouped as statements, questions, exclamations or commands.

A statement is said to be "in the declarative mood".

See *also* **mood** (of a verb) • **question** • **sentence**

statement of opinion

(Also called a ***statement of position***) An introductory paragraph that states the writer's opinion, as used in an argument. The text then goes on to present reasons for that opinion.

Children Should Be Given the Vote

Statement of opinion

In a democracy it is often said that "everyone has a vote". Surely "everyone" should include children.

See *also* **persuasion**

statement-question

A sentence that looks like a statement (there is no question mark) but is really a question.

Surely you don't mean that.
= Do you really mean that?

See *also* **question**

stationary or *stationery?*

- ***stationary*** means "not moving"
- ***stationery*** means "writing or drawing materials"

The train remained ***stationary***.
Pencils and paper are ***stationery***.

storyboard

A visual text in which a series of events are presented as a number of images each in a separate box. The boxes are numbered in the order in which they should be read, forming a sequence.

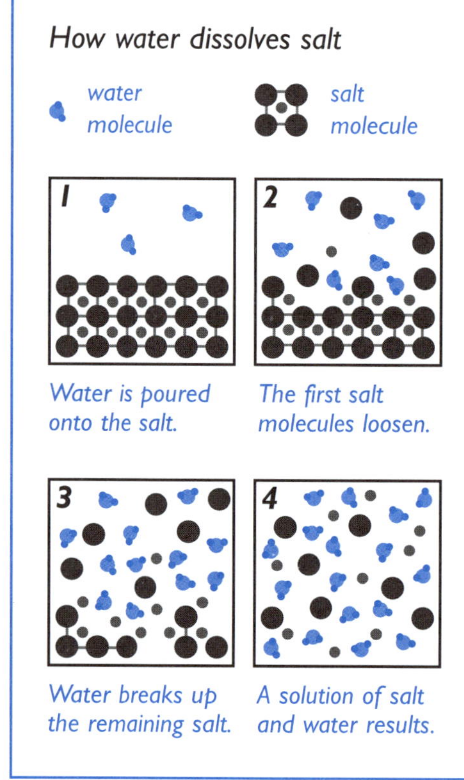

Storyboards are used to plan narrative sequences in film and television. They enable the director and camera operator to visualise each scene before shooting begins. Other uses for storyboards include:

- procedures, such as a recipe
- factual recounts, such as a record of a science experiment
- explanations of processes ("how things work")
- recounts of historical change

See also **explanation • factual recount • procedure**

story line

See **narrative**

story map

A visual text that tells a narrative or recount in a form loosely resembling a map or flow chart.

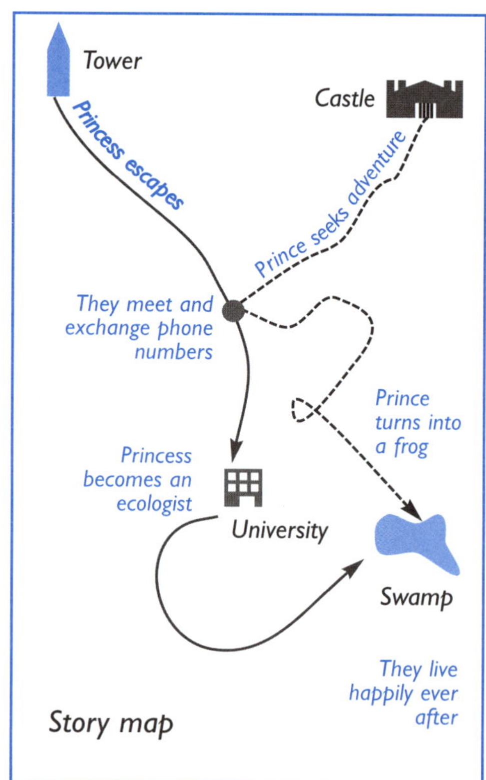

Although this kind of text looks like a map, it is not concerned with exact distances or positions. It is more like a flow chart than a true map.

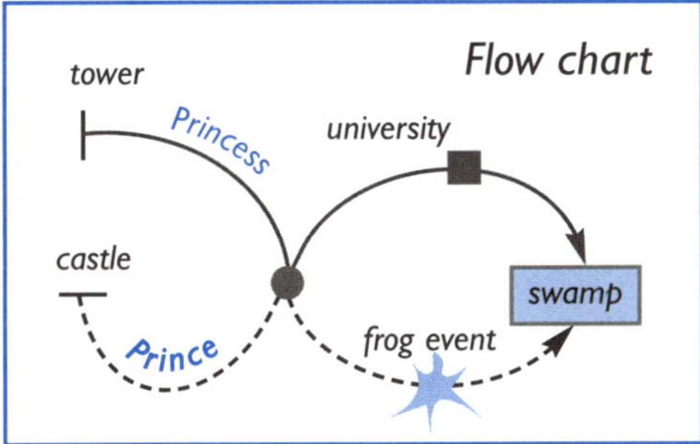

See also **flow chart** • **map** • **narrative** • **recount** • **time line**

style

Style includes ***personal*** style, ***publishing*** style and ***word processing*** style.

Personal style

Traditionally "style" refers to the more personal aspects of how we *choose* to write. Style can convey the writer's personality or may suggest the period when s/he wrote.

In *The Catcher in the Rye* Salinger wrote in a conversational ***style*** typical of teenagers in the 1940s.

Personal style includes such qualities as tone of voice and choice of words (formal, chatty, ironic, intimate and so on).

Publishing style

(Also called ***house style***) The writing conventions used by a publishing house, including:

- spelling and punctuation
- where to hyphenate or when to capitalise a word
- how to arrange lists, tables, diagrams and other visual texts
- how indexes, bibliographies and glossaries are compiled
- how to design a book or website

Many of these style "rules" have been devised by publishing companies so that their books are written consistently. With the rise of desktop publishing and word processing, students are increasingly expected to know the basics of book and website publishing style.

Word processing style

In a word processing program ***style*** refers to the appearance of the type, including the type's size, font, colour, alignment, spacing and so on.

To change the appearance of the highlighted text click on ***Style*** in the menu bar.

See **alignment** of text • **font** • **front matter** and **end matter** • **graphic design** • **menu**

S

subheading

A ***heading*** is a word or phrase that indicates the topic of the paragraphs that follow. Headings can be of different levels, indicating different degrees of importance.

A ***main heading*** is sometimes followed by a subheading which is less important and belongs "under" the main heading:

> ***Living and non-living***
> The world can be seen as made up of living and non-living things.
>
> Living things
> There are five main groups of living things: animals, plants, fungi, bacteria and protists.

When planning or editing a text with many headings and subheadings a ***nested list*** can sometimes be used.

See also **heading • nested list**

subject (of a sentence)

Usually the first part of a sentence. In many sentences the ***subject*** is the agent (the "doer" of the verb's action):

> ***He*** picked up the camera.

All of the sentence that is *not* the subject is called the *predicate*:

> ***He*** *picked up the camera.*

The subject of a sentence is said to be "in the ***nominative case***".

Not all subjects start a sentence. In some sentences there is a ***grammatical subject*** and a ***logical subject***.

Grammatical subject

A grammatical subject is always the first part of the sentence even when it is not the "doer" of the verb's action. In the following sentence ***Our TV*** did not "do" anything:

> ***Our TV*** was stolen.

Logical subject

The logical subject is always the "doer" of the verb's action. It does not always come at the front of the sentence:

> ***Someone*** stole our TV.
> Our TV was stolen by ***someone***.

See also **agent • case • predicate**

subject-verb agreement

See **agreement**

subjunctive mood

See **mood** (of a verb) **• mood and residue**

subordinate clause

See **clause**

subordinate conjunction

A ***word or phrase*** that introduces a subordinate clause.

The girl ***who*** lives opposite us has a new dog.

You can stay ***as long as*** you wish.

See *also* **clause**

subplot

See **narrative**

substitution

See **ellipsis** and **substitution**

such as or *like?*

See ***like, as, as if*** or ***such as?***

suffix

See **prefix** and **suffix**

superlative degree

See **degree**

syllable

IN SPEECH

A sound usually made with a single pulse of air from the lungs.

IN WRITING

The written expression of this:

Once | u | pon | a | time |

Cin | der | el | la . . .

In English a syllable is said to have only one vowel sound but it can have one, several or no *consonants*:

sprock | et
ciao!

in | ter | na | tion | al | i | sa | tion

However, some syllables seem to have a consonant and no vowels:

Middling can be pronounced
mid | ling or *mid | **dl** | ing*

In practice it is often difficult to hear where one syllable ends and the next begins. Some words seem to have only one pulse (as in ***going***) yet are said to have two grammatical parts (the base ***go*** + the suffix ***-ing***). This causes disagreement about where to hyphenate words.

See *also* **hyphenation**

syllabi or *syllabuses*?

Both words are plurals of ***syllabus*** and both are accepted.

See *also* **plural nouns** • **regular and irregular nouns**

symbol

A symbol is anything that stands for an idea.

Symbols in narratives

In an allegory a symbol is a thing or person that represents an idea, belief, value or attitude.

> Frodo's ring has been described by some readers as a ***symbol*** of the dangers of personal power.

Symbols in maps

In a map a symbol is a simplified picture (or icon) which stands for an idea just as a word does. Colours can also be given symbolic meanings in a map.

Typical map symbols

- *water*
- *airport*
- *bicycle path*
- *information*

See *also* **allegory** • **icon** • **map**

synonym

A word with the same (or almost the same) meaning as another word. The following words are synonyms of each other:

> to lift up   to raise   to elevate

However, very few words are *exact* synonyms. They can be swapped in some sentences but not in every sentence:

> They raised his salary.
> ≠ They lifted up his salary.
>
> His style is too elevated for me.
> ≠ His style is too raised for me.

See *also* **antonym** • **chain**

synopsis or *script*?

See ***script, synopsis*** or ***treatment?***

syntax

(1) The order of words in a sentence.

(2) The study of word order in sentences.

See *also* **pre-modifier** • **word order**

system diagram

See **flow chart**

table

A visual text that arranges information in columns and/or rows. The columns and rows are identified by headings.

	Group 1	Group 2
Aspect 1		
Aspect 2		
Aspect 3		

Each column arranges items into one group, and each row treats a separate aspect of the groups.

Tables are useful when planning an information report that classifies a topic (by sorting the facts or examples into groups and aspects to be discussed).

Column table

The simplest kind of table is a series of lists. Each list is arranged as a column with its own heading. There are no rows.

Group 1	Group 2

All items in a column belong to its heading. Usually they are specific examples of a more general category named in the heading.

Row-and-column table

Most tables have both rows and columns. Where a row and column meet, they form a cell.

	Group 1	Group 2
Aspect 1		
Aspect 2		cell
Aspect 3		

In a row-and-column table each cell belongs to *both* its row heading and its column heading. These connections form meaningful statements.

	Bats	**Bees**
Legs	2	6
Wings	2	4
Eyes	**2**	**5**

= ***Bats*** have **two eyes** but ***bees*** have ***five***.

See *also* **cell** (in a table) • **column** (in a table) • **information report** • **row** (in a table)

T

table of contents

(Also called the ***contents page***) A list of chapters in a book showing the page number of the beginning of each chapter.

Contents

The table of contents is placed among the ***front matter*** of a book, usually after the title page and acknowledgements page but before the list of illustrations and preface.

A table of contents is used differently from an index.

Table of contents
A table of contents lists only the main headings (chapters) and arranges them in the order they appear in the book. This allows the reader to survey the general topics (or main events) of a book.

Index
An index arranges many small details in alphabetical order and is used to search for these details in the text.

The website equivalents of a table of contents are a ***menu***, ***browse page*** or ***site map***:

- a ***menu*** provides chapters or main topics as a list of hyperlink "buttons"
- a ***browse page*** provides a (usually more detailed) list of hyperlinks
- a ***site map*** sets out all topics arranged as a nested list

The hyperlinks are provided instead of page numbers.

See also **browse**, ***find*** *or* ***search?*** • **front matter** and **end matter** • **hyperlink** • **index** • **menu** • **nested list** • **site map**

tag question

(Also called a ***tag***) A question that follows a statement asking for agreement.

That's right, ***isn't it?***
Frogs aren't reptiles, ***are they?***

A positive statement is followed by a negative tag:

it is, ***isn't it?***

A negative statement is followed by a positive tag:

they aren't, ***are they?***

tautology

See **redundancy**

template

In word processing a template is a page that has already been formatted. Layout and typography have been "built in".

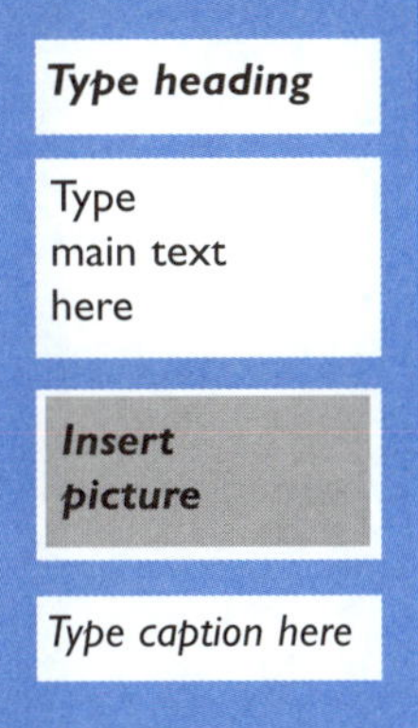

See *also* **formatting**

temporal conjunction

IN FUNCTIONAL GRAMMAR

A way of joining clauses or sentences. A temporal conjunction links events that have a time connection.

They were seated ***when*** I arrived.
She came in ***after*** I had sat down.

See *also* **cohesion**

tenor

See **text** and **context**

tense (of a verb)

The form of a verb that indicates whether the action happens in the present, past or future.

Present tense:	I ***catch*** the bus.
Past tense:	I ***caught*** the bus.
Future tense:	I ***will catch*** the bus.

Tenses can indicate other information about the time of the action:

Continuous present tense:	I ***am catching*** the bus.
Continuous past tense:	I ***was catching*** the bus.
Continuous future tense:	I ***will be catching*** the bus.

In English the tense of a verb is not always shown by these forms. Sometimes only the context can tell us whether a verb is past, present or future:

Looks like present tense but is really future:
I ***am catching*** the bus tomorrow.

Looks like past tense but is really future "conditional":
If I ***caught*** the bus tomorrow …

Looks like present tense but is really "timeless" (past, present and future):
I (always) ***catch*** the bus on Mondays.
Cats ***catch*** mice.

See *also* **continuous tenses • future tenses • past tenses • present tenses**

text

Any meaningful communication. Some texts do not include words. Other texts are formed by combining words with other kinds of communication, such as symbols, images, gesture or tone of voice.

Wordless texts

These include mime, painting and sculpture, signing (or sign language), symbols on street signs and icons on computer screens and other technology.

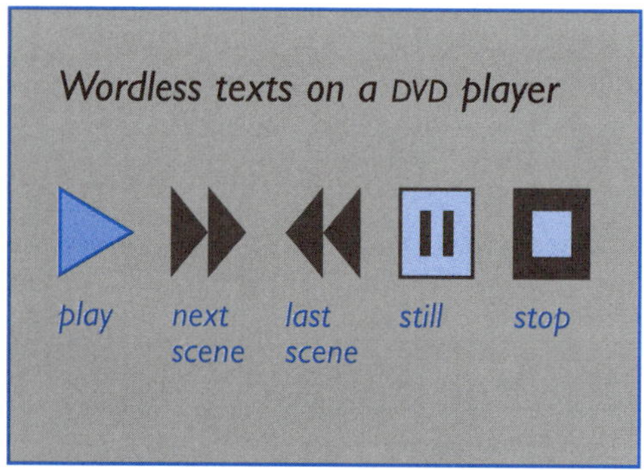

Texts combining words, gesture and tone of voice

An actor uses gesture and tone of voice to convey additional meanings or to say the opposite of the words' apparent meaning. Irony and sarcasm use tone of voice to reverse the apparent meaning of the words.

Visual texts

Many visual texts (such as maps and diagrams) combine words and images to make their meaning.

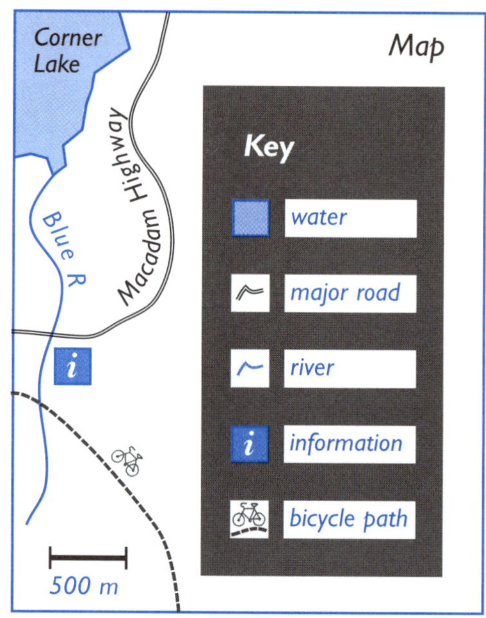

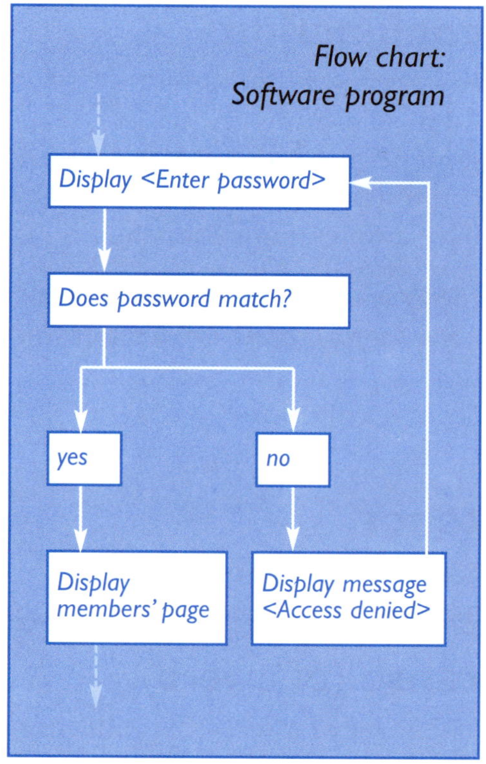

Other visual texts (such as tables, flow charts and time lines) arrange words in a meaningful relationship without putting them into sentences. Rules, arrows, boxes or columns help the user to read the text in a sequence that makes sense.

Texts can be grouped as:

- ***fiction*** or ***non-fiction***
- ***printed*** or ***electronic***
- ***lexical*** or ***visual***

Fiction and non-fiction texts

Fiction is said to be imagined while non-fiction is said to be true or factual. However, these categories can overlap. For example, a biography may include dialogue that the author has invented. Non-fiction is also called information or ***factual text***.

Printed and electronic texts

Printed texts

Texts that (traditionally) are printed onto paper using a machine such as a printing press or typewriter. Printed texts now include those produced by a computer printer or a photocopier. Paper is not the only medium for a printed text. Metal road signs and cardboard or plastic packaging are also printed texts.

Electronic texts

Texts that are conveyed or accessed electronically. Electronic texts include film and video, illuminated signs and digital texts. Digital texts include documents, emails, digital photos or movies, CDs and DVDs, mobile text messages and websites. A printed copy of a digital text is a ***hard copy***.

Lexical and visual texts

A ***lexical*** text is one made up of words or sentences only. A ***visual*** text combines images (or graphics) with words. A lexical text might be a paragraph or a novel. A visual text could be a diagram or an atlas.

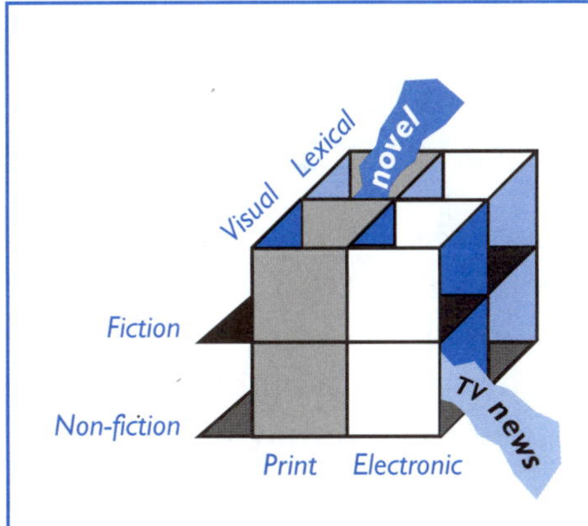

A novel is fiction, lexical, print.
TV news is non-fiction, visual, electronic.

See also **fiction • factual text • graphic • hard copy • lexical text • *irony* or *sarcasm?* • text and context • visual literacy**

text and context

IN FUNCTIONAL GRAMMAR

The relationship between what is said or written and the context in which the language occurs.

Context

The circumstances in which a text occurs is its context. This might be:

- a branch of science studied at school or university
- a railway platform where people are trying to board a crowded train

In each case the context affects the kind of language (or the text) that is produced.

There are said to be four aspects of context: ***purpose***, ***field***, ***tenor*** and ***mode***.

Purpose (why are they communicating?)

Functional grammar focuses on the purposes of language. The people involved may intend:

- to understand how animals breathe
- to board a train

Field (what is involved?)

The field (or circumstances) of the text may include:

- the subject of biology; a classroom; a textbook
- train delays and a football match that is about to start

Tenor (who is involved?)

Tenor is the relationship between the people who are communicating. These may be:

- the author of a textbook and her readers (who never meet)
- football fans and other commuters, most of them strangers to one another

Mode (how is the language used?)

The "communication channel" may be speech or writing. The language may be:

- written; a form of reflection (explaining or understanding a biological process)
- spoken; a form of negotiation (persuading others to let you board a crowded train)

Here is another example:

Context	a job interview
Purpose	to get a job; to fill a vacancy
Field	a supermarket; a job vacancy
Tenor	relationship between a supermarket manager and a student looking for work
Mode	spoken; a form of action and decision-making

Text

Text is any meaningful form of communication. Context has an effect on the ***register*** of the text and the ***genre*** in which the text is spoken or written.

Register
Register includes all the language qualities that are a mark of a particular context. Distinctive registers include the language that is typical of lawyers, bureaucrats, TV news, school teaching, sports commentators, advertising, street signage, chat rooms and so on.

Genre (or text type)
The kind of text, or genre, is also a product of context. A biology textbook may include ***explanations*** of how we breathe; ***information reports*** that classify branches of biology; ***recounts*** of key discoveries; and ***procedures*** for laboratory experiments.

Other information genres are ***persuasive texts*** (such as letters to newspapers) and ***discussions*** of various points of view (such as newspaper editorials). ***Literary*** genres include poetry, drama and fiction.

See also **description • discussion • explanation • factual recount • genre • information report • narrative • personal recount • persuasion • procedure**

text type

IN FUNCTIONAL GRAMMAR
Another word for *genre*.
See **genre**

than me or ***than I***?

Some writers concern themselves with whether it is correct to use constructions such as:

She is older than ***me***

or

She is older than ***I***.

Both are accepted. The first is used in all contexts, whereas the second is found only where the speaker or writer is trying to demonstrate his or her learning or adherence to snob grammar.

Writers who use ***than I*** argue that the expression is "short for" the clause ***than I am***. Since it is the subject of the verb ***to be***, the pronoun should be ***I***. This idea began in the eighteenth century when grammarians wanted English to conform to the rules of Latin. In Latin there is no exact equivalent of ***than me***.

However, writers who use ***than me*** argue that the phrase is not short for anything, and that this form is widely used in English and other modern languages.

See also **hypercorrection • snob grammar**

that, who or ***which***?

See ***which, who*** or ***that?***

their, *they're* or *there*?

- ***their*** means "of them"
- ***they're*** means "they are"
- ***there*** means "that place" or "in/to/at that place"

They're taking ***their*** bikes ***there***.

theme and rheme

IN FUNCTIONAL GRAMMAR

The two parts into which most sentences can be divided.

Theme

The first participant, process or circumstance of a clause. The **theme** is the "main point" and comes first in the clause.

Participant as theme

The milk is heated only after it has been stirred in.

Process as theme

Heat the milk only after you have stirred it in.

Circumstance as theme

Only after it has been stirred in can the milk be heated.

Rheme

The rheme is <u>all of the rest of the clause</u>:

The milk <u>is heated only after it has been stirred in</u>.

Heat <u>the milk only after you have stirred it in</u>.

Only after it has been stirred in <u>can the milk be heated</u>.

there, *their* or *they're*?

See ***their*, *they're*** or ***there***?

they after *everybody/everyone*?

See **everybody/everyone** + ***is*** or ***are***?

they after *he or she*?

See **he or she** + **they**?

they're, *their* or *there*?

See ***their*, *they're*** or ***there***?

third person

See **person**

though or *although*?

See ***although*** or ***though***?

through or *thru*?

See **advertese**

till or *until*?

Both words mean "up to the time of". ***Until*** is sometimes more formal than ***till***.

Dinosaurs remain in the fossil

record ***until*** the Cretaceous.

"I won't see you ***till*** Thursday."

Another spelling is ***'til*** which is a contraction of ***until***.

Note that ***'till*** is a misspelling.

See also **contraction**

timeless present

See **present tenses**

time line

A visual text in which events are arranged in chronological order along an ***arrow of time***. The time line is marked in equal time units, such as hours, weeks or centuries.

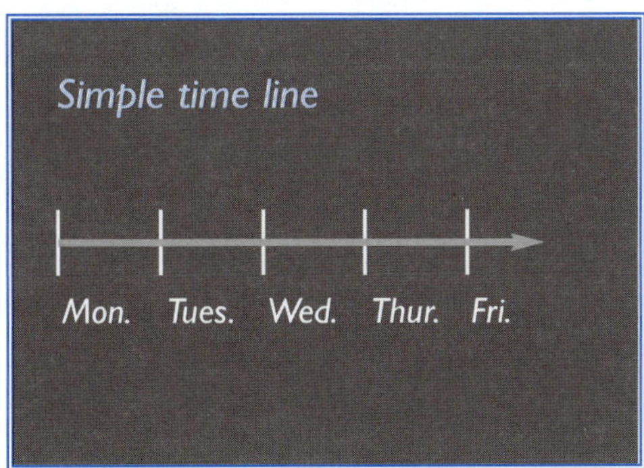

The time units are accurately shown, so that elapsed time can be measured exactly.

A ***multiple time line*** has two or more ***life lines***, which can be placed beside each other to show events that may be related.

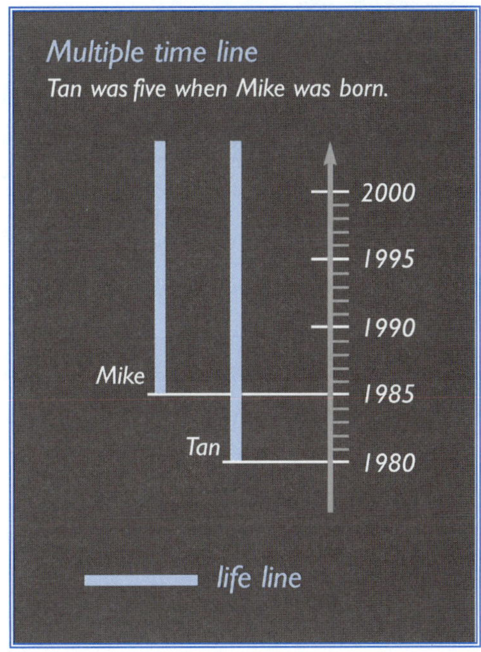

Time lines can take other forms. The following time line shows the planet Pluto's journey since 1930. This time line resembles a flow chart or story map.

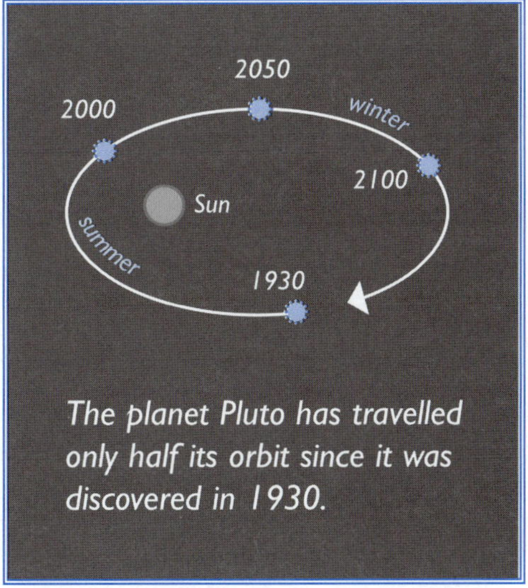

The planet Pluto has travelled only half its orbit since it was discovered in 1930.

Time lines can be found in recounts, procedures and explanations, where events need to be sequenced in order to be understood.

See also **life line • multiple time line • story map • visual text**

title bar

A horizontal banner on a web page that names the main subject of the page. A title bar on a website performs a similar role to a chapter heading in a printed book or a headline in a newspaper.

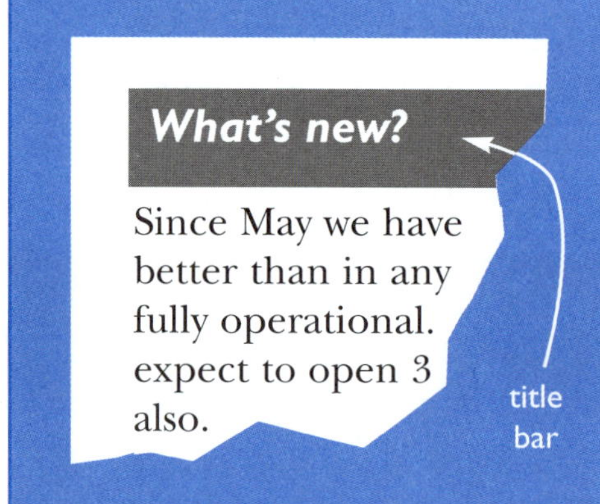

title page

The page at the front of a book which carries the book's title. A title page is always on a recto (right-hand) page.

Some books also have a ***half-title page***. This page shows the title in smaller print, without the author's name or publisher. A half-title always precedes the title page.

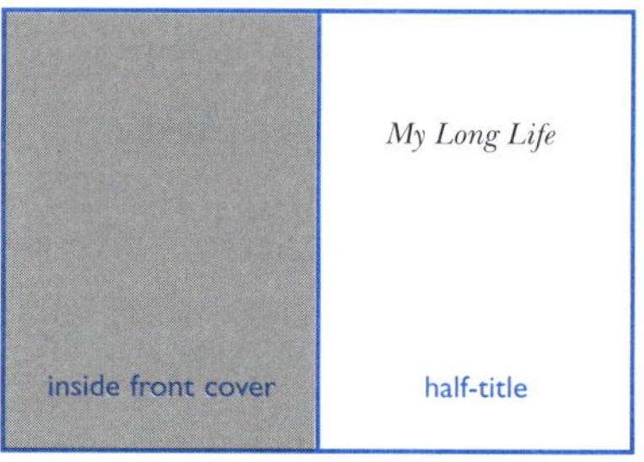

My Long Life

MAY B. TEDIOUS

back of half-title

title page

See also **front matter** and **end matter • *recto*** *or* ***verso****?*

to *ending a sentence?*

Some writers try to avoid ending a sentence with the preposition **to**.

> ***Who*** does this belong ***to***?
> = ***To whom*** does this belong?

Both of these expressions are widely accepted.

To whom does this belong?
is viewed by some writers as a hypercorrection and an example of snob grammar.

See *also* **hypercorrection** • **preposition** *ending a sentence?* • **snob grammar** • ***who*** *or* ***whom?***

to-infinitive

See **finite verb** and **non-finite verb** • **split infinitive**

toolbar

A collection of icons in a computer program. Each icon when clicked performs a function, such as to cut, paste, print or find a text.

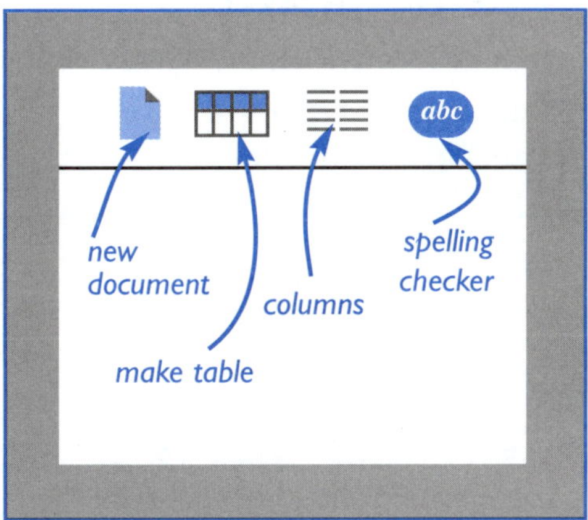

to whom or *who ... to?*

See ***to*** *ending a sentence?*

tracking shot

A movie effect produced when the camera is moved along rails. A tracking shot is often used when the camera needs to follow (and keep up with) an actor or a moving object such as a car.

Tracking shot *or* ***dolly shot?***
A ***tracking shot*** requires the camera to be moved along rails that look like a small railway track. A similar effect can be produced when the camera is mounted on a wheeled platform called a ***dolly***. However, a ***dolly shot*** does not require rails. A dolly can also be used to raise the camera high above the action.

See *also* ***pan*** *or* ***zoom?***

traditional grammar

Traditional grammar looks at the relationship between words in sentences.

The first traditional grammarians believed that there are strict rules about "correct" and "incorrect" grammar. These rules were based not on how English is commonly used but how Latin grammar works. Traditional grammarians believed that English should behave like Latin, a language once spoken by the ancient Romans.

Traditional grammar was first developed in the eighteenth century and for two hundred years it was the only grammar taught in schools.

Traditional grammar has become less concerned about prescribing and more concerned with describing the English language.

See also • **functional grammar** • **grammar**

transitive verb and intransitive verb

A verb which has a direct object is ***transitive***.

Subject	*Verb*	*Direct object*	*Indirect object*
We	***took***	the car	to the beach.

A verb that does *not* have a direct object is ***intransitive***:

Subject	*Verb*	*Direct object*	*Indirect object*
We	***went***		to the beach.
We	***swam***.		

The same verb may be transitive or intransitive in different sentences:

Transitive

Subject	*Verb*	*Direct object*	*Indirect object*
We	***lost***	the game.	

Intransitive

Subject	*Verb*	*Direct object*	*Indirect object*
We	***lost***		to Hawthorn.
We	***lost***.		

See also **object** (of a sentence) • **verb**

treatment (in film writing)

See ***script, synopsis*** *or* ***treatment?***

tree diagram

A visual text in which topics are broken down into groups and sometimes examples.

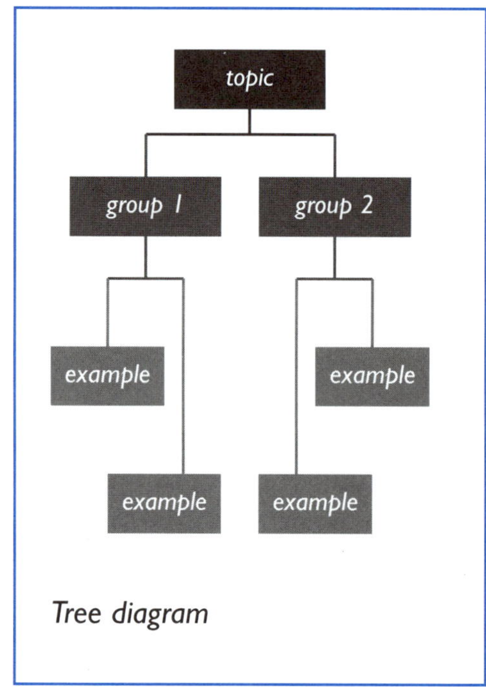

Tree diagram

Leader lines are used to connect parts of the diagram. Where a line divides, the new topics or groups "belong to" the first topic.

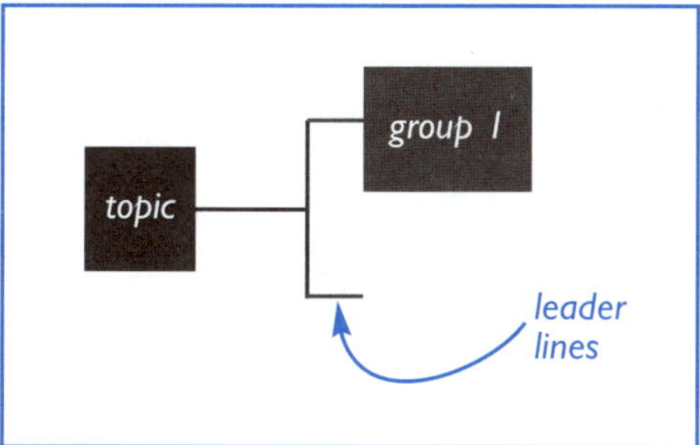

A tree diagram can be seen as a tree with branches (*1*), or as a tree that is "upside-down" (2).

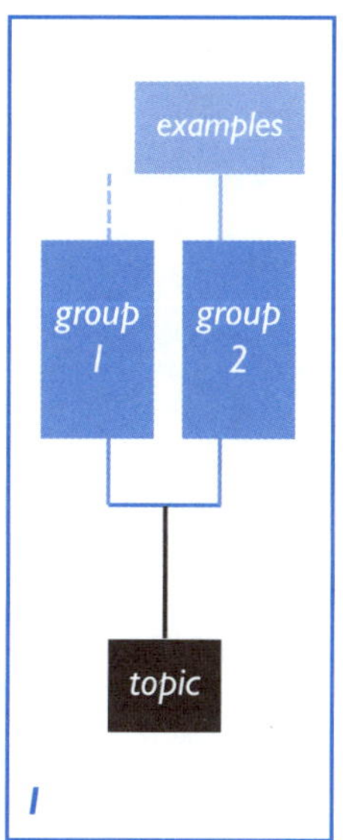

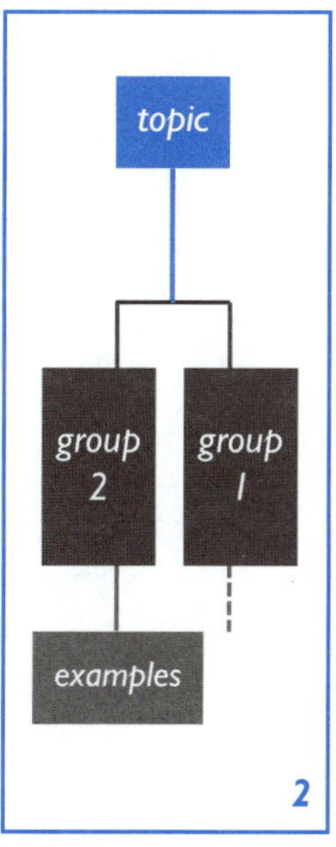

1 Standard tree diagram: "branches" at top
2 Inverted tree diagram: "trunk" at top

Tree diagrams are useful when arranging a topic as a hierarchy. A hierarchy organises groups into smaller groups. This kind of diagram is used to plan an information report which divides main topics into subtopics. ***Nested lists*** serve a similar purpose.

See also **information report • leader line • nested list**

try to *or* try and?

Some writers prefer **try to**. There are two reasons offered for this:

• the **to** in **try to** is really part of the following verb (it is part of a to-infinitive):

> I ***tried*** to reach the top shelf.

• only one action is involved, not two: we do not try *and also* reach the shelf (we may try but *fail* to reach it):

> I ***tried*** to reach the top shelf.
> ≠ I ***tried and also*** I ***reached*** the top shelf.

See also **to-infinitive**

two

T

two-shot

In film and television writing, a scene in which only two actors (usually only their heads) are seen is called a two-shot.

See *also* **close-up shot** • **wide shot**

typeface

See **font**

types of + plural?

See ***kinds of*** + plural?

typo

A keyboarding mistake, where the wrong keys have been struck.

> We used to live in ***Syndey*** but now we live in ***Meblourne***.

A ***typo*** is different from a spelling mistake. It is possible (and very common) for someone who knows how to spell a word conventionally to produce a typo of that word.

The word ***typo*** is an abbreviation (clipping) of the phrase ***typographical error***.

See *also* **abbreviation**

typography

See **graphic design**

underlining or *italic*?

Generally underlining is used in handwriting, whereas italic is used in keyboarding.

Underlining in handwriting

Handwritten words can be underlined to highlight them—or to show that they are the names of books, films or plays.

Bilbo may be the main character in The Hobbit, but he's not the most interesting character.

Italic in keyboarding

When keyboarding the same text, *italic type* is used instead of underlining:

Bilbo may be the *main* character in *The Hobbit*, but he's not the most *interesting* character.

See *also* **font** • **names**

under or *in the circumstances*?

See ***circumstances***: ***in*** or ***under***?

uninterested or *disinterested*?

See ***disinterested*** or ***uninterested***?

until or *till*?

See **till** or **until**?

upon, on or *up on*?

• ***upon*** and ***on*** mean the same thing and both are accepted; sometimes ***upon*** sounds more formal (and possibly more pompous) than ***on***:

> New responsibilities were placed ***upon*** the government.
> = New responsibilities were placed ***on*** the government.

• ***up on*** is used where ***up*** is a particle that belongs with a verb:

> We were carried ***up on*** the ski tow.

See *also* **compound verb** • **particle**

upload or *download*?

See ***download*** or ***upload***?

upper case and lower case

See **lower case** and **upper case**

U

URL

(**U**niform **R**esource **L**ocator) The internet address of a file, web page or website.

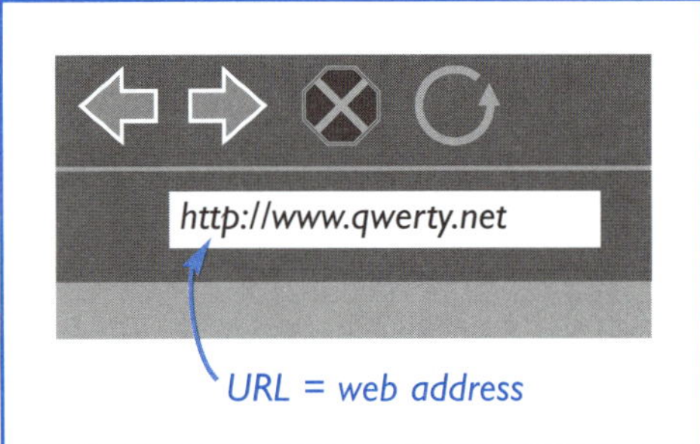

The URL *http://www.qwerty.net* is made up of two parts:

Protocol name
http://www

Domain name
qwerty.net

In a bibliography a website address or **URL** is written within angular brackets (< >):

< xyz.info.au >

These brackets work like quotation marks. When typing the URL into a browser the brackets must be omitted.

See also **angular brackets • bibliography • domain name**

usage

The various ways in which words or phrases are used. "Accepted" usage depends on the social context. Formal usage is not always the appropriate usage.

Usage often involves deciding on the most appropriate word or phrase.

What is the difference in meaning between ***uninterested*** and ***disinterested***?

Do I understand how and where to use ***complement*** and ***compliment***?

Usage is different from grammar and style. ***Grammar*** is a description of a language system that attempts to explain how the language works. ***Style*** includes personal style (such as tone of voice and choice of vocabulary), publishing style (spelling, punctuation, layout and design) and word processing style (fonts and basic design).

See also **grammar • style**

Venn diagram

A diagram in which groups or sets are seen to overlap. Items placed in the overlapping section belong to both groups.

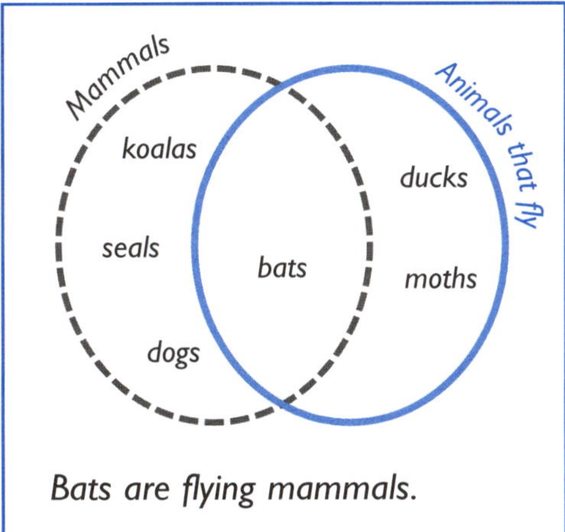

Bats are flying mammals.

Venn diagrams are useful when planning ***information reports*** where items belong to more than one group. A Venn diagram manages this better than a table, which does not highlight items that belong in more than one group, such as *bats*:

Mammals	*Animals that fly*
koalas *seals* *bats* *dogs*	*ducks* *bats* *moths*

A Venn diagram is also useful when planning a ***discussion*** to locate where conflicting opinions may sometimes agree (overlap).

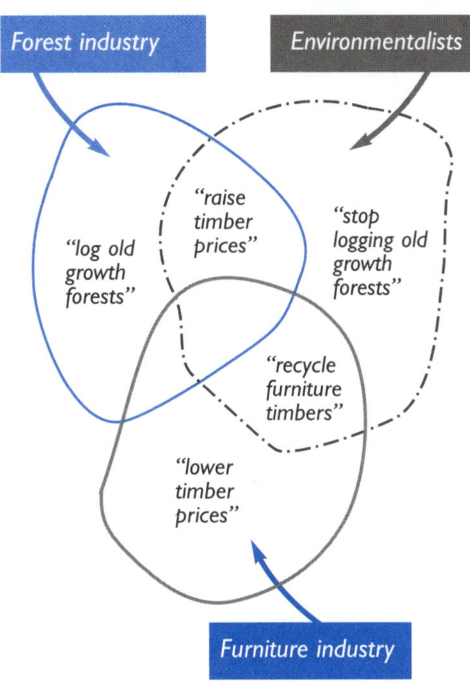

See also **discussion • information report**

verb

A word that usually stands for a ***state*** or an ***action***.

> I ***am*** sure that your dog ***chased*** our cat.

A verb is said to be essential to a clause:

Phrase:	to the Summit
Clause:	We ***walked*** to the Summit.

Verbs can be ***lexical*** or ***auxiliary***. Some auxiliary verbs are called ***primary*** verbs. Verbs can also be ***finite*** or ***non-finite***.

Lexical and auxiliary verbs

Most verbs are lexical verbs, while others are auxiliaries. The auxiliary verbs are said to "support" the ***lexical*** verbs:

We ***walked*** there.
We could ***walk*** there.
We ought to ***walk*** there.

Primary verbs

Some writers treat the verbs ***to be***, ***to do*** and ***to have*** as part of the auxiliary group. Others treat them as a separate group, the ***primary*** verbs:

Lexical:	We ***walked*** there.
Primary:	We ***have*** walked there.
	We ***are*** walking there.
	We ***do*** walk there.
Auxiliary:	We ***should*** walk there.
	We ***can*** walk there.

A primary verb can work either as an auxiliary or as a lexical verb:

As auxiliary verb:
We ***are*** walking there.
We ***have*** taken the tents.
We ***did*** walk 5 km yesterday.

As lexical verb:
We ***are*** here.
We ***have*** the tents.
We ***did*** it.

Finite and non-finite verbs

Verbs can be finite or non-finite. A ***finite*** verb indicates person (who did it), number (how many) or tense (when it happened). A ***non-finite*** verb does not indicate any of these three things.

See *also* **auxiliary verb** • **clause** • **finite verb** and **non-finite verb** • **lexical verb** • **number** • **person** • **primary verb** • **tense** (of a verb)

verbal noun

See **gerund**

verbal process

See **process**

verb group

A group of words based on a verb. A verb group is the ***lexical verb*** + its auxiliaries.

They had been ***coming*** here for years.

We should have ***finished*** by now.

See *also* **auxiliary verb** • **lexical verb**

verbosity

Using many words, or using too many words.

I deeply and sincerely regret my action. = I'm sorry I did it.

The verbosity of the sentence I deeply and sincerely regret my action is not a "fault". The writer has used many words to say something more forcefully and expressively.

Where it is said that "too many" words are used, verbosity may be called ***redundancy***, which is using unnecessary words to say something:

> ***Finally*** and ***in conclusion*** I ***would like to finish*** by saying …

See *also* **redundancy**

verb-subject agreement

See **agreement**

verso *or* recto?

See **recto** *or* **verso**?

viewing

See **visual literacy**

virgule [/]

See **slash** [/]

virtually, literally or *metaphorically?*

See ***literally, virtually*** *or* ***metaphorically***?

visual element

A meaningful unit of a visual text. In a visual ***text*** such as a map, the visual ***elements*** may include a scale, compass rose and grid.

The meaning of any one visual element (such as a map symbol) is supported by other items (such as a key which defines the symbol). Some common visual elements are:

Visual text	*Visual elements*
diagram	leader lines, labels, scale, key
table	columns, rows, cells
storyboard	boxes, number labels, captions
map	symbols, colours, arrows, scale, key, compass rose, grid

See *also* **visual grammar • visual literacy • visual text**

visual grammar

A description of visual literacy that attempts to explain how ***visual texts*** and ***visual elements*** make meaning.

Grammar of a visual text

The grammar of a visual text such as a map would discuss:

- the meanings of shapes and colours on a map, and the use of a key to define them
- the functions of a map (such as

to locate places, to define distances and relative positions or to trace journeys)

Grammar of a visual element

The grammar of a visual element such as an arrow would discuss (for example) its uses:

- to indicate the direction of a flow chart
- to link labels to details in a diagram
- to show journeys in a map
- to show enlargement in a nested diagram

See also **arrow • diagram • flow chart • map • nested diagram • visual element • visual text**

visual literacy

The ability to interpret and produce visual texts. Visual literacy includes many "literacies":

- the ability to read and draw visual texts such as maps and diagrams
- an understanding of film and video techniques
- the building of computer graphics and websites
- interpretation of the visual performance arts (acting, mime, dance) as well as set design, costume and lighting
- the visual arts (such as painting, sculpture, gallery installations, architecture and design)

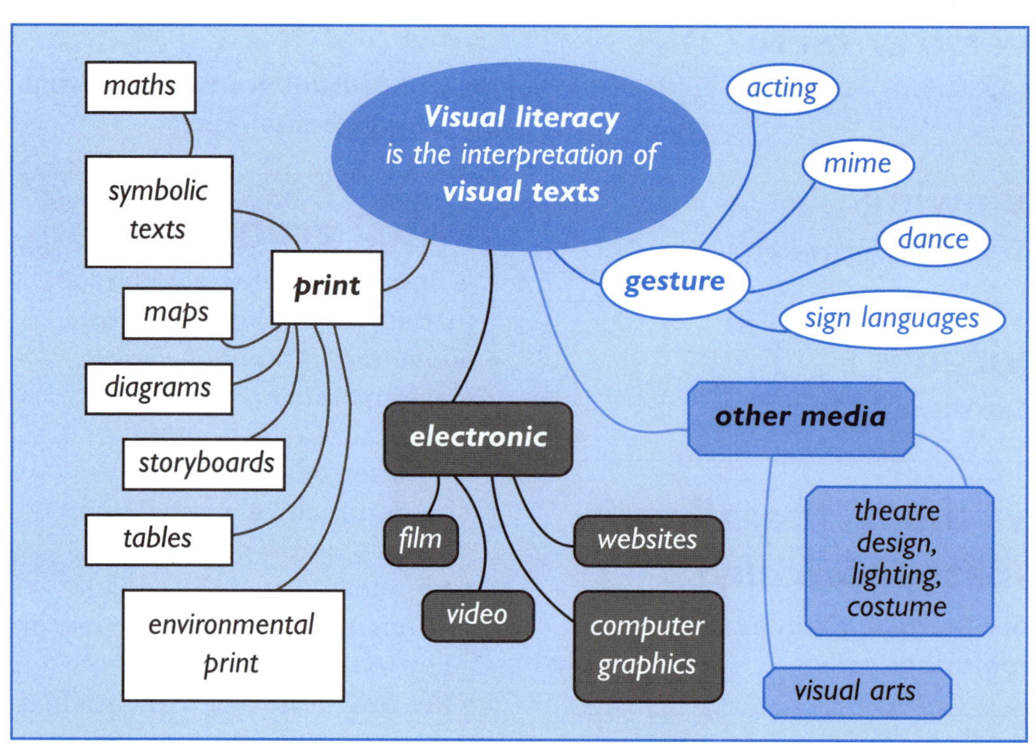

• the use of icons on street signs, computer toolbars, mobile phones and other technologies
• the ability to sign (use a sign language)
• the ability to use a symbol system such as mathematical symbols

Visual literacy is sometimes called ***viewing***, which is contrasted with reading words and sentences. Some people link viewing to drawing, just as we can link reading to writing. Others see visual literacy as a branch of reading.

Visual literacy is sometimes contrasted with ***lexical literacy***, which is a literacy employing only words and sentences.

See also **icon • lexical literacy • toolbar • visual grammar • visual text**

visual text

Any form of communication that conveys all or part of its meaning visually. Visual texts can be printed, electronic or performed, and they can be ***informational*** or ***imaginative***.

Informational texts

These visual texts include maps, diagrams, tables, graphs, time lines, storyboards, flow charts,

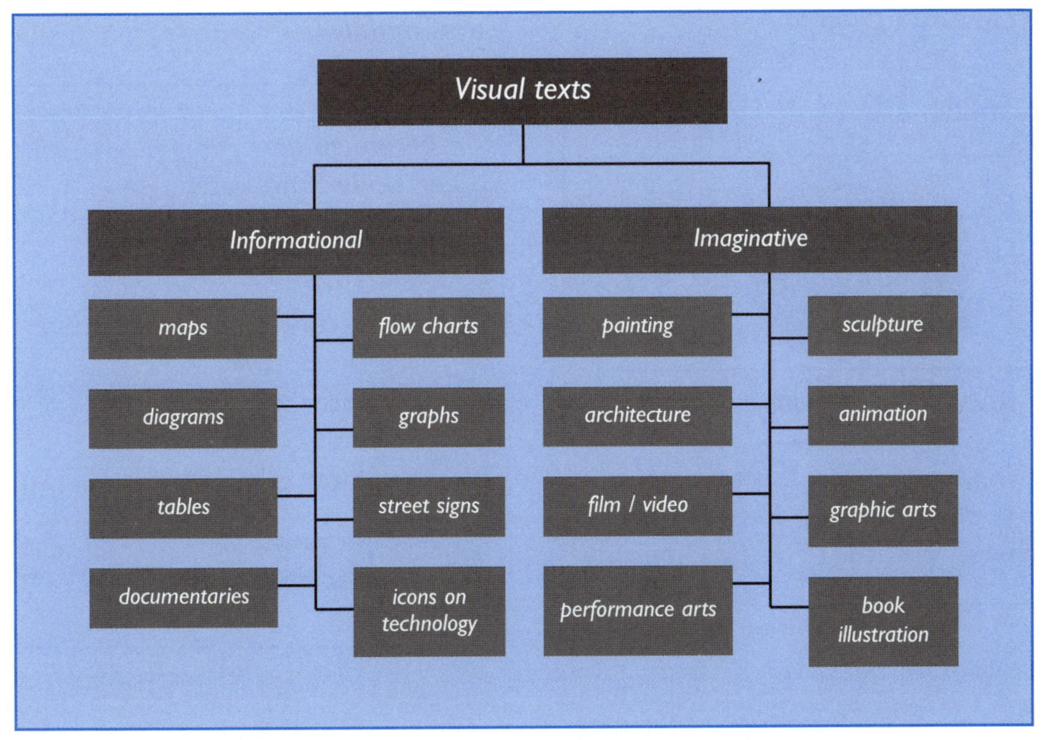

☞

street signs, toolbars on a web browser, icons on a DVD or VCR remote, TV documentaries, etc. Some of these texts give information; others give instructions or warnings; still others are used as tools.

Imaginative texts

These visual texts include movies, animation and digital video; plays and other performance arts; painting, sculpture, architecture and interior design; narrative book illustration, etc.

Visual texts often include *both* pictorial elements *and* lexical elements (words or sentences). The pictorial part could be called the ***graphic***.

Graphic	*Labels*

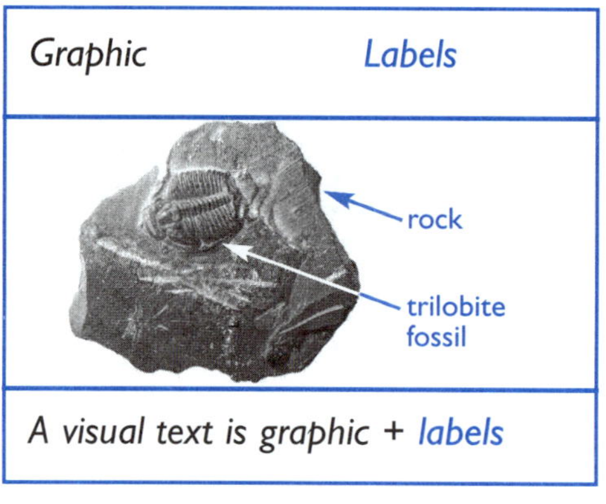

A visual text is graphic + labels

See *also* **graphic** • **lexical text** • **visual element** • **visual literacy**

vocative

The case of words used when speaking to a person or thing.

"Hey, ***Tony***, are you still there?"

"And now, ***my friends***, would you please welcome our speaker . . ."

In traditional grammar the words ***Tony*** and ***my friends*** are said to be "in the ***vocative case***".

See *also* **case**

voice (of a verb)

Verbs can be grouped according to how the action is seen, and whether the agent or the effect is to be stressed. There are said to be three voices: ***active***, ***passive*** and ***middle***.

- ***Active voice:***
  Lee ***boiled*** the water.
- ***Passive voice:***
  Full passive:
  The water ***was boiled*** by Lee.
  Agentless passive:
  The water ***was boiled***.
  Get-passive:
  The water ***got boiled***.
- ***Middle voice:***
  The water ***boiled***.

In these sentences the agent (the cause of the process) is Lee and the effect (the thing affected by the process) is the water.

In the active voice, the agent Lee is stressed, because it is placed first in the sentence. In the other voices the water is stressed by being placed first, and the agent Lee can sometimes be omitted altogether.

See also **active voice • middle voice • passive voice**

voice-over

In film and video, a voice that does not belong to anyone currently in front of the camera. In a movie a voice-over can be used for narration or to establish a scene or a character. In a documentary a voice-over usually provides the main text and explains or gives context to what the images show.

The tone, pitch and accent of the speaker's voice can be varied to suggest attitude or "authority". For example, in a documentary some viewers may experience deeper voices and "educated accents" as "more authoritative" than higher-pitched or more casual voices.

vowel and consonant

A ***vowel*** is a speech sound made with the vocal chords, or a letter that stands for that sound. All the other speech sounds and letters are *consonants*.

Aa *Bb Cc Dd* ***Ee*** *Ff Gg*
Hh ***Ii*** *Jj Kk Ll Mm Nn*
Oo *Pp Qq Rr Ss Tt* ***Uu***
Vv Ww Xx Zz

The letter **y** can be used as either a vowel or a consonant:

As a vowel	*As a consonant*
eye, sky	yellow

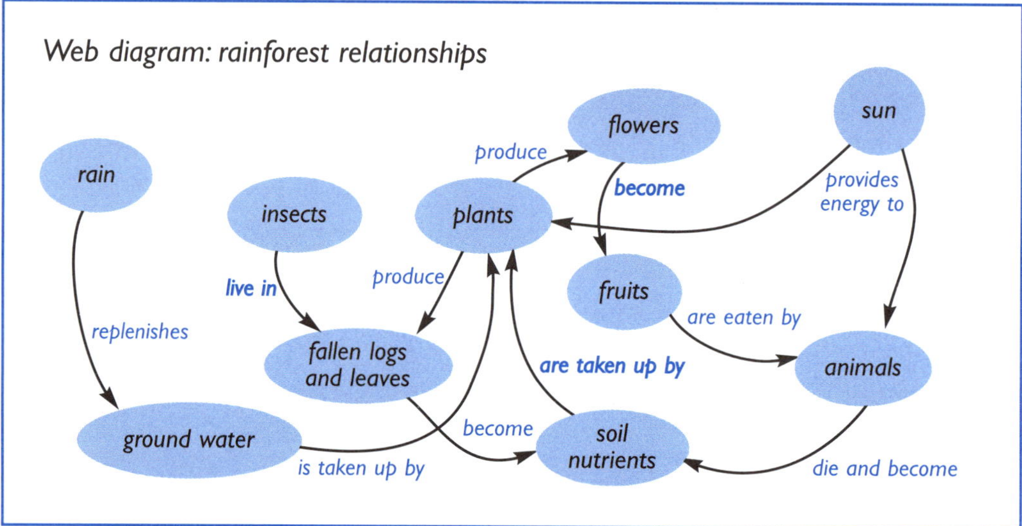

web diagram

(Also called a ***concept map***)
A visual text in which people or things are connected with arrows which show the relationships between them. A web diagram that is about people is sometimes called a sociogram.

Web diagram or flow chart?

A web diagram looks similar to a flow chart. However, the arrows on a flow chart show the flow of a process through a system (such as water flowing through the environment in a water cycle diagram).

See also **flow chart • sociogram**

web *or* net?

See ***internet*** *or* ***world wide web****?*

web page

A page on a website. A page is everything that can be viewed on one screen, including that part which can be viewed only by scrolling.

Web pages do not have page numbers. Instead they are accessed by hyperlinks.

Every page on the one website is linked to at least one other page on that site. Web designers recommend that every page be no more than two or three "clicks" (or links) from the home page.

The organisation of all the pages on a site can be planned or viewed as a ***site map***.

See also **hyperlink • site map**

website

(Also spelt ***web site*** or ***Web site***; also called a ***site***) All the web pages that can be accessed from the one home page and usually operated by the one owner. The **URL** of all pages on the one website start the same way:

> Our home page is <***neveronline.name***>
>
> and you can contact us at <***neveronline.name****/contact_us*>

See also **home page** • **names** • **URL** • **web page**

---

wh- question

See **question**

---

wh- words

See **interrogative words**

---

what (omitted)?

See ***as a good as*** *(what)?*

---

what or which?

In the following sentence ***what*** means ***the one that***:

> Choose ***what*** you like.
> = Choose ***the one that*** you like.

NOT

> Choose ***the one what*** you like.

---

which, who or that?

- ***which*** is used for things
- ***who*** is used for people
- ***that*** can be used for either people or things

> The trees ***which*** grow here . . .
> All the students ***who*** came . . .
>
> The trees ***that*** grow here . . .
> All the students ***that*** came . . .

Some writers also make a distinction between:

- ***defining "that"***
- ***non-defining "which" / "who"***

Defining "that"

Some writers reserve ***that*** for clauses that define or describe the preceding word:

> The books ***that*** are on this shelf are overdue.
> The people ***that*** you met are from Canberra.

Non-defining "which" / "who"

The same writers reserve **which** and **who** for clauses that do *not* define the preceding word:

> My computer, ***which*** I need for writing my essays, has crashed.
> My father, ***who*** has just come back from China, works as a chef.

However, not all writers observe this "defining/non-defining" distinction.

while or *whilst*?

- ***while*** means the same as ***whilst***
- ***whilst*** is said to be more "old-fashioned" and some writers avoid it for this reason

who or *whom*?

- ***who*** is the subject of a verb
- ***whom*** is the object of a verb

Max ***who*** likes swimming …

Max ***whom*** I hardly know …

Writers sometimes use ***whom*** where ***who*** is correct. This is caused by confusion about which verb belongs with ***who***:

(*a*) Mr L—, ***whom*** I know, is ill.

(*b*) Mr L—, ***who*** I KNOW is Mike's father, is ill.

In (*a*) ***whom*** is the object of the verb know.
In (*b*) ***who*** is the subject of the verb is. It is *not* the object of the verb KNOW.

See *also* **agent** • **effect** • **subject** • **object**

whose or *who's*?

- ***whose*** means "the … of whom"
- ***who's*** means "who is"

Max, ***whose*** family has left for Europe, is staying with us.
= Max, ***the*** family ***of whom*** …

"***Who's*** he?" she asked.

wide shot

In film and TV a distant and general view that shows the setting. Used to establish the context of an event or character.

See *also* **close-up shot** • **two-shot**

will or *shall*?

See ***shall*** or ***will***?

word chain

See **chain**

wordiness

See **verbosity**

word order

The order in which words occur in an English sentence has an important effect on meaning.

Subject (agent)	*Verb (process)*	*Object (effect)*
The dog	bit	the man.

is not the same as:

The man	bit	the dog.

The usual word order in an English statement is:

subject—verb—object

or

agent—process—effect

Some words relate only to the word they follow or precede:

He ***only*** sells cars
(= he does not buy them)

is not the same as

He sells cars ***only***
(= he does not sell trucks).

The study of word order is called ***syntax***.

See *also* **active voice** • ***only*** • **passive voice** • **pre-modifier**

word origin

See **etymology**

word wheel

A diagram in which related items are connected to the one topic.

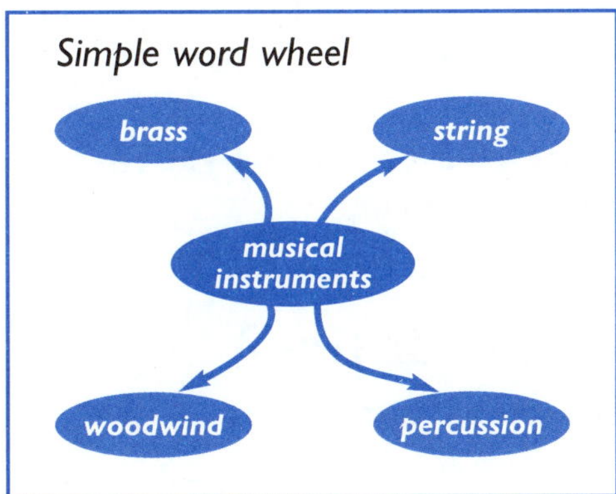

A word wheel can be extended to show subtopics.

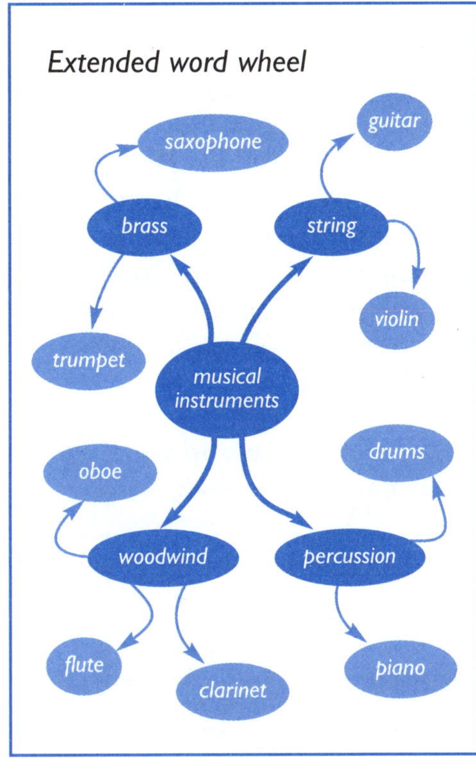

Word wheels are useful when summarising or planning a description or an information report.

See *also* **description** • **information report** • **tree diagram**

world wide web *or* ***internet?***

See ***internet*** *or* ***world wide web?***

world wide web or *World Wide Web*?

Some writers say that, because there is only one world wide web, it is a proper name and should have capitals: ***W**orld **W**ide **W**eb* (or *the **W**eb*). Others argue that the web is just another information medium like television and radio, so it needs no capital: ***world wide web*** (or ***the web***).

They're on the ***world wide web***.
= They're on the ***web***.

The usual abbreviation is ***www***.

See *also* **internet** *or* **Internet***?* • **internet** *or* **world wide web***?*

would have, would've or *would of*?

See **could have, could've** *or* **could of***?*

-x plural

A form of plural used in some French words. Some English words borrowed from French may keep the French plural.

one plateau, two plateau***x***

See *also* **plural nouns**

-y, -ies and -ied

Words ending in ***-y*** usually change to ***-ies*** or ***-ied***:

tr*y*	tr*ies*	tr*ied*

Words ending in ***-ay***, ***-ey*** or ***-oy*** simply add ***-s*** or ***-ed***:

betr***ay***	betr***ays***	betr***ayed***
pr***ey***	pr***eys***	pr***eyed***
destr***oy***	destr***oys***	destr***oyed***

Proper nouns ending in ***-y*** usually add ***-s***.

We invited the Smiths and the Barry***s***.

See *also* **proper nouns**

yes/no question

See **question**

you or *one*?

See **one** *or* **you***?*

your or *you're*?

- ***your*** means "belonging to you"
- ***you're*** means "you are"

Bring ***your*** backpack if ***you're*** walking with us.

zoom or *pan*?

See **pan** *or* **zoom***?*